D0989806

THE JUDGEMENTS OF JOAN

JOAN OF ARC. THE TRIAL by M. Boutet de Monvel
(From the W. A. Clark Collection, the Corcoran Gallery of Art, Washington, D.C.)

The Judgements of Joan

JOAN OF ARC

A STUDY IN CULTURAL HISTORY

BY

CHARLES WAYLAND LIGHTBODY

M.A. (OXON)

LONDON

GEORGE ALLEN AND UNWIN LTD

RUSKIN HOUSE   MUSEUM STREET

FIRST PUBLISHED IN 1961

PRINTED IN GREAT BRITAIN
in 12pt. Fournier type
BY SIMSON SHAND LTD
LONDON, HERTFORD AND HARLOW

PREFACE

This book forms part of a larger research project, which has already, in the main, been completed. The author hopes to present his further conclusions in a succeeding volume, or volumes, which will amplify the story of the *Judgements of Joan* from 1456 to the present day, sketched in mere outline in the *Epilogue* of the present work. In a later volume, it is planned to publish a Bibliographical Note.

The writer would like to acknowledge gratefully the tangible help received in his work from Mr R. B. McCallum, Master of Pembroke College, Oxford; from Mr John Hale, Fellow of Jesus College,Oxford; from Dr Crane Brinton, McLean Professor of Ancient and Modern History, at Harvard University; from Dr Frederick G. Marcham, Goldwin Smith Professor of English History, and Dr Mario Einaudi, Professor of Government, at Cornell University; from Dr C. W. de Kiewiet, President of the University of Rochester; from Dr Thomas J. Wilson, Director of the Harvard University Press; and from Dr Geoffrey Bruun. All of these gentlemen have read this work, or a portion of it, in manuscript, and made valuable suggestions, but for all errors, and all opinions expressed, the writer is, of course, alone responsible. He would like also to acknowledge the assistance and encouragement of Dr George Sabine, Professor Emeritus of Philosophy, and former Vice-President and Dean of the Graduate School of Cornell University; of Henry Rees, QC, and Walter Francis, QC, LL.D, of Saskatoon, Sask., Canada; of Mrs Charles Taft Ennis of Lyons, New York; of Dr and Mrs J. M. Minifie, of Washington, DC; of the Provost and Fellows of Worcester College, Oxford, who have hospitably provided him with quarters in college in which to carry on his work; of the authorities of the University of Saskatchewan; of the Humanities Research Council of Canada, which provided a grant-in-aid; and of the staffs of the New York Public Library, of Widener Library at Harvard, of the British Museum Library, of the Bibliothèque Nationale, as well as of the Bettmann Archive in New York City, and the Corcoran Gallery of Art, in Washington. In particular, he would like to mention the help of Dr Brinton, under whose auspices the original plan of this work was conceived, and who has helped with it throughout; of the late Dr Carl Becker, John Stambaugh Professor of History at Cornell University; and, not least, of the Master of Pembroke College, Oxford, his former tutor, who has been adviser in connection with publication plans. As a Canadian, the writer of this book cannot but be deeply sensible of the kindness with which he has been received at various centres of learning, in the United States, in Great Britain, and in France.

It remains for him to mention, in conclusion, the invaluable assistance of his wife, both in the earlier preparation of the manuscript and in the provision of illustrations. It was this assistance which made the book possible.

May, 1960   CHARLES W. LIGHTBODY

CONTENTS

PREFACE   page 9

I. Prologue   15

II. *La Pitié Qui Estoit en Royaume de France*   36

III. The Witch of the Armagnacs   58

IV. A Simple Shepherdess   85

V. Ashes in the Seine   98

VI. Witch Unwitched   118

VII. Epilogue   154

CHRONOLOGICAL APPENDIX   172

INDEX   177

ILLUSTRATIONS

Joan of Arc: The Trial	frontispiece
Reputed portrait of Joan of Arc	facing page 16
Joan of Arc: The vision and the inspiration	17
Joan of Arc: Her appeal to the Dauphin	32
Joan of Arc: The turmoil of conflict	33
Joan of Arc on horseback	48
Joan of Arc and standard	49
Charles VII	64
Maid of Orleans, the burning of the saint	65
Joan of Arc's house at Domrémy	80
Joan of Arc at the Coronation of Charles VII	81
Pierre Cauchon, Bishop of Beauvais	96
Portrait of the Duke of Bedford	97
Joan of Arc at Domrémy	112
Joan of Arc monument	113

I

PROLOGUE

'History is, after all, nothing but a parcel of tricks that we play upon the dead,' said Voltaire.[1] In this study we shall indeed be concerned to look, as far as may be, into the eyeless sockets of men long dead; and we shall seek to do so by studying the thoughts that they have left behind them about a dead girl, who left no eyeless sockets, but only a handful of dust to be cast into the Seine, along with a heart that was not consumed.

'You have heard the last of her,' says the Executioner to the Earl of Warwick, in Mr George Bernard Shaw's play, *Saint Joan*; to which pious reassurance Warwick responds, with wise caution: 'The last of her? Hm! I wonder!'[2] In a later scene, the Executioner himself admits his failure: 'I could not kill the Maid. She is up and alive everywhere.'[3] And Joan makes a claim which is characteristically self-confident, but hardly exaggerated: 'I shall outlast the cross. I shall be remembered when men have forgotten where Rouen stood.'[4] In an equally emphatic celebration of her immortal fame, Mark Twain remarks of her title, 'Maid of Orleans': 'Between that first utterance and the last time it will be uttered on this earth—ah, think how many mouldering ages will lie in that gap!' Or, as one of her more recent American biographers has expressed it: 'Her life was the shortest, her active career the briefest and most striking in achievement, while her fame remains

---

[1] François Marie Arouet de Voltaire, *Corr. Oeuvres* (Bâle, 1784–1790) LXVI, 17.
[2] George Bernard Shaw, *Saint Joan: A Chronicle Play in Six Scenes and an Epilogue*, London, 1924, p. 139.
[3] *Ibid.*, p. 155.
[4] *Ibid.*, p. 147.

the greatest and most enduring of any woman signalized in secular history.'[1]

After the lapse of more than five centuries, every detail of her life, her visions and her achievement remains significant to countless numbers of our contemporaries, alike in her own country and in many other parts of the globe. This peasant girl who never got out of her teens, who had an active career of little more than two years, whose life ended in heroic martydom at an age when girls today leave school—this peasant girl left such an impress upon the history of her time that many members of each succeeding generation of Western civilized men have thought it worth while to record, often at full length, their varied comments upon her, in countless histories and biographies, dramas, poems, pictures, works of music, even upon medals and upon playing cards! To some preliminary discussion of these comments, this volume is devoted.

This is not, therefore, an essay in historiography in the conventional sense. Our task is to write the history of a reputation; we are not here concerned directly with the events of Joan's life, for our story, properly speaking, begins with the day of her death. We wish to trace the mutations of her fame, and to analyse the causes of those mutations.[2] It is a task which will require more than one volume.

'Of the making of books, there is no end'; and certainly the pages of several thousand tomes have fluttered down upon her non-existent tomb,

Thick as Autumnal leaves that strow the Brooks
In Vallombrosa, where th'Etrurian shades
High overarch'd imbour.[3]

It is a literature which affords a wide panorama of the whole of modern intellectual history; it bristles with unsolved problems. Certainly, the total bibliography passes the limits of usefulness; in 1901[4] Mrs Catherwood found it to include more than 2,000

[1] Michael Monahan, *My Jeanne d'Arc* (New York, 1928), p. 8.
[2] See Appendix, for a chronological summary of the career of Joan of Arc.
[3] *Paradise Lost*, I, 301–3.
[4] Mrs Mary Catherwood, *The Days of Jeanne d'Arc*, Preface (New York, 1901).

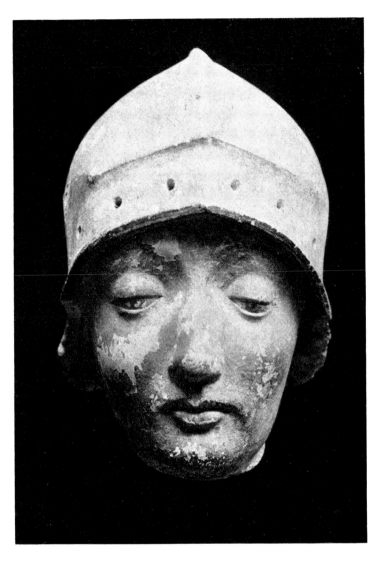

2. REPUTED PORTRAIT OF JOAN OF ARC. From the original, formerly in the Church of St Maurice, Orleans
(*Musée Historique, Orleans*)

3. JOAN OF ARC: THE VISION AND THE INSPIRATION by M. Boutet de Monvel
(*W. A. Clark Collection*)

volumes, and a more recent estimate, in 1931, stated it to number in excess of 3,000 items. The impression exists in some quarters that there was comparatively little interest in Joan of Arc before the nineteenth century;[1] but an examination of such a catalogue as that of the British Museum, or Lanéry d'Arc's *Livre d'Or de Jeanne d'Arc*,[2] is sufficient to demonstrate the fallacy of this view. Certainly, from the beginning of the nineteenth century, in France especially, the Joan of Arc literature flows in an unbroken stream, watered by tributary rivulets from every phase of intellectual life. Each junction point in the stream, each great book, releases a turbulent flood of lesser books, all the more so as it usually marks some peak of interest in the subject, owing to extraneous circumstance, political or religious. Many of the books, of course, are largely imitative and repetitive; the student of the subject is reminded of the maxim that history does not repeat itself, but historians repeat each other.

Long and various as the record is, of what men have thought about Joan, preserved in the books which the centuries have left to us, the subject remains far from exhausted, and continues to attract writers of talent and genius—just as the role of Joan of Arc appeals to so many leading tragediennes, in London or Paris or New York, as a supreme test of their skill. The kaleidoscopic theme of the *via triumphalis* and *via dolorosa* of the sainted Maid has a phenomenal faculty of revealing, from time to time, ever fresh facets of attraction.

The study of Joan of Arc in intellectual history is, in fact, the study of a series of transformation scenes, such as one might see projected by an old-fashioned magic lantern; our heroine appears successively under lights of many different colours. Each generation, each new grouping of creative spirits, even each historian, poet or artist, if of an independent and original turn of mind, sees her in a different light. One might also say that each generation recreates Joan of Arc in its own image. She is immortal, because in

[1] Guy Endore, *The Sword of God, Jeanne d'Arc* (New York, 1931), p. 474.
[2] Pierre Lanéry d'Arc, *Le Livre d'Or de Jeanne d'Arc. Bibliographie raisonée et analytique des ouvrages relatifs à Jeanne d'Arc* (Paris, 1894).

each succeeding age she is born again, in a new guise. Personal temperament, conviction, experience, and environing climate of opinion are the determinants of these individual or group images. Like a great work of art, Joan has always new meanings—different for royalists and for revolutionists, for Catholics and for Protestants, for feminists and for traditionalists, for classical antiquarians and for Gothic revivalists, for radical nationalists and reactionary chauvinists, for stern realists and fervent romanticists. Every conceivable theory about her has been propounded, along with some that one might have thought inconceivable. As Coley Taylor[1] remarks, 'Every book about her adds to the controversy'. In fact, at times the original Joan seems quite lost to view beneath the successive coats of grime and whitewash, warpaint and plaster-of-Paris sanctity which have been applied to her.

Of course, it is in the last century above all that Joan of Arc has found her apotheosis. One of the major ironies of history is the tendency of humanity to make icons of rebels and heretics and revolutionary trouble-makers, once safely dead. The career of Joan of Arc is one of the best examples of this tendency. It might be suggested that to understand her role requires an effort of the historical imagination of which many of those who have written about her have been incapable; or they have been so much involved with contemporary politics that they have not been concerned to exercise that imagination. Thus, an Anatole France can so manipulate[2] historical evidence as to represent her as the mere minion of feudal forces, essentially agreeing in this with the monarchists he is attacking. It requires a transformation of her personality into its opposite, to make M. France's bewildered and saccharine saint out of Joan. The real Joan, the peasant Maid, was strong-minded and puissant of limb, beloved of the people of the King's good towns. She violated all the laws of feudal war to turn over to

---

[1] Wilfred Philip Barrett (translator), *The Trial of Jeanne d'Arc* ... with an essay 'On the Trial of Jeanne d'Arc' by Pierre Champion, translated from the French by Coley Taylor and Ruth H. Kerr (New York, 1932), Preface, p. vii. (This work is hereafter cited as 'Barrett-Champion'.)

[2] Anatole France, *The Life of Joan of Arc*, a translation by Winifred Stevens, 2 vols. (London, 1908), *passim*.

burgher justice the Burgundian freebooter Franquet d'Arras, and she incurred in this and in other ways the widespread mistrust and censure of the nobles and higher clergy of France.

M. France does not like Joan the icon, but he accepts her as real; others exalt her, and make of this bloodless plaster figure a messiah and culture-god. 'Joan of Arc—Maid of France!' says Albert Bigelow Paine, one of her best-known American biographers, 'burned as a heretic and witch, long regarded as a half legendary figure, today she lives again, patron saint of her nation's armies, divine symbol of love and sacrifice, not only in France but throughout Christendom'.[1]

In fact, the *a priori* assumption of the great majority of historical students who deal with Joan is that, since she was always right, anyone who opposed her can only have been wrong. The presence, in any historical narrative, of a hero or heroine tends to throw the whole out of ordinary perspective. In any case, it is usual for Joan's historians to accept Joan'e evaluation of all persons about her—Cauchon, Richemont, Alençon, and all the rest—and to judge all of them only in the single term of their relationship to her.

The development of the cult of what we may choose to call 'Johannolatry', to the point where it becomes the central and dominating point in the history of fifteenth-century France, is a good example illustrative of the generalization enunciated by Mr Allan Nevins:[2]

All champions of the enslaved, the dispossessed and the downtrodden are served well by time. Their own generation may see that their ideas are crude, their methods are violent and wrong, their examples dubious. . . . But men feel a natural desire to exalt the protectors of the oppressed; we forget their faults and errors, and think only of the magnificence of their intentions.

[1] Albert Bigelow Paine, *The Girl in White Armor: The True Story of Joan of Arc* (New York, 1927), p. 274. In another, more serious work, Paine expresses himself even more extravagantly: 'Five hundred years have passed, and Joan remains a living, breathing presence, when those others of her day have become little more than names, a museum of labelle d shadows. Stepping down the centuries, she leads us on. Symbol of a super-faith and high-hearted valour with righteous resort to arms, in Joan of Arc, if anywhere today, lies the hope of the world.' A. B. Paine, *Joan of Arc* (New York, 1925), II, 327.

[2] Allan Nevins, 'The American. A Middle Western Legend by Howard Fast,' *New York Times Book Review*, July 21st, 1946.

The brave and the chivalrous, and the prominent and the respectable, delight to defend the good name of St Joan—bishops and marquises, the marshals of France and the members of the French Academy, are among her champions, as a glance at her bibliography will testify; nor must we omit to mention her eminent Anglo-Saxon defenders, like the doughty Scottish mystic, Mr Andrew Lang. We may well wonder, however, whether, if this strange girl were to return to earth again, to play, *mutatis mutandis*, a part similar to that which she played in the fifteenth century, many who now revere her would not be the first to repudiate her. The remark of Nathaniel Howe, 'the way of this world is to praise dead saints, and persecute living ones,' is trite indeed, but applicable to Joan as to many another historical personage.

It is, of course, true that Joan could not have attained her immortal fame without having sustained the crowning glory and terror of a particularly cruel martyrdom; it is this, we cannot but realize, that burns her name into the pages of history in letters of fire. If imprisoned, she would have been released in time, self-repudiated, discredited and with her influence extinguished; the psychiatrists even give us some reason for believing that her mental condition would steadily have deteriorated. Pierre Champion, the leading twentieth-century student of Joan of Arc, puts it thus;[1]

It was the stake which was, in truth, her first altar, a prophecy of that upon which the piety of man has today placed her. As the excellent Michelet has said: 'She no longer understands salvation in the material sense as she had until then; she sees clearly at last, and leaving the shadows she obtains that which was lacking to her of light and sanctity.'

She becomes a light-bringer, one who gives her life that the tribe may prosper. She becomes a symbol of mankind's propensity for destroying those who are the agents of its advance; she becomes an illustration, indeed, of the truth that genius is at home only with posterity, and that, too often, its own era casts it forth with fire and cross.

[1] Barrett-Champion, pp. 534–5.

A nineteenth-century French writer, James Darmesteter, can compare her explicitly to Christ;[1] it is not certain that she would have been surprised at this, for her self-confidence was sublime, and she was sure that she was the daughter of God. Her trial has been described as 'a trial that has become second in importance only to the trial of Christ'.[2] In fact, she has had a whole series of trials; again and again, from the assembly of the doctors at Poitiers in the spring of 1429, through the long trial at Rouen and the rehabilitation proceedings twenty years later, to the canonization process dragging through half a century, solemn gatherings of ecclesiastics have met to pass judgement upon her; and she is still on trial. She still divides opinion, expecially French opinion, as she did in her lifetime; she is still called devil and saint, and she remains, in the twentieth century, a factor in contemporary politics and war. She is not dead, but lives, and on a flaming battle-field, as hotly contested as any that she knew during her brief sojourn on this planet. Her life is the chosen tourney ground of fiercely contesting parties, ecclesiastical and political, and it has been so throughout the modern history of France. The standard which she loved so much has fluttered in every breeze of controversy, since it flew at Orleans, before Paris and at Compiègne. When her ashes were dropped into the unquiet Seine, it carried them out into a billowy sea of political, religious and cultural contention.

Every one of the formal trial proceedings which we have mentioned was a move in the propaganda battle that centred about her. Armagnac and Burgundian, *Ligeur* and Huguenot, Monarchist and Republican, Catholic and Freemason, Gaullist patriot and Vichy collaborator—all of them have found her memory at once a weapon and a ground of contention in their quarrels.

She has often been identified with Church and Crown, though the one is held by many to have condemned her to death, and the other, as many have thought, abandoned her. To the French Crown she was certainly devoted, and that loyalty was most

---

[1] James Darmesteter, *English Studies*, 'Joan in England' (London, 1896), pp. 70 ff.
[2] Coley Taylor, introduction to Barrett-Champion.

useful to it, during her lifetime and for centuries thereafter. Above all, she has been a symbol of French nationalism and patriotism, of resistance to the foreign invader, and especially of hostility to England, long the hereditary enemy of France. It was this tradition, and her connection with clerico-monarchism, that made her useful even to Vichy. More and more, however, she has been claimed as the child and champion of the people. But how the peasant lass, who despised clerks, would have laughed at all the research that has been lavished upon her, and all the varying conceptions of her which have been presented to the public through the centuries!

'Political excursions by prominent French writers have been rare in the past,'[1] says an American journalist, in speaking of the intense political controversy that in our day has prevailed in France. Nothing could be further from the truth; although it is true that French writers have often had the subtlety to disguise their political excursions beneath a specious appearance of neutrality and impartiality, thereby rendering their propaganda manoeuvres all the more effective. Certainly, most of the passion which has entered even into debate on minor points concerning Joan of Arc may be traced to the fundamental clashes of religion and politics. The dictum of Pascal, 'All our reasoning can be traced back to an emotion,' is pertinent here. Benedetto Croce has said that all history is contemporary history; most of all is this true of the historiography of Joan of Arc, which has played such a part in the contemporary history of each later generation since her time.

Joan of Arc has been extravagantly extolled by modern English and American writers; less attention has been paid to the point of view of her critics—perhaps less attention than they deserve. Some of them have been German, some, in former times, English, but it is notable that some of the most adverse opinions have come from among her own people. It is because she has never really died and been embalmed that her own countrymen have been, at times, so rough with her. In each generation, she

[1] George Slocombe, editorial page, *New York Herald-Tribune* (August 22, 1946).

has been burned again, as Jesus has been crucified again. We shall trace in this study and its sequel a more or less continuous negative tradition, often ignored, or ignorantly denounced—from the Burgundian Chronicles to certain Renaissance writers, French and English; thence to the sceptics of the eighteenth-century *Aufklärung*, and on to some of the modern scholars who have studied the subject. Monstrelet, Du Haillan, Shakespeare, Voltaire, Anatole France, Mahrenholtz, Murray— the roll of critics is not without its varied eminences, and it has, as shall show, its continuity, no less than the tradition of 'Johannolatry'. Joan encountered a feudal opposition in her own time and an opposition from middle-class critics later; in our time, new critical approaches have been opened up.

She has been held, at various periods, an impostor, or self-deceived, or a puppet of designing men. Her abjuration and relapse have been accepted as proved. Some, of old, and again in our time, have held her to be a witch or a trafficker in witchcraft, proud, disdainful, bloodthirsty, given to display, a coarse soldier or an ignorant peasant without judgement. No man's life, nor that of any woman, if narrowly scrutinized by an unfavourable criticism, can fail to afford ground for accusation, and we shall not be surprised to find that Joan's critics, no less than her defenders, can quote the scripture of source materials to their purpose. Every saint must have his *advocatus diaboli*, equipped with the weapons of science.

Along with her detractors have been those who have held her guilty as charged, of heresy, if not of witchcraft, but have glorified her in her guilt, and have defended her nationalist and popular rebellion against certain constituted authorities.

We might have grouped all our discussion as a case for the prosecution and a case for the defence in an ever-recurring trial before the tribunal of time and history; but the two sides interact and interpenetrate so subtly that to do this would be to organize our subject in a forced and arbitrary manner.

If Joan of Arc has incited the historian, the biographer, the writer of monographs, the philosophic student of politics, to endless debate with his peers, it is no less true that she has fascinated recurrently the poet, the playwright, the romancer, the painter, the sculptor, the composer of music, the weaver of tapestries. The pageant of Joan's life has itself the unity and simplicity of a great work of art; and perhaps this is one reason it has inspired so many works of belles-lettres.

Shakespeare, in *Henry VI, Part One*, presented the Maid of Orleans as a subject of dramatic art. He had at least one predecessor, the author or authors of the interminable mediaeval *Mystère du Siège d'Orléans* produced by the faithful city which Joan had saved from the English. Later dramatists have not allowed the theme to rest. It has been like one of those Greek myths at which every tragic dramatist in ancient Athens tried his hand, finding in it, or putting in it, always new meanings.

The pageant of Joan's life runs through these works like the theme of a piece of music, repeated always with variations. Since 1815, it has been a rare year in France which has not produced at least one play about Joan, though not all of these have reached the stage, and many which did so have not long survived the experience. Joan the peasant maid, Joan the leader in the struggle for a nation's freedom, continues to interest even those in our generation who are less concerned with Joan the mystic and *dévote*, Joan the saint who was burned as a witch, and Joan the military chieftain who preserved a virginal purity. The puzzling aspects of her character are absorbing even to those relatively indifferent to her military and political career.

An historical theme, of course, involves the artist in special problems. He cannot usually have complete freedom with his material—though surely it cannot be denied that, permissibly or not, great dramatists, like Shakespeare and Schiller and Voltaire, have taken enough liberties with Joan! In modern France, however, and even to lesser extent in other countries, the Joan legend is so familiar that the artist's freedom in dealing with it is limited by the expectations of his public. He may select and arrange, as

---

[1] See François Guessard and Eugène de Certain (eds.) 'Le Mystère du Siège d'Orléans' (Paris, 1862) in *Recueil des documents inédits relatifs à l'histoire de France.*

even the historian must do; he may seek to find what Henry James called 'the figure in the carpet'; but he may not modify the accepted sequence of events too drastically.

A work of art upon such a familiar historical topic involves a kind of creative struggle with the material, very interesting to analyse; the artist must battle within rigid limitations to make his subject come to life, to reveal its inner meanings for our age, and to evoke the emotional responses which he desires. He is as confined as the mediaeval religious artist was confined by a tradition inviolably maintained, or the neoclassic poet or playwright by the severe rule of Aristotle and Horace, as interpreted by Longinus and Boileau, with their unities, their prescriptions, their rigidly defined prosody. Some influential critics have thought, especially in France, that Joan of Arc was beyond the reach of the poet, because of the greatness of the subject, and the restrictions imposed by public taste upon its treatment. Unfavourable comments upon the works actually produced have not been lacking. For instance, Lord Ronald Gower,[1] writing in 1893, suggested, 'The Maid of Orleans [though a more poetical figure cannot be found in history] has not been more fortunate at the hands of the poets than at those of the historians'. More weighty is the judgement of the great French critic, Charles Augustin de Sainte-Beuve. In his *Causeries du Lundi* he speaks of her literary vicissitudes: *sans sortir de cercle de l'horizon littéraire, que de retours soudains, que de mésaventures!*[2] Again he returns to the subject.[3]

Pauvre Jeanne d'Arc! elle a eu le malheur dans ce que sa mémoire a provoqué d'écrits et de compositions de diverses sortes. Elle a inspiré de grandes poètes tragiques, aux Shakespeare et aux Schiller eux-mêmes des inventions odieuses ou absurdes; elle a inspiré au plus bel esprit et à la plus vive imagination une parodie libertine qui est devenue une mauvaise action immortelle;[4] elle est en possession de faire naître, depuis Chapelain, des poëmes épiques qui sont synonymes d'ennui, et que rien ne décourage, qui recommencent de temps en

---

[1] Lord Ronald Charles Sutherland Gower, *Joan of Arc* (London, 1893), p. 301.

[2] Charles Augustin de Sainte-Beuve, *Causeries du Lundi*, 'Procès de Jeanne d'Arc' (Paris, 1852–1885), II, 313.

[3] C. A. de Sainte-Beuve, *Nouveaux Lundis* (Paris, 1878–1885), III, 417, citing Guessard and Certain.

[4] This refers, of course, to Voltaire's *La Pucelle*.

temps et s'essayent encore ça et la, même de nos jours, sans arriver jusqu'au public, soyez bien sûrs qu'à l'heure ou je vous parle il y a quelque part un poëme épique de Jeanne d'Arc sur le métier.

It must be conceded that the quest for originality in dealing with a mine much worked, like the Joan story, becomes too often a vapid quest of novelty, far indeed from the immortal novelty of great art. It would be easy to illustrate this point from the literature of the Joan of Arc cycle, especially in the nineteenth century. None the less, we venture to think that the critics have been too severe. Restraints, such as the Joan material imposes, have often stimulated artists to greater excellence; and if there be restraints, there are also great opportunities. Even Sainte-Beuve, for all his clarity and lucidity, for all his relative independence of judgement concerning Joan of Arc, was influenced by the climate of opinion of his own age, by its perfervid French nationalism and romanticism, by its consequent iconizing attitude toward Joan, by its comfortable middle-class smugness. A student in our time, therefore, may be permitted to find him less than just to Schiller and to Shakespeare, not to speak of Voltaire.

We have sought, then, to give some idea of the character of the Joan of Arc literature; it remains to consider the nature and scope of his study, its general approach and 'inarticulate major premises'. This work is, of course, but an essay; a thorough work in the Teutonic manner would require twenty volumes, and several lifetimes, to complete. It would be utopian, therefore, to attempt to exhaust the subject; the reader, and the writer, would be exhausted long before that were accomplished. The only complete summary possible within reasonable limits would be a purely bibliographical one. Yet we must summon our courage for an attempt upon a subject which carries us to the heart of the question as to the nature of history and literature. In pursuing this study, in this volume and in its projected successor, we are enabled to compare styles, techniques, ideologies, noting the infinitely varied approaches to a single historical moment. To account as best we can for changes in approach is to come near to the core of the problem of the historian, near to the core of the problem of the artist, and to cut close to the heart of reality itself.

As we have not wished to present any mere Homeric 'catalogue of the ships', any schematized and superficial outline, we have had perforce to concentrate a good deal of attention upon certain key works, certain turning-points. It has been necessary to subsume various works under categories; but we have sought, so far as in us lay, to avoid diversion from the thing itself, *wie es eigentlich gewesen*, and to avoid, also, being so absorbed with congeners that we ignore differences and distinctions. If, in places, we have seemed compelled to summary judgement, without being able to marshal all the evidence which had led us to our view, it is because of the limitations of time and space. Prolonged immersion in a subject inevitably leaves one with awarenesses, the evidence for which cannot be summed up on demand.

Although, as we have indicated, we think the critical approaches to Joan deserve more attention than they have sometimes received, we shall not engage in any futile and ungenerous 'debunking' attempt to deprive her of her hard-earned and immortal laurels; we cannot doubt that she deserves her deathless fame. The world will always admire Joan of Arc, because it admires nothing so much as supreme courage; and the French people will always commemorate her because, as a soldier in humanity's war of liberation, she expressed their needs and underlying wishes. It is in order to accord her the reverence which is her due that each age has had to reshape her in accordance with its own ideal. She belongs to universal history, in the sense in which Lord Acton used that phrase when he said: 'by universal history I understand that which is distinct from the history of all countries, and is not a burden on the memory but an illumination of the soul.'

Most works on Joan display far more propensity for moral judgements than they do for the analysis of causes; they do not heed Quintilian's injunction, *Scribitur ad narrandum non ad probandum*, and still less Virgil's *Dulce est cognoscere rerum causas.* We shall be content to leave moral preference to the philosopher and the theologian; and at the same time, we shall remember, with Lytton Strachey, that

facts relating to the past, when they are collected without art, are compilations; and compilations, no doubt, may be useful, but they are no more history than butter, eggs, salt and herbs are an omelette.

History is concerned with facts seen in their varied concatenations with other facts; it is concerned with events seen against the background of human motives, as well as of more impersonal forces.

While, however, we retain our modern analysis of cause and effect, we must make the effort of the historical imagination required to enter into the spirit of the age of Joan of Arc, and of later periods which we shall consider. We must, temporarily, unlearn all that we know of modern politics, war, cosmography, in order to enter into the atmosphere of the fifteenth century. 'The historian must alternately contract his horizon and widen it.'[1] So many values of Joan's age—moral attitudes, feudal class-distinctions, attitudes to witchcraft and visions—appear to us ever increasingly remote!

It is not possible to discuss intellectual history merely in terms of the influence of one idea upon another. History is made by men and groups of men, not by abstract ideas; ideas influence them in the making of it, and out of their experiences and conditions of life emerge new ideas. No idea, therefore, can be fully explained apart from its historical meaning, its place in a setting. Ideas have social causes, are used as social instruments, and also reflect social phenomena directly. To place them in a social setting clarifies their meaning; it does not explain them away. The various specialists have sunk their exploratory shafts; the intellectual historian seeks to find perspective by linking these shafts together to form a gallery.

Our ultimate task, then, is nothing less than an intellectual and spiritual biography of the modern world, in terms of its treatment of Joan of Arc. We must cut a road through five centuries of intellectual history. Such tasks have been too long neglected; and

[1] Anatole France, *op. cit.*, I, lxviii.

they will always have to be done anew. 'One barber shaves not so close but another finds work.'

What are the values which a study such as this seeks to realize? In the first place, it deals with a material that is fascinating in itself. We must not allow familiarity to obscure to us the unique and amazing character of the story of Joan of Arc. It is a strange, romantic, half-incredible tale—wholly incredible in many of its versions! The 'facts', in so far as we can ascertain them, are more remarkable than the legends that have overlaid and obscured them; and their minute study in every detail through hundreds of volumes reflects the truth that this is a series of events without exact counterpart in human history. As T. Douglas Murray[1] says, Joan accomplished 'in short months . . . more than Alexander and Caesar accomplished in so much time, and at an age when even Alexander had as yet achieved nothing'. No wonder that the marvel echoes down the centuries, of this career so comet-like in its brilliance and in its fiery extinction!

There is a perennial morning freshness about the tale of the simple peasant maid who became a leader of armies, at home in the feudal pomp of camp and court, the central figure in the gorgeous ceremonial of a coronation, and who then, caught in the maelstrom of war and high politics, after a grimly spectacular trial, was burned as a witch; it is a record touched with the splendours of courage and genius and faith, the lights of high romance, the stark outlines of tragedy. It is stranger than any poet's fancy in its dramatic confrontations, its heroes and its villainies, its historical significance, its appeal to our sympathies, its overture of idyllic simplicity, its background of the occult, the supernatural, and the mysterious, visions and voices apparently not of this earth, strange, dark, lurking spectres of mediaeval witchcraft.

---

[1] T. Douglas Murray, *Jeanne d'Arc, Maid of Orleans, Deliverer of France* (New York, 1902), p. viii. [Hereafter cited as 'T. D. Murray'—an incomplete, but accessible version of the Rehabilitation Proceedings is available here.] It is true that Charles XII of Sweden defeated Denmark and Russia at eighteen; but he was a prince, trained for political and military leadership, whereas Joan was an unlettered village maiden, however quick her apprehension, and however intuitive her genius.

The more we study Joan, the more, in some respects, does she become an enigma. She has the charm of an enigma, of a sphinx whose riddle many of the greatest minds of more than five centuries have tried to read. The famous smile which crossed her face as she made her mark upon her paper of abjuration is like the smile of the Mona Lisa in Leonardo's painting—to some it is a sneer, to others the vacuum of an exhausted and vacant mind, to yet others, eternal wisdom. Each artist, poet and scholar has tried his turn at fathoming its depth of meaning.

The copious proceedings of the original trial and Rehabilitation provide us with that abundance of detail which lends such interest to the whole story. Few historical source-materials there are which develop such an intensity of psychological conflict; says Henri Blaze de Bury:[1]

> Ce chapitre, disons mieux, ce livre des interrogatoires, vous passionne comme le plus beau drame; on se sent ému ,enlevé à chacune de ces ripostes qui partent fulgurantes au choc de la question.

Aside from the interest of the sources, a subject whose raw material comprises so many masterpieces has its own obvious attractions! It is alive with the effort of many minds to solve problems which are fundamental in man's struggle for awareness of himself and his world; for the history of the Maid of France raises the basic scientific and philosophical problems. If some have thought it a dry or a sentimental tale, that is because their impressions were formed from dull and inaccurate textbooks, mawkish religious tracts, or patriotic allocutions—of which there has been an infinite number.

If the original history itself be ceaselessly interesting—often told, and yet, in a sense, a story that has not yet been told—the history of the contradictory judgements which have been passed upon Joan is one no less curious and moving than the story of her life. With the development of psychology and the social sciences, we have new instruments with which to explore both these histories; and each has a special meaning for our time, distracted as it is by ideological conflicts as violent as ever were those of

[1] Baron Henri Blaze de Bury, *Jeanne d'Arc* (Paris, 1890), p. 372.

Armagnac and Burgundian. Each has a special meaning for France, which in our day again has experienced foreign invasion, a threat to national survival, a collaborationism which misused Joan's name, a 'resistance movement', a crusade of liberation and a national rebirth which were inspired by the memory of her.

In the course of this study the writer's view of Joan of Arc will emerge, at least in shadowy outline, from his comments upon her varied treatment by others. As one watches the evidence sifted and resifted, one's convictions on moot points take form and a new biography writes itself in one's mind. Our understanding of Joan is enriched as we see her from many different angles; the truth probably is that Joan was a complex personality, and that, more or less, all the different Joans can be found in her, just as all can be sustained from the 'sources'. The various writers who have discussed her resemble the seven blind savants of Hindustan, each of whom grasped a part of the elephant, and gave a different description of it; each description of Joan, each theory about her grasps some element of the truth. Were she to return to earth and meet a gathering of the scholars and artists who have discussed her, doubtless each would find in her what he was seeking, and would say that he was not surprised. Certainly, contemporary comment anticipated all later views—witch, virago, genius, warrior, camp-follower, impostor, puppet, saint, myth, saviour of France, sold and betrayed for thirty pieces of silver—she was all of these things, and more, in the chroniclers and poets of the fifteenth century, and the later views of her can all be traced to these fountainheads.

As we survey the 'Joan literature', we are reassured to find that, though the reputations of men and books fluctuate, and, in our own day, ephemeral reputations are made or broken by 'high-powered publicity', those works which have been accorded the most 'long-run' prestige, seem generally to us to deserve it— even when, as in the case of Voltaire's *Pucelle*, they have been in eclipse for a period.

Their lasting and deserved reputations have, in the case of historians, usually been earned as much by their success in clearing away outmoded and useless lumber, as by any striking new discovery. The historian is often an angel with a flaming sword, who comes not to fulfil but to destroy—or to fulfil by destroying. He sweeps away legends that have come to stand in the path of human advance, even though once they have been useful. As Benedetto Croce indicated, with Hegelian insight into the interaction of all aspects of a time, men construct a history that they can use; and we may add that this involves the elimination of forms no longer useful. So the Renaissance historians, and those of the Enlightenment, sought to destroy the mediaeval myth about Joan of Arc; the French Republicans sought to destroy the myth of the Monarchists; some English and some German historians, as well as some internationalists, have sought to destroy the French nationalist myth. With this destruction, creation goes hand in hand. 'It is desire that creates life, and the future is careful to realize the dreams of philosophers.'[1]

'But of what use will my book be when it is finished?' asked James Boswell, of Dr Johnson; to which the Great Cham replied, with characteristic testiness: 'Never mind the use. Do it!' Yet the question arises. History, of course, has its interest, which is its own excuse for being; and it has primary value in giving us perspective upon the events of our own time, and understanding of the relationships between events in the world of economics and politics, and events in the world of ideas. A study such as this may hope for an especial value in that it may develop a certain saving scepticism, a modesty which will not assume that our own truth is absolute when we have seen that others' truth is so extremely relative. As we learn how men have manipulated historical events in the past in most various ways, to suit their purposes, we may be put on our guard, and become less susceptible to future propaganda campaigns couched in historical terms, and more aware of the arduousness and subtlety of the historian's research. Our minds may be thus liberated from prejudice and dogma and doctrinaire approaches.

The process may be a painful one. 'We are covetous enough

---

[1] Anatole France, *op. cit.*, I, lxvii.

4. JOAN OF ARC: HER APPEAL TO THE DAUPHIN by M. Boutet de Monvel

(*W. A. Clark Collection*)

5. JOAN OF ARC: THE TURMOIL OF CONFLICT By M. Boutet de Monvel
(W. W. Clark Collection)

PROLOGUE

of such knowledge as may furnish weapons to our hand or tongue; as may serve our vanity or gratify our craving for power; but self-knowledge, the criticism of our own appetites and prejudices, is unwelcome and disagreeable to us,' says Amiel.[1] Disagreeable, perhaps, but extremely salutary. It is most valuable to us to realize how much all human observation depends upon the observer, his unarticulated values or prejudices. An open mind, tinctured with Humeian scepticism, is not a tactic to elude social pressure; it is one of the first qualifications of the historian, and, in its full development, is the ripe fruit of a lifetime of historical study.

We see, then, that there are no final value-judgements of time or history, but always new judgements, reflecting new conditions surrounding those who do the judging. Even the rebels are shaped by the age against which they rebel. *Primum vivere, deinde philosophari.* Life's necessities form the mould of thought. How intimately, indeed, are all aspects of the culture of any period linked together by a thousand ties! We cannot envisage Voltaire's *Pucelle*[2] except as an eighteenth-century Minerva, from one of the magnificent Gobelins at Versailles, armed cap-à-pie in plumed helmet of pseudo-antique design, and long cuirass to match. As for Lebrun des Charmettes,[3] his beauteous heroine is skirted to the ground, a belle of the Restoration. And so it is with all the others. That most astute of art historians, Émile Mâle, expressed this truth in generalized form with his usual felicity:

Au fond la moindre ligne est d'essence spirituelle; le jet d'une draperie, le contour qui cerne une figure, le jeu des lumières et des ombres peuvent nous révéler la sensibilité d'une époque tout aussi clairement que le sujet d'un tableau.[4]

It is because of this that the beauties and the ideas of another age

[1] *Amiel's Journal: The Journal Intime of Henri-Frédéric Amiel.* Translated by Mrs. Humphrey Ward (A. L. Burt Company, n.d.) P. 305 (Feb. 6, 1877).

[2] François Marie Arouet de Voltaire, *La Pucelle d'Orléans, passim* (Paris, 1832; *nouvelle édition*).

[3] Philippe Alexandre Lebrun des Charmettes, *Histoire de Jeanne d'Arc, surnommée la Pucelle d'Orleans, tirée de ses propres déclarations, de cent quarante-quatre dépositions, de témoins oculaires, et des manuscrits de la Bibliothèque du roi et de la Tour de Londres* (Paris, 1817), *passim.*

[4] Emile Mâle, *L'Art Religieux de la Fin du Moyen Age en France* (Paris, 1908), p. vii.

C

33

are often so strangely dead, though, if they have in them sufficient of life and style, they may transcend their own time, and break through to a more universal significance, while retaining their local garb of time and place.

Great historical figures live in the minds of the peoples, however, in a state of constant transformation, always being clothed in new thought and new sentiment. Books about them which do not suitably revise their attire of feeling and passion, are not likely to be written, or published, or widely and significantly read. So historians must recognize that the 'facts' are indeed dumb, and will not speak for themselves; historians can make history, using documents, in a manner almost analogous to that in which judges, as modern students of jurisprudence have taught us to see, make law, using legal precedents.

'What is truth?' said jesting Pilate, and, no doubt wisely, he did not stay for an answer. It is surely elusive! Perhaps there is no final truth, but only truths, a different one for each generation, for each angle of vision within it. The prisms of our minds refract truth into a thousand lustres. Even the canonization did not settle the affairs of Joan of Arc, save for devout Roman Catholics, and to judge by the works of Raymond de Rigné,[1] these are not settled in opinion about her, aside from a formal façade of agreement. Historians continue to engage in their elaborate quarrels, major and minor, concerning her; it is probably true that what we call historical perspective is at least partly an illusion, produced by the fog of years, and the indifference of the lay public. We never expect to agree about the events of our own time; of course, in some ways we know less about them, if in other ways so much more, than we do about events distant in time; and our passions are more directly involved. But it is impossible to think that these contemporary controversies are all finally settled by the historian. As Jacoby says:[2]

---

[1] R. de Rigné, *Jehanne d'Arc, Héroine du Droit; La vraye istoire de Jehanne-la-pucelle* (Paris, 1929), *passim*.

[2] J. Jacoby, 'Jeanne d'Arc a-t-elle été trahie?' *Revue de France*, February 1935, *Année* 15 I, 3, 445.

PROLOGUE

On a souvent parlé du tribunal de l'histoire; figure de mauvais rhétorique, car l'histoire est un procès en continuelle révision.

As long as men continue divided in belief, there will be, not a history of Joan, but histories; she cannot possibly appear the same, for instance, to a French Roman Catholic and a French *libre-penseur*. Many of the great societies, institutions and associations with which Joan was involved—England, France, the Church—remain very much alive, and so the dust of controversy concerning her cannot even begin to settle. But, all institutions aside, men will always be explaining her in new ways.

II

LA PITIÉ QUI ESTOIT
EN ROYAUME DE FRANCE

In the arresting phrase which heads this page,[1] Joan of Arc, at her trial, described the state of France in her time, the condition which formed the background of her career and its main motivating force. In 1429, when she so suddenly moved to the forefront of the historical stage, France was in a state of utter devastation and distraction; the Hundred Years' War with England had been in progress, with intervals of quiet, for almost a century, and it had been conducted entirely on the soil of France.

It was, in reality, that most destructive and terrible form of war, a civil war. England, the smaller, less wealthy and populous of the two countries, was able to wage aggressive war against France only because of that country's internal divisions, and in particular because of the power and self-assertiveness, vis-à-vis the Crown, of the great French feudatory princes.

In 1429, the national cause centred on the dauphin Charles, who was supported by the interest of the Duke of Orleans, and who held most of France south of the Loire; his followers were called Armagnacs, after the county of Armagnac in the south of France. Leading the opposition to him was the powerful Duke of Burgundy, Philip the Good, who controlled most of the north and east of France, including the rich cloth towns and trading centres of the Low Countries, and who was yoked in a somewhat

[1] Jules Etienne Joseph Quicherat, *Procès de Condemnation et de Réhabilitation de Jeanne d'Arc, dite la Pucelle: Publiés pour la première fois d'après les manuscrits de la Bibliothèque royale, suivis de tous les documents historiques qu'on a pu réunir et accompagnés de notes et d'éclaircissements*, 5 vols. (Paris, 1841–1849), I, 170. [Hereafter cited as '*Procès*'.]

uneasy alliance with the English foeman of his *soi-disant* liege lord, the dauphin Charles, who claimed the style and title of King of France.

All Gaul, then, was divided into the two parts, Armagnac and Burgundian; and the reaction to Joan of Arc's meteoric career was divided strictly upon these party lines. To Armagnacs generally, she was a saint of God, sent to bring about the coronation of the lawful heir to the throne in the cathedral at Rheims. Burgundians were equally sure that she was the child of the Devil, a witch, or at best a brazen impostor, doing the Devil's work by aiding the vicious and cruel Armagnacs, the ravishers of France and treacherous murderers of John the Fearless, father and predecessor to Duke Philip, upon the bridge at Montereau. As for Charles, they looked upon him as a worthless fellow, bastard son of an infamous mother, Isabel of Bavaria, conceived during one of the worst fits of insanity of his mad 'father', King Charles VI, and having, therefore, no true hereditary title to the throne he sought to seize.

In view of this state of opinion, we are not surprised to find that contemporary French chroniclers of Joan's career fall as sharply into two camps as did contemporary opinion generally. Foreign chroniclers, mainly Italian and German, are more detached; as Beckmann says, about one-third of all the chroniclers believe in Joan, another third deny her, and the remaining third is in doubt.[1] In this and succeeding chapters, we propose to consider these chroniclers, and other fifteenth-century discussions of Joan. In addition to the original record of her famous trial and Rehabilitation,[2] certain official contemporary records, account books, and the nine letters of her dictation which have come down to us, the contemporary chronicles are, of course, the sources upon which all later accounts of her are based.

The chronicles of the Armagnac party, of the period 1430–70, all, needless to say, favourable to the Maid, are, after the record of

---

[1] P. Beckmann, *Forschungen über die Quellen zur Geschichte der Jungfrau von Orleans* (Paderborn, 1872).

[2] *Infra*, Chapter VI.

the trial and Rehabilitation, the sources chiefly relied upon by modern historians of Joan of Arc, although, in spite of all the research which has been devoted to Joan, they have, perhaps, never been analytically studied as fully as they deserve; and there are many differences of opinion about their dates, origins, probable sources of information, and relative values. Some of these differences are not without their basic significance for the whole approach to the subject. The study still invites the hand of some thorough scholar, of the quality of M. Pierre Champion, who, according to report, proposed to devote himself to the task. It calls for scholarship of the type that 'higher critics' have lavished on the Gospels.

The student who approaches these documents for the first time cannot but be immediately struck by their confusions and contradictions. Almost every detail of an event so much discussed in them as the siege of Orleans, for instance, is beset with dispute and controversy; in despair, one is tempted to conclude that history, so far from being an exact science, is indeed, as Voltaire said, *une fable convenue*. Even of the lilies, Annunciation, et cetera, on Joan's banner, we have surprisingly varied accounts.[1] We can understand the plight of the unfortunate Abbé Vertot, who, Ireland tells us, 'wrote the siege himself' because he found the chronicles so confused.[2]

Joan moves through the chronicles of her own party, moreover, surrounded from the beginning by a kind of nimbus of miraculous happenings, like the cloud of white butterflies which some thought they saw fluttering about her standard.[3] In the Burgundian chronicles, on the other hand, this nimbus becomes a sinister penumbra of suggestions about witchcraft.

Even when friendly, the chroniclers often give scant details of Joan's life; to them, she is only one of the actors in a great drama. The chroniclers of the period were often paid chroniclers, one of

[1] *Cf.* T. D. Murray, p. 31.

[2] William Henry Ireland, *Memoirs of Jeanne d'Arc, Surnamed la Pucelle d'Orleans; with a History of Her Times* (London, 1824), I, 232.

[3] Anatole France, *op. cit.*, I, 477. 'Behold her,' says M. Anatole France, 'from the first and perhaps forever, enclosed in a flowering thicket of legends'.

them attached to every great baron, as in the case, which we discuss below, of Perceval de Cagny, or of Guillaume Gruel; so we find one Tringant saying that his master did not spent any money in order to obtain mention in the chronicles, and, therefore, was omitted from them.[1]

The chronicles do contain much vivid detail of the time, lovingly recorded; they give us its very flavour, as when, in recording the role at the siege of Orleans of the primitive cannon then in existence, they bring home to us their exciting charm of novelty. But Joan, herself, in the *Urkunde*, is already a plaster saint very different from the proud, bold, gay, saucy, sometimes even impudent *gamine de France*, whom we glimpse in the trial report. There is no effort to understand her, or to make her intelligible or credible; she stands forth suddenly in her full armour, like Minerva from the head of Jove. One moment she is romanticized as an humble and simple shepherdess, and the next, full of courage and high emprise, she is a *pucelle* 'of such high chivalry that there was no knight in Christendom whose fame overshadowed hers'. No wonder her more romantic, idolatrous and hagiographical historians have found in these chronicles a mine of material, and are ready to say with Mrs Florence Caddy, one of the many English ladies who have devoted their talents to this subject:[2]

> There is wide variation among the different historians in matters of detail, but all the old chroniclers agree right well as to the principal facts. The chain of evidence is splendid.

To a more sceptical student, it will seem that these materials, as dubious as they are copious, must be used with the greatest caution. If we did not have the trial, and had only these, Joan of Arc would be indeed a vague, half-legendary figure. It is true that even a liar may speak the truth now and then, but it is hard to know when he does so. The modern worship of 'original sources' may easily lead us to overrate the value of chronicle evidence; there is truth in the dictum of Plutarch:

---

[1] Fabre and Lecestre (editors), *Le Jouvencel*, II, 283.
[2] Mrs Florence Caddy, *Footsteps of Jeanne d'Arc; A Pilgrimage* (London, 1886), p. 221.

The contemporary records of any actions and lives, partly through envy and ill-will, partly through favour and flattery, pervert and distort truth.

The earliest of the Joan of Arc chroniclers is apparently Perceval de Cagny, whose work, which dates from 1436, was brought to light by Jules Quicherat, the greatest of the Joan of Arc scholars,[1] who never wrote a biography of Joan, but expressed his views on the more controversial points in his *Aperçus nouveaux*, published in 1850, after he had completed a careful editing of the sources in his huge five-volume *Procès de la condamnation et de la réhabilitation de Jeanne d'Arc* [1841-9]. Quicherat's views of the subject were heavily influenced by De Cagny, whom he found terse, but exact—the best informed, the most complete, the most sincere, and the earliest of the chroniclers of the Maid;[2] and as almost all the innumerable biographers of Joan in the late nineteenth century and since have followed Quicherat rather slavishly, the influence of De Cagny upon them has been tremendous. Even the judicious Sainte-Beuve accepted Cagny as *son historien le mieux informé*,[3] and the freethinking Fabre also esteemed highly his care for historical truth.[4] His influence remains great, especially in the more orthodox and conservative treatments of the subject—clerical, French nationalist, or romantic.

Perceval de Cagny was master of the horse to the Duke of Alençon, one of the powerful princes of the blood royal of France, who was married to the daughter of the Duke of Orleans, the poet-duke who had been a captive in England since Agincourt. As Alençon's relationship with Joan was a close one, De Cagny is most favourable to the Maid. He was with the Alençon family forty-six years, and it would appear that he kept a journal. He does not know much about the Maid save when Alençon is involved. He was present at the coronation campaign, but after

---

[1] See Jules Quicherat, *Aperçus nouveaux sur l'histoire de Jeanne d'Arc* (Paris, 1850), p. 36 (hereafter cited as *Aperçus*).

[2] *Procès*, IV, 1 ff., (De Cagny).

[3] Charles Augustin de Sainte-Beuve, *Causeries du Lundi*, 'Procès de Jeanne d'Arc' (Paris, 1852-1885), II, 320.

[4] Joseph Fabre, *Jeanne d'Arc, libératrice de la France* (Paris, 1896), p. 266 (hereafter cited as *Libératrice*).

the autumn of 1429, when Alençon and Joan were separated, his chronicle becomes hearsay.

Doubtless Joan's close connection with Alençon, portrayed in the pages of Cagny, was only part of her generally close connection with the House of Orleans. So many of her associates— Rabateau, Boucher, the Bastard Dunois, her page Louis de Coutes, as well as Alençon—were associated with that House. Joan felt deeply the cause of the captive Duke, whose city of Orleans was being so unchivalrously attacked by the English;[1] and she considered his release from captivity, as well as the rescue of his beleaguered city, to be part of her mission.[2] Like Charles VII, he was to her a symbol of France. She wore the livery of Orleans, as a costly gift from the Duke—a *huque* or cloak of dark green, worn with a *lévite*, or long flowing sleeved mantle of fine crimson Brussels cloth lined with white satin, the whole worn over her armour. 'Thus they made of her,' says Anatole France, 'a kind of herald-at-arms or heraldic angel'.[3]

De Cagny directly attributes to Joan's friendship and good will for the Duke of Orleans, and to the fact that he was a part of her mission, her friendliness to his son-in-law, Alençon.[4] When he first met her, Alençon gave her a horse, because she won his heart by her gracious horsemanship and her handling of the lance. Many writers have attributed to Alençon the most chivalrously romantic sentiments towards her.[5] Alençon was certainly devoted to the Armagnac cause, the cause of the splendid ducal house into which he had married; after his capture at Verneuil, he had spent five years in captivity at Le Crotoy rather than accept liberty without ransom on condition that he desert that cause. Finally, he had secured his liberty, in 1427, by means of the pledge, with hostages for security, of a ransom of 200,000 *saluts d'or*; in order to raise it, even with royal help, he had sold lands, and become

---

[1] Andrew Lang, *The Maid of France, Being the Story of the Life and Death of Jeanne d'Arc* (London, 1908), p. 72.

[2] *Procès*, IV, 10 (De Cagny).

[3] Anatole France, *op. cit.*, I, 357.

[4] *Procès*, IV, 10 (De Cagny).

[5] See Michael Monahan, *op. cit.*, p. 101; Andrew Lang, *op. cit.*, p. 98; Percy Wallace Mackaye, *Jeanne d'Arc, a Drama* (New York, 1907), *passim*.

'the poorest man in France'. He was naturally of the 'forward' or war party, of which Joan was at least the figurehead, if not the leader. He was eager to recover estates in Normandy which were in the hands of the English. 'Faithful to France, having nothing to lose and everything to gain,' M. Pierre Champion describes him with his usual perspicacity.[1] That, at least, was his attitude in his youth, in the period prior to Joan's appearance.

De Cagny gives us a picture of the pleasant social relationship of Joan with the Duke and Duchess of Alençon, who made much of her; her standard was prepared, it would seem, in the course of a visit at their château of St Florent, near Saumur. Doubtless they aided tactfully in her tutelage for her place at court. At Jargeau, we have Joan telling the duke to advance, reminding him that she has promised the duchess to protect him:

'*En avant, gentil duc!*'
'*Ah! gentil duc, times-tu? Ne sais-tu pas que j'ai promis à la duchesse de te ramener sain et sauf?*'

On one occasion, she did save his life, by pointing to a cannon aimed at the spot where he stood; another man was killed on the same spot a moment later. Good understanding with the duchess, affectionate condescension to the duke; he is even represented as a sort of aide-de-camp to her, and her page, Louis de Coutes, testified at the Rehabilitation, 'Many times when the Duke of Alençon swore or blasphemed before her, I heard her reprove him'.[2] Albert Bigelow Paine cites her orders to Alençon, who was in nominal command, to advance to the assault at Meung, as proof that she was the real commander-in-chief.[3] De Cagny portrays her as sending messengers to each garrison to summon them: 'Surrender to the King of Heaven, and to the noble King Charles.' If they refused, she went in person against them. Our chronicler vividly portrays the enthusiasm she aroused. In his pages alone do we find her sole oath, 'Par mon martin,' referring to the baton she always carried; an oath she is said to have offered La Hire as a

[1] Barrett-Champion, p. 402.
[2] T. D. Murray, p. 264.
[3] A. B. Paine, *Joan of Arc* (New York, 1925), I, 213, note.

substitute for more violent expletives.[1] The *Journal du Bourgeois de Paris*, an unfriendly chronicle, tells us about the large baton which she carried, and with which she struck any who displeased her; but this detail would hardly fit with the saintly portrait De Cagny presents.

De Cagny's central theme is that the Maid performed miracles, and would have done more had she not been thwarted by the cowardice, sloth, weakness, stupidity, jealousy of the King and his council, especially its dominant figure, Georges de la Trémoïlle. It is primarily from De Cagny, and Quicherat following him, that this prevalent modern picture has been derived. French and American republican attitudes toward monarchy, English willingness to maximize French blame for Joan's misfortunes, and clerical desire to concentrate on secular factors in her woes, have doubtless all contributed, so we may conjecture, to the acceptance of De Cagny's thesis, which undoubtedly reflects the views of Alençon and the 'war party' at court. We do know from Joan's own letter to the city of Rheims that she viewed with mistrust the royal policy of truce with Burgundy after the coronation; and De Cagny is, so far, confirmed. Typical is his picture of Joan's distress because the King dallied at Compiègne, instead of attacking Paris at once:

> *Quaint le Roy se trouva audit lieu de Compiengne, la Pucelle fust moult marrie du séjour que il ly voulloit faire; et semblait a sa manière que il fust content à icelle heur de la grace que Dieu lui avoit faicte, sans autre chose entreprendre.[2]*

De Cagny is Quicherat's favourite source for the events of the unsuccessful attack on Paris, which De Cagny attributes to the frustration of the Maid's designs by hostile intrigues.[3] The army, according to him, had fallen to half its number, because of a wavering policy, and lack of supplies; the King prevented a promising renewal of the attack on Paris by breaking an essential bridge. There follows a disorderly and unnecessary retreat, with the

[1] *Procès*, IV, 4 n (De Cagny); *ibid.*, III, 206; *ibid.*, IV, 469.
[2] *Ibid.*, IV, 24 (De Cagny).
[3] *Ibid.*, IV, 24-28 (De Cagny).

Maid's prestige shattered; 'And thus was broken the will of the Maid, and the army of the King'.[1] It seems that at this time the Count of Clermont replaced Alençon as lieutenant-general; the commission was dated September 7, 1429.[2] Alençon presently planned a campaign in Normandy, and desired Joan's help in raising forces for this; he had previously suggested an attack on the English base in Normandy as preferable to the coronation campaign, and was continuously concerned with the recovery of his estates there. The Royal Council would not allow Joan to accompany him to Normandy;[3] De Cagny blames this on Gaucourt, Le Trémoïlle and Regnault de Chartres, the able, avaricious, clever and ruthless diplomatist who was Archbishop of Rheims.

It is from De Cagny that we learn that the failure of Joan at La Charité, in the winter of 1429–30, was owing to lack of supplies. His evidence on this, as we have seen, is only hearsay; and this is the case also with the famous 'flight from Sully', of which we are informed by De Cagny. He tells us that in March, 1430, when the King and court were at La Trémoïlle's château of Sully-sur-Loire:[4]

La Pucelle qui avoit veu et entendu tout le fait et la manière que le roy et son conseil tenoient pour le recouvrement de son royaulme, elle, très-mal contente de ce, trouva manière de soy départir d'avecques eulx; et sans le sceu du roy ne prendre congé de lui, elle fist semblant d'aler en aucun esbat, et sans retourner s'en ala à la ville de Laingni-sur-Marne . . .

There are grounds for supposing that this dramatic account is a legend, wishful thinking on the part of De Cagny. The King had every reason to wish to harass the enemy into renewed negotiations; two months later, we find Joan at Compiègne with ten or twelve thousand *écus* of the king's money, and she also spoke of

---

[1] *Procès*, IV, 29. The phrase is vivid enough in English to deserve translation.
[2] G. L. E. du Fresne, marquis de Beaucourt, *Histoire de Charles VII*, 6 Vol. (Paris, 1881–1891), II, 239.
[3] *Procès*, IV (De Cagny), 30; see also *Chronique de Berri, Procès*, IV, 48.
[4] *Ibid.*, IV, 32 (De Cagny).

asking supplies of him.[1] Surely this indicates his approval of her expedition!

In fact, De Cagny's whole account represents the differences which undoubtedly existed between La Trémoïlle and Alençon in a manner most unfavourable to La Trémoïlle, and to the King. We must recall that the late-mediaeval monarch was the rallying point of the common people, especially the town-dwelling middle class, in their struggle to find prosperity and security from feudal oppression under a strong government. The King usually had good reason to be jealous of 'overmighty subjects' and he inevitably preferred, as more reliable, officials of less exalted birth. Charles VII certainly had cause to mistrust powerful princes, like Richemont, and Brittany, and Burgundy, and Alençon, who was a nephew of Richemont and Brittany;[2] apparently, he found La Tremoïlle, who was of somewhat lower rank, more dependable. Charles VII's long and successful reign proves that he was no fool. Was there not some reason in public policy to detach Joan of Arc, so influential with the people, from Alençon, who may have swayed her greatly while humouring her claims? Joan's unwavering loyalty to Charles VII at her trial shows clearly that her attitude to her King was not De Cagny's, nor that of Alençon as later revealed.

A consideration of Alençon's later history will discount the heroic Sir Galahad image of him usually presented in accounts of Joan of Arc, and will show him in his true, fully formed character, as a typically insubordinate, rebellious, adventurous feudal noble, turbulent, jealous, violent and fiery, contemptuous in his attitude towards the King, useful to the royal and national cause only if kept under firm control. He seems to have dabbled in witchcraft, and was rather credulous, vain and flighty. In 1429 he was still in his graceful youth, but De Cagny reflects his outlook at a somewhat later period (1436), the date the chronicle was completed.

---

[1] W. P. Barrett, *The Trial of Jeanne d'Arc* (London, 1931 edition, English translation, hereafter cited as 'Barrett'), pp. 96, 204. Barrett has been cited repeatedly in this work as a reliable, and much the most easily accessible, version of the Trial Record. On the point here in question, see also A. B. Paine, *Joan, op. cit.*, II, 29–30; also note, p. 336.

[2] Francis Cabot Lowell III, *Joan of Arc* (Boston, 1896), p. 118.

He was to live to be tried twice for treason and to be charged with seeking 'powders to dry up the king.'[1] In 1440, along with the Duke of Bourbon, the Count of Vendôme and even the Count Dunois, Bastard of Orléans, Alençon, Joan's 'beau duc', was one of the leaders of the fierce feudal revolt against Charles VII, called the *Praguerie*, in which self-seeking nobles waged ardent war against the Crown, at a time when the struggle with England was still going on. In 1442, Burgundy, Orléans, Alençon, and Bourbon tried again to seize the government and restore 'the old regime of pension, plunder and privilege';[2] they resented, not merely the position in the government of Anjou and constable Richemont, whom the King had been able to detach from the feudal party, but also they resented even more the growing role of the middle class, and of the royalist official bureaucracy of humbler rank—men such as Des Ursins, Brézé, and the banker, Jacques Coeur. Alençon was condemned to death, after a secret correspondence with the English was discovered. Finally his sentence was commuted to life imprisonment, and for some time he was confined in a tower of the Louvre.[3] In short, his later record does not incline us to accept his estimates of affairs at court, nor those of his henchman, Perceval de Cagny. The twenty-seven chapters of a few lines each which De Cagny devotes to the Maid are, moreover, often very vague and unreliable, especially on military matters; and perhaps the best that can be said for this chronicle is that, whatever its weaknesses, those of the other Armagnac chronicles are even more glaring. All of them belong to hagiography more than to history.

Certainly this is true of the ostentatiously titled *Chronique de la Pucelle* which once was regarded as the earliest and best of these chronicles, but is now dated after 1467. It was first printed by Denis Godefroy in 1661;[4]

[1] A. France, *op. cit.*, I, xii, 183, 185; Jules Michelet, *Histoire de France*, (Paris, 1846), V, 382; Dupuy, *Procès de Jean II, duc d'Alençon, 1458–1474*, (Paris, pub. 1658 in 4to).

[2] Lowell, *op. cit.*, p. 363.

[3] A. B. Paine, *Joan, op. cit.*, II, 323.

[4] Denis Godefroy (*historiographe de France*), *L'histoire du Roi Charles VII contenant les choses memorables de 1422 à 1466* (Paris, 1661).

LA PITIÉ QUI ESTOIT EN ROYAUME

Buchon,[1] Petitot[2] and Quicherat[3] reprinted it, and Michelet[4] used it. Vallet de Viriville[5] brought out a scholarly edition in 1859.

Viriville, who attributed great value to the *Chronique*, thought it the work of Guillaume Cousinot of Montreuil (an important figure in the defence of Orleans, and chancellor to the Duke of Orleans) and his son (some say his nephew) of the same name; the original core was the work of the father; the *Chronique dit de la Pucelle* was produced by the son, with additions to and subtractions from the father's work, and thus a general chronicle, containing the work of both, was elaborated.[6] Quicherat had already argued it was a hybrid product, and had traced part of it back to the *Gestes des nobles françoys . . . (MS.* 10297 Bib. nat.)[7] a history which has been attributed to the elder Cousinot; it commences its tale with Priam of Troy. More recent study has cast doubt on the authorship of the *Chronique de la Pucelle* by the Cousinots,[8] and has tended to show it to be largely derivative, from the Rehabilitation testimony, Jean Chartier, and the *Journal du Siège*.[9] Samaran, by printing the Chronicle in parallel columns alongside its sources, demonstrates conclusively that the work is a hodgepodge.

This Chronicle, in fact, is contradictory, repetitive, and it ends abruptly with the King's return to the Loire valley after his defeat at Paris. 'En nom Dieu' replaces 'Par mon martin' as Joan's favourite exclamation here; the change is indicative of a piety of tone which has made this source a favourite with clerical histor-

[1] J. A. Buchon, *Collection des Chroniques nationales françaises* (Paris, 1827), (*tome XXXIV*) *Chronique et procès de la Pucelle d'Orléans.*

[2] Claude B. Petitot, *Mémoires concernant la Pucelle d'Orléans, dans lesquels se trouvent plusieurs particularités du règne de Charles VII* (*Collection complète des mémoires relatifs à l'histoire de France . . . Sér le tome* 8) (Paris, 1819), etc., 8vo.

[3] *Procès*, IV, 203 ff. (*Chronique*).

[4] Michelet, *op. cit., passim.*

[5] A. Vallet de Viriville, *Professeur adjoint à l'École des Chartes*, member of the society of Antiquaries of France: *éd., Chronique de la Pucelle, ou Chronique de Cousinot* (Paris, 1859, 16mo.), *Bibliothèque Gauloise.*

[6] *Ibid.*, p. 4.

[7] *Procès*, IV, 203–4 (*Chronique*).

[8] Anatole France, *op. cit.*, I, xiv; see also Beckmann, *op. cit.*

[9] Charles Samaran, 'La Chronique de la Pucelle,' *Ann. Bulletin de la Société de l'Histoire de France* (Paris, 1926), p. 194.

47

ians. The conscientious, somewhat pedestrian M. Wallon follows it closely,[1] and Father Ayroles regards it with enthusiasm.[2] From this chronicle are derived many of the quaint stories traditional with biographers, such as the anecdote of the English soldiers disguising themselves in priestly robes before capture during the siege of Orleans, and thus saving their lives, thanks to the good-natured intervention of the Maid.[3] The chronicle is generally, however, fiercely chauvinist in its attitude toward the English; it tells us that Glasdale had threatened to kill every man, woman and child in Orleans, and that whereas, before the Maid came, two hundred Englishmen used to chase five hundred Frenchmen, after her coming two hundred Frenchmen used to chase four hundred English.[4]

This chronicle contains the report of the conversation with Dunois[5] in which the Maid indicates that her mission is accomplished, and that she wishes to go home, although she implies, as Quicherat points out, that God will not let her return home.[6] The *Journal du Siège* has the same tale, which is perhaps copied by the author of *Chronique de la Pucelle* from this source. This story of her divine mission being accomplished at the coronation was formerly generally accepted, and it afforded a convenient excuse for the Maid's later failures. Villaret,[7] followed blindly by many other writers, for several centuries to come, transposed the conversation to Rheims, with Charles VII and Dunois the parties to it, with the Maid asking release and Charles refusing; we can see that the onus of later disasters is thus placed squarely on the shoulders of that unfortunate and long-suffering monarch. But Dunois' own account of her conversation with him says nothing of her mission being accomplished,[8] and we may believe this idea

---

[1] Henri Wallon, *Jeanne d'Arc* (Fermin-Didot, Paris, 1876; hereafter cited as 'Wallon'), *passim.*

[2] J. B. J. Ayroles, *La Pucelle devant l'Eglise de son temps* (Paris, 1890), xvi.

[3] *Procès*, IV, 224, (*Chronique*).

[4] *Ibid.*, IV, 221 (*Chronique*).

[5] *Ibid.*, III, 4 (Rehabilitation testimony).

[6] Quicherat, *Aperçus*, pp. 37 ff.

[7] M. Villaret, *Histoire de France* (Paris, 1764), *tome XIV.*

[8] *Procès*, III, 14 (Rehabilitation testimony).

6. JOAN OF ARC ON HORSEBACK. Equestrian statue by Anna Hyatt
Huntington
(*From the Bettmann Archive*)

7. JOAN OF ARC AND STANDARD. Contemporary drawing from the
Register of Clément de Fauquembergue, Notary of the Parlement
of Paris
(*Bettmann Archive*)

to be a later interpolation; the Chronicle presumably draws the conversation, directly or indirectly, from the Rehabilitation testimony, and distorts it in so doing. Actually, Joan's mission was only half accomplished at the time of her death; it included not only the relief of Orleans, and the coronation of the King, but also the liberation of the Duke of Orleans, and the expulsion of the English from France.[1] Quicherat conclusively established this (see *Aperçus*, cited above) though the contrary view is still occasionally encountered in more sentimental narratives. Beyond that, she had ambitious plans for a crusade. One cannot believe that she would ever willingly have gone home to her native village and turned her back on the 'pride, pomp and panoply of glorious war', her very element. We know that she had leased a house in Orleans, which doubtless she intended as her head-quarters. Less than a month before her death, she said she would take woman's dress when her mission was fulfilled 'ce pourquoy je suis envoyée de par Dieu'.[2] The date of fulfilment, we may well surmise, was adjourned to the Greek kalends. It is not psycho-logically credible that she wished to give up her immensely exciting career, however longingly she may have spoken occasion-ally in some mood of nostalgia, of a return to the sheep and cattle of her native village

The *Chronicle* of Jean Chartier[3] was compiled in the decade 1440–50, and published, apparently, in 1449, before the Re-habilitation. Chartier, precentor of St Denis, had been appointed by Charles VII to be chronicler to the Kings of France—not 'historiographer royal' as Andrew Lang thought, for that title only comes into existence a century later. Chartier's chronicle undoubtedly reflects court opinion, and we can trace in it evidence of the great embarrassment to the Crown of France which was caused by the burning of Joan as a heretic and witch—evidence which leads us to believe, despite all the historians' diatribes

---

[1] *Procès*, III, 99, 205—for more limited and less adequate accounts of her mission, also in the Rehabilitation testimony, see III, 20, 74, 115.
[2] *Ibid.*, I, 394 (Trial).
[3] *Ibid.*, IV, 51 ff. (Chartier).
[4] Lang, *op. cit.*, p. 346.

against his faithlessness, that Charles VII would have prevented the burning if he could have done so. Although he has little to say about events after September, 1429, Chartier is most anxious to state[1] that Joan was burned without trial. What can he mean? Can he mean that she was burned without formal secular sentence by the *Bailli* of Rouen? This is, after all, a merely technical point. Her ecclesiastical trial was prolonged for months before a tribunal of theologians as august as any that could have been assembled in Christendom. Her burning was, he says, cruelly done, seeing the life and rule she lived, for every week she confessed and received the body of our Lord, as beseemeth a good Catholic. The English are thus reproached for burning 'a good Catholic' without semblance of justice.

Chartier thinks Joan lost her magical powers by breaking St Katherine's sword over the back of a prostitute—an event which he places at Auxerre,[2] although Alençon, an eyewitness, says it occurred at St Denis. He credits Joan with an important share in the military victories with which she was associated, and with a causal role in regard to the coronation campaign; the royal army at Gien was 'formed by the counsel of the said Maid'. Obviously, by the time he wrote, her legend had had time to grow.

Chartier is frank about the futility of various royal advisers, who by 1449 were mostly dead or out of office, and without friends at court. He says that the captains and army leaders were very angry at La Trémoïlle and others of the Royal Council on the occasion of the bargain for the surrender at Auxerre.[4] This may well be true, but we may remark, parenthetically, that the resentment of young hotheads in the army, or even of the sainted Maid, does not prove that the suave diplomacy of the Council was either traitorous or unwise—even though it has exposed the long-deceased advisers of Charles VII to a belated but murderous attack from Joan's modern historians.

[1] Jean Chartier, *Chronique de Charles VII, roi de France, nouv. éd., rev. sur les manuscrits, suivie de diverses fragments inédits, etc. par* Auguste Vallet de Viriville (Paris, 1858), I, 122.
[2] *Ibid.*, p. 122.
[3] *Ibid.*, p. 87, also p. 97.
[4] *Procès*, IV, 72 (Chartier).

Quicherat called Chartier a 'mauvais écrivain', noting his care-lessness about details; he gave the chronicler, however, credit for honest intentions, and regarded the *chronique* as the most circum-stantial that we have, on the subject of the 'coming' of the Maid.[1] Some recent criticism has tended to show that the chronicle is a poor copy of better sources; Anatole France, for instance, finds Chartier 'extremely weak-minded and trivial'.[2]

The *Journal du Siège d'Orléans et du Voyage de Reims* was printed in 1576 by Saturnin Hotot from a manuscript prepared 1468, or thereabouts, by notary Soubsdan (Soudan). The oldest copy dates from 1472 (*MS. fr.* 14665). Quicherat states, however, that the *Journal du Siège* is evidently copied from a register pre-pared in the presence of events[3] and this opinion has not been successfully challenged. The *Journal* remains, therefore, one of the better chronicle sources.

The *Journal*, a manuscript conserved in the archives of the city of Orleans, incorporated the Orleans tradition about the Maid. It formed a basic source for the celebrated *Mystère du Siège d'Orléans*, and for the *Chronique de la Pucelle*. It is full of vivid detail of the siege, giving us a description, for instance, of the new instruments of war which were used. Always a central figure is the miraculous Maid. The *Journal* gives us a wonderful picture of her entry into the city—the picture immortalized in Scherrer's famous painting.[4] We have here portrayed scenes of marvellous enthusiasm, of people carried away by fanaticism, no longer afraid of anything, drunk with religion and war; amazed always at Joan's courage and knightly skill, and ready to obey her without question. Here we have the image so dear always to the hearts of the people of Orleans, Joan's own city—the city which from 1429 almost un-

---

[1] *Procès*, IV, 51–2 (Chartier).

[2] Anatole France, *op. cit.*, I, xii.

[3] *Procès*, IV, 95 (*Journal*).

[4] J. J. Scherrer, *Entrée triomphale de Jehanne d'Arc dans Orléans* (Musée d'Orléans), reproduced in Abbé Albert Le Nordez, *Jeanne d'Arc racontée par l'image d'après les sculpteurs, les graveurs, et les peintres* (Paris, 1898; hereafter cited as 'Le Nordez'); facing p. 168; also in Boucher and Clarke, French edition of Andrew Lang, *Maid of France* (Paris, 1911), facing p. 144.

interruptedly to the present day has expressed grateful devotion to the memory of the heroine by a ceremony on each May 8th anniversary of its liberation from the English besiegers.

The *Journal* comes to an end with September, 1429; and the section after May 8th of that year is apparently drawn from Jean Chartier, the Herald of Berri, and the Rehabilitation proceedings. Material about Joan's career prior to the siege is unskilfully interpolated; alleged facts are occasionally cited which contradict the financial records of the town, and the miraculous tinge of the story testifies 'to an advanced stage of Jeanne's legend'.[1] The tale of Joan's miraculous prediction of the Battle of the Herrings it to be found here, and from this source, apparently, the *Chronique* and the *Mystère* borrowed it. The Abbé Dubois (1752–1824) who studied the siege of Orleans for many years, and summarized his conclusions in a manuscript work published in 1894,[2] at a time of growing interest in the subject, claimed that Soudan had omitted from the *Journal* all that might offend the captains who were in command of the city. This is a sweetened picture, not free from what Fabre called *un certain parti pris de froide idéalisation*.[3]

The *Chronicle* of Gilles le Bouvier, called the Herald of Berri, was formerly attributed to the court poet and secretary, Alain Chartier. Its author, King-of-arms of the province of Berri, was forty-three years old in 1429,[4] and his chronicle has, as we should expect, a certain judiciousness, though its chronology is confused and there are manifest errors. Quicherat thought quite highly of it,[5] but, as this chronicle covers the period from 1402 to the death of Charles VII, its account of Joan is more summary than that of some of the other chronicles, too lacking in detail to be of much real value. Its author is well-informed on military matters, and it is significant that he denies Joan much military role, even in the coronation campaign.[6]

[1] Anatole France, *op. cit.*, I, xiii.
[2] F. N. A. Dubois, *Histoire du siège d'Orléans* (Orléans, 1894).
[3] Fabre, *Libératrice*, p. 266.
[4] Anatole France, *op. cit.*, I, xi.
[5] *Procès*, IV, 40 ff. (Herald of Berri).
[6] *Loc. cit.* It is the Herald of Berri, with an eye for all that concerns heraldry, who gives us the interesting information that Joan's herald at Orleans was held in the English camp,

The 'Abbreviator of the Two Trials' composed (1500) on the command of King Louis XII, and on the instigation of Mallet de Graville, a summary narration drawn from various chronicles, from the record of the original trial, and from the Rehabilitation proceedings.[1] Here we find the first account of the miraculous revelation by Joan of the King's secret prayer—a revelation made as a sign to the King in a private interview with him. Here, also, we find an early reference to the betrayal of the King by Guillaume de Flavy. Both ideas are developed further in later chronicles, for instance Pierre Sala's *Hardiesses des grandes rois et empereurs* (1516), Alain Bouchard's *Croniques, l'Histoire et discours au vray du Siège*, (1621), the *Livre de la Pucelle natifve*, etc. (1581), the *Annales d'Aquitaine*[2] and Jacques Meyer's *Annales de Flandre*.[3]

The 'Abbreviator' gives John of Luxemburg the credit of long resisting proposals for the sale of the Maid, his captive, to the English:

'*À quoy icellui de Luxembourg ne voulloit entendre, et ne la voulloit la bailler à nulle fin.*'[4]

Alain Bouchard's *Les Grandes croniques de Bretagne*, an 'histoire un peu naïve', first printed in 1514, went through five editions before 1541.[5] Its author, advocate at the *parlement* of Rennes, the Breton capital, and counsellor to Francis I, composed his work from the ducal archives opened to him by the queen, awaiting the authority of the University of Paris to burn him, and that he was found later by the French in the camp, after the English had given up the siege of Orleans, and had withdrawn.

[1] Pierre Champion, *Guillaume de Flavy* (Paris, 1906), p. 285; *Procès*, IV, 254 ff.

[2] *Ibid.*, IV, 94, 255, 536 (*histoire, livre, Annales*).

[3] This sixteenth century work is not Burgundian, as might be expected from its place of origin; it follows Basin, and treats the Pucelle as the envoy of God. Meyer, however, follows Massaeus in saying that the Pucelle could beat the English but was never able to conquer the Burgundians; he is thinking of Compiègne, and her capture. *Ibid.*, IV, 350.

[4] *Ibid.*, IV, 262 (Abbreviator).

[5] Pierre Champion, *Guillaume de Flavy*, p. 283. Champion points out that the *Mirouer des femmes vertueuses* (*Procès*, IV, 267-276), very popular in its day, unites the Griselidis of Boccaccio with an extract regarding Joan of Arc, drawn from Bouchard. Its ideas influenced later writers, such as Belleforest, *Histoire des neuf Charles*, Nicolas Gilles, *Les Grandes annales et histoires generalles de France* (Paris, 1579), and Eudes de Mézerai, *Histoire de France* (Paris, 1685). In the seventeenth century, its story of betrayal became an accepted version of the tale of the Maid.

Anne of Brittany. It is a collection not yet studied as critically as it deserves. Its author apologizes for his French, on the ground that Breton and French are very different languages, and Breton is his mother tongue.

The *Relation of the Notary (Greffier) of la Rochelle*[1] is an extract made in the sixteenth century from the registers of the town hall of La Rochelle. The author also made use of other chronicles, particularly the *Chronique de la Pucelle*. It is noteworthy for the light it throws on Joan's sword with five crosses, found in the church of St Katherine of Fierbois. The *greffier* says it was found in a reliquary within the great altar, which had not been opened for twenty years or more;[2] this is more reasonable than the accounts of other chronicles, which state that it was buried in the earth. The sword was clearly one of the many votive offerings in the church; had it been in the earth long, it would have been eaten away by rust. Doubtless the sword matched some general description given by the Maid, who, by her own admission, had heard three masses at the Church of St Katherine,[3] though some of the chronicles deny she was there.

The *Chronicle of the City of Tournai* was formed from the official record of a city in which the common people, at least, were always faithful to the French Crown. It reiterates the opinion that the French captains, out of jealousy, conspired with the English to bring about the death of Joan.

With Thomas Basin, we move past the year 1470, in our glance at the source materials on Joan; but some facts may be gleaned even later than 1470, where the writer mentions good sources of information. Thomas Basin, Bishop of Lisieux, wrote a Latin history of the events of his time, when he was in exile at Trèves in 1471;[4] it covers the reign of Charles VII and carries us into that of his successor, Louis XI, towards whom Basin entertained an

---

[1] *Relation sur Jeanne d'Arc, extraite du livre noir de l'Hôtel de Ville de la Rochelle,* Orléans, 1879, edited by Jules Quicherat. See also, *Revue historique,* IV, p. 327 *et seq., Relation du Greffier de la Rochelle.*

[2] See Lang, *op. cit.,* p. 109.

[3] Barrett, pp. 71, 161.

[4] *Cf.* Marius Sepet, *Jeanne d'Arc* (Tours, 1891) p. 528.

enmity which caused him to treat Charles rather leniently.[1] Joan, to whom he devoted several chapters, he regarded with some reserve;[2] he dared not pronounce absolutely upon the value of her revelations, although he composed a memoir supporting her cause at the Rehabilitation. He did affirm absolutely Joan's sincerity, her belief in the visions which were her motive force in accomplishing that which was apparently impossible, and, thereby, winning deathless fame and glory.

Mathieu Thomassin, one of Louis XI's principal counsellors, devotes to Joan several pages of his *Registre Delphinal*, well stocked with miracles. This work is, of course, written from a point of view preoccupied with the affairs of Dauphiné, and Thomassin is our authority for the statement that the situation a the time of the siege of Orleans was so desperate that the royal council meditated a retreat to Dauphiné if Orleans fell.

A number of other Armagnac chronicles contain useful references; among them we may mention the *Chronicle concerning the deliverance of Orleans and the holiday May 8th*,[3] the *Chronicle of Mont-Saint-Michel*,[4] the *Chronicle of Lorraine*, and the *Chronicle of Arthur de Richemont*, by Guillaume Gruel.

The *Chronicle of Lorraine* dates from the reign of Charles VIII, and it has been suggested that it is derived from a poem;[5] at any rate, it is entirely fabulous. The story of Joan is transformed *en une sorte de chanson de geste ou de roman d'aventures*;[6] popular legends are mingled in it, and perhaps the memory of the false Pucelle. In this chronicle, the Duke of Lorraine arms Joan, and she engages in a tourney on the castle ground of Nancy. In truth, Joan, already the *egregia bellatrix* of Renaissance poetry, here performs all the great feats of arms that were accomplished in the whole long victorious reign of Charles VII; she takes Bordeaux, Bayonne, all the towns of Normandy save Rouen, and finally

---

[1] Lowell, *op. cit.*, p. 359.

[2] *Procès*, IV, 350 (*Basin*). Fortournai Chronicle, *ibid.*, IV, 301; V, 125.

[3] See Caxton Society Publications, (8) *Chronique du siège d'Orléans et de l'établissement de la fête du 8 mai 1429*. See also *Procès*, V, 285–99.

[4] *Chronique du Mont-Saint-Michel*, Siméon Luce edition (Paris, 1879–83).

[5] Marius Sepet, *op. cit.*, p. 529.

[6] *Loc. cit.*

disappears beneath the walls of that town.[1] We are left in doubt as to whether she was burned by the English, or put to death by jealous army chiefs.

Guillaume Gruel's chronicle,[2] the work of an historian in the pay of Richemont,[3] has important information on Richemont's relations with Joan; although it portrays her dealings with that proud nobleman entirely from his point of view, as when it tells us, rather improbably, that Joan knelt to him.

There are some other items, not without significance, from the Armagnac side. Quicherat verifies the date of Joan's arrival at Chinon as March 6th from the contemporary chronicle, or journal, of Guillaume de Nangis.[4] Calmet, in his *History of Lorraine*[5] prints the so-called *Chronicle of Metz*, which extends the story of the false Pucelle.

We must not omit to mention, also, the famous Latin letter to the Duke of Milan written by Perceval de Boulainvilliers, counsellor and chamberlain of the French King, and seneschal of the Duke of Berri.[6] Boulainvilliers is a careless writer, who misdates his own letter, and misdates the battle of Patay; but he is our sole authority for the alleged date of Joan's birth, January 6, 1412. The date is surrounded with apocryphal details, some of them so picturesque and beautiful and appropriate that we wish we could accept them for sober history. Thus we learn that the Gallic cock greeted Joan very suitably, with much flapping and crowing in the middle of the night; 'the cocks as heralds of a new joy, against their wont, burst forth in songs not heard before, and with flapping wings for more than two hours appeared to foretell the coming of a new thing'. Here we have the origin of that idyllic

---

[1] *Procès*, IV, 329–338 (*Chronique de Lorraine*).

[2] Guillaume Gruel, *Histoire d'Artus III, duc de Bretagne, comte de Richemont et connestable de France, 1393–1458, conténant ses memorables faicts, depuis l'an 1413 jusques à l'an 1457, mise en lumière par* Théodore Godefroy (1580–1649). In Petitot, Claude B., éd *Collection complète des mémoires relatifs à l'histoire de France,* . . . (Paris, 1819–20), sér. 1, t. 8, 1819, pp. 403–568. See also *Procès*, IV, 315 ff.

[3] Lang, *op. cit.*, p. 160.

[4] *Procès*, IV, 313 (De Nangis).

[5] Dom Calmet, *History of Lorraine*—the chronicle, the work of the doyen of St Thibaud of Metz, extends to the year 1445. (*Procès*, IV, 321 ff.)

[6] *Procès*, V, 114–21 (Boulainvilliers).

childhood of Joan, beloved of romantic poets, in which the lambs she tended were marvellously spared from the wolves. There is also the story of her miraculously speedy running, and of the mysterious youth who tells her, falsely, that her mother wants her, just before her 'Voices' appear for the first time; strangely enough, she takes him to be her brother, or one of the neighbours' children. All of this is in contradiction to her own testimony at the trial.[1] After all these tales, we are not surprised that Boulainvilliers depicts her as the real director of the army, and as sustaining a miraculous lack of losses at Patay.

Another letter, written at the end of July, 1429, is generally attributed to the King's secretary, Alain Chartier, the court poet, author of *La Belle Dame sans Merci*—several centuries before Keats found in the same title a notable inspiration. In it, Joan is extolled in ecstatic terms, and all the powers and virtues, military and civil, are attributed to her. Chartier tells us of the King's 'shining face' as he listened to Joan's reassurances.[2]

A French clerk in Rome added a note to an historical compilation he had edited under the name of *Breviarum historiale*. He gives us the tale of the King bequeathing his kingdom to Joan, who transferred it to God, and then, on the order of God, reinvested Charles with the kingdom by a solemn act—an unlikely story, and an obvious piece of mediaeval war propaganda, but significant as reflecting the growing prestige of the King, and the development, at least in germ, of the idea of his special divine right, independent of all other authorities on earth. Such a story reminds us that the career of Joan of Arc marks a watershed between the mediaeval and the modern world.

---

[1] *Barrett*, pp. 54-5, 149.
[2] *Procès*, IV, 133 (Alain Chartier).

III

THE WITCH OF THE ARMAGNACS

We shall turn our attention now to the chronicles of the Burgundian party. Contemporary French opinion about Joan of Arc was, as we have seen, profoundly divided along party lines. It continued to be so divided, more or less, until the Rehabilitation proceedings, twenty-five years after her untimely death, restored a formal façade of official unity. This unity was not to be lasting, for the old controversies later reappeared in new forms.

Before the close of the fifteenth century, the Burgundian interest no longer existed in France as a separate party, because of the triumph of the centralizing power of the French monarchy, especially personified in Charles VII's son, Louis XI; but the view of Joan of Arc set forth by the Burgundian chroniclers lived on in the pages of English chroniclers, such as Holinshed, and in Shakespeare's historical play, *Henry VI, Part One*. The tradition did not wholly die out until the nineteenth century in England, and in our own day it has been revived in a new form.[1] On the continent, too, the Burgundian tradition flows along submerged and completely neglected by observers, like a subterranean river. Commencing with the shrewd sceptic, Monstrelet, who saw Joan soon after her capture, it comes up again, as we have observed, in the Renaissance, in the Enlightenment, and in twentieth-century anticlericalism. We shall trace its course.

Modern French historians usually feel a patriotic contempt for the Burgundian chroniclers, as being traitors in league with the

---

[1] See Margaret Alice Murray, *The Witch-Cult in Western Europe, A Study in Anthropology* (Oxford, 1921), and *The God of the Witches* (London, 1933).

national enemy—'fifth columnists' as we should say today—and so, though essential to a rounded view, they are seldom cited. Most English and American writing, influenced by French models, has likewise adhered closely to the Armagnac tradition, clerical, conservative or monarchist, nationalist or romantic. Historians have seldom recognized two sides to the 'Joan question'. The growth of humanitarian horror at 'cruel and unusual punishments', the decline of the sort of supernaturalism expressed in the belief in witchcraft, as well as the decline of feudalism and the growth of the national state, have undermined many of the bases of the Anglo-Burgundian position.

Yet, though they find few defenders in the court of current public opinion, the Burgundian chroniclers include a number of the most important fifteenth-century historiographers. Some of them have a sceptical, cynical realism that seems curiously 'modern' in tone. Perhaps we may find an explanation of that in the fact that the Anglo-Burgundian territory included the richest, most 'advanced' and urbanized sectors of France—the great towns of Flanders, Rouen, above all Paris, then as now the focus of the political, economic and cultural life of the country. The Burgundian tradition contains inaccuracies, no doubt, and leaves much unexplained, but it may also contain truths which the orthodox version neglects.

The Burgundians, of course, did not regard themselves as traitors. Charles VII, aside from his doubtful legitimacy, had been barred from the succession for complicity in the foul murder of Jean sans Peur, Duke of Burgundy. Charged with the murder before the *parlement* of Paris, and failing to answer the charge, Charles of Valois was 'proclaimed' on three successive days at the celebrated table of marble in the Palais de Justice; at the sound of the trumpet and by public proclamation *et, après tout l'ordre judiciaire à ce requis et observé, il est, par arrest, déclaré indigne de succéder à la couronne.*[1] In addition, by the treaty of Troyes, Charles's own parents, King Charles VI and his queen, Isabel of Bavaria, had repudiated the claim of their son, and this repudiation

---

[1] Étienne Pasquier, *Les Recherches de la France* (Paris, 1596), *Livre* VI, *Chap.* IV

had been ratified by the *parlement* and by the estates of the realm. Moreover, we must remember that Charles's sister Katherine was the mother of the young English King, Henry VI; that the English royal house had long had an hereditary claim of sorts to the French throne, and that the English aristocracy after the Norman conquest had been French in culture. Legally and morally, the Burgundian party felt that it had good reason for its attitude towards the Armagnac freebooters; and law and morality were forcefully seconded by the economic interest of the wool towns of the North, whose merchants saw in England a market and a source of raw materials. Law and morality were forcefully seconded, too, by the economic ties of the wine merchants of Bordeaux, who traded with England, or of the wine merchants of Burgundy, who traded with Flanders, as well as by the class interest of the clergy and of many feudal nobles, opposed to a dominant centralized monarchy.

The Maid's visions, so exalted in the eyes of the Armagnacs, become 'foolish fantomries' or imposture in the eyes of the Burgundians. They point out that her prophecies were not always fulfilled, and sometimes grievously misled her followers. They usually recognize Joan's courage, and her influence on the course of events, but they tend to see it as something fearful, monstrous, unnatural. Her conduct seems to them vicious and immoral, vain and cruel, and she herself a lowborn pretender to divine inspiration—a detestable woman, the laughing stock of her sex, the scandal of men. Whereas Armagnac tradition sees her as a sweet, saintly heroine, combining the utmost in feminine charm, humanity and sensibility with the utmost in achievement in the most characteristically masculine realm, the Anglo-Burgundian tradition tends to see Joan as a man-woman, *hommasse*, a sort of virago.

In Joan's turning over the Burgundian military chieftain, Franquet d'Arras, for trial and execution, this tradition sees a shocking and cruel violation of the laws of (feudal) warfare, and a suitable precedent for her own treatment later. Her defence against this charge is, that Franquet d'Arras had been legally convicted of murder and outrage by the *Bailli de Senlis* and a jury of citizens of Lagny;[1] but he was doubtless no worse than a hundred or a thousand others on both sides, and we may see in her handling of his case a revelation that Joan represents new anti-feudal and national codes of values, new social forces rising from the bottom of society. The trial of Franquet d'Arras breaks new ground, just as the Nuremberg trials break new ground in our own day, by branding aggressive war as a crime; and contemporary conservative opinion, even among the Armagnacs, was shocked by the trial of Franquet d'Arras, just as Senator Taft of the United States, for parallel reasons, was shocked by the Nuremberg trials. Established law, usage, and feudal privilege were outraged by the verdict on Franquet; if this became precedent, no longer was the common soldier-prisoner to be massacred with impunity and the noble held to ransom, no matter what outrages against humbler folk he had committed.

There is no doubt that the principal Burgundian chronicle is that of Enguerrand de Monstrelet.[3] This extensive work was produced a few years after Joan's death—apparently about 1440, at any rate after the Treaty of Arras, by which Charles VII and the Duke of Burgundy were reconciled (1435).[4] John Richard Green, the eminent English nineteenth-century liberal historian, regarded Monstrelet as the leading authority for this whole period.[5] Monstrelet was at Compiègne when Joan was captured,

---

[1] Barrett, pp. 117, 183.

[2] Senator Robert Taft, at the Conference on the Heritage of the English-speaking Peoples at Kenyon College, Gambier, Ohio, in 1946, in debate with Mr Harold Laski declared the Nuremberg verdicts unjust, on the ground that they were based on legal principles which were not law at the time that the alleged crimes occurred.

[3] *Chroniques, éd. Buchon* (Paris, 1826-7). See also *The Chronicles of Enguerrand de Monstrelet; continuing an account of the cruel civil wars between the houses of Orleans and Burgundy; of the possession of Paris and Normandy by the English, their expulsion thence; and of other memorable events that happened in the kingdon of France, as well as in other countries . . . Beginning at the year MCCCC, where that of Sir John Froissart finishes, and ending at the year MCCCCLXVII, and continued by others to the year MDXVI.* tr. by Thomas Johnes (London, 1853).

[4] *Cf.* Égide Jeanné . . . *L'Image de la Pucelle d'Orléans*, etc. (Paris, 1935), Introduction, p. 5, citing Rapin de Thoyras.

[5] John Richard Green, *Short History of the English People* (New York edition, 1900), I ,334.

and his account of some of the events he described has, therefore, the prestige that attaches to the record of the eyewitness. He did not know a great deal about Joan, but much that he did know is extremely significant, though most modern historians are reluctant to use him for more than the barest facts, because of his critical approach. Actually, he seems more 'modern' than most of those 'moderns' who traduce him: he is conscientious, orderly, rational, and remarkably fair, reflecting, no doubt, the dawning rationalism of the Renaissance. To the eye grown accustomed to the mediaeval gloom of the Armagnac chronicles, his light seems almost painfully bright. Yet he had the misfortune to be on the side which later French history was to adjudge the wrong one—certainly, the losing one. Already, in the sixteenth century, nationalist patriotism has blackened his name, along with that of his party; the great Rabelais calls him *ce tabellion plus baveux que ung pot de moutarde*.[1] His merits, perhaps, have seldom since received their due.

Monstrelet, as we should anticipate, has scant appetite for Joan's miracles; he either explains them away or passes over them without mentioning them. He cannot accept her undeniable equestrian skill as a miraculous endowment; he says:

laquelle Pucelle Jehenne fut grant espace de temps chamberière en une hostellerie. Et estoit hardie de chavaulcher chevaux et les mener boyre, et aussi de faire appertise que jeunes filles n'ont point accoustumé de faire.[2]

The Burgundians and the English had generally circulated the story that she had learned to ride as a chamber-wench at the inn at Neufchâteau, and that she had lost her virginity there.[3] Joan herself admitted at her trial that 'for dread of the Burgundians' (doubtless at the time of a Burgundian raid on Domrémy) she stayed 'about a fortnight'[4] at the inn at Neufchâteau, a fortified town in Lorraine, and at that time assisted its proprietress, a woman named *La Rousse*. Rehabilitation witnesses from Domrémy

---

[1] Rabelais, *Pantagruel*, Book III, Chap, XXIV.
[2] Monstrelet, *op. cit.*, III, 314.
[3] *Cf.* Andrew Lang, *The Monk of Fife*, p. 156.
[4] Barrett, p. 54.

essayed to cut down her stay at Neufchateau to four or five days, in July, 1428, and to maintain that she was accompanied thither by her parents;[1] doubtless the episode was thought to be a humiliating one, minimizing the heroine's social status, in a society where such matters were all-important, affording ground for the propaganda of the enemy, and casting doubt upon her virginity. We may dismiss that doubt, for even her trial judges, who had verified her virginal status by causing her to be examined physically by the Duchess of Bedford and her ladies, did not dare to question it, though to have done so would have been much to their advantage in proving her guilt, since there was a prevalent belief that the Devil could not make a pact with a virgin.[2] Joan was undoubtedly virginal; but she may have stayed at the inn longer than she admitted at the trial.

Despite the general assumption of historians that Joan's words are infallible, there is really no reason whatever to assume that she told her judges the truth, the whole truth, and nothing but the truth. She herself cautiously said to them that there was a saying among little children: 'Men are sometimes hanged for telling the truth.'[3] When first exhorted to take oath to speak the truth, she answered, 'Perhaps you might ask such things that I would not tell'.[4] Finally, she swore to tell the truth 'concerning matters of faith'. Next day, after swearing the same oath, very reluctantly,

[1] *Procès*, II, 416, 419 (Rehabilitation testimony).

[2] See Barrett, pp. 100, 101, 187, 192, 228, 232, 304 for Joan's vow of virginity, as attested by her at her trial. It was alleged (Art. IX of the *Twelve Articles*, p. 228) that Joan had said 'that her soul would be saved if she preserved the virginity she had consecrated to them when she first saw and heard them' (her saints here indicated).

Another passage seems to involve a tacit admission of her virginity on the part of her judges. They asked 'whether it had not been revealed to her that she would lose her good fortune if she lost her virginity, and that her voices would no longer come to her, she answered, "That has not been revealed to me".' (Barrett, p. 128.)

Joan is, however, accused of kissing, embracing and 'entering into familiarity with' the spirits who visited her. (*Ibid.*, p. 191.)

Accused of wishing to 'employ only men whom she made serve in the private office of her room and in her secret affairs, a thing unseen and unheard of in a modest or devout woman' (*Ibid.*, p. 204), she replied, 'where she lodged or slept at night, she usually had a woman with her; when she was fighting, she would lie fully dressed and armed, if there was no woman to be found.'

[3] Barrett, p.63.

[4] *Ibid.* (February 21, 1431), p. 50.

she said to Beaupère: 'You may ask me such things, that to some I shall answer truly, to others I shall not.'[1] Admonished 'to speak the simple and absolute truth on the questions put to her, and to make no reservation to her oath,' she refused, saying, 'By my faith, you could ask things such as I would not answer'. And again, 'Perhaps I shall not answer you truly in many things that you ask me, concerning revelations . . .'; and later, 'She said that of her coming to France she would willingly speak the truth, but not the whole truth . . . .'[2] Ultimately, she swore[3] 'to speak the truth of what I know concerning the trial', a sufficiently limited and ambiguous undertaking! Similar altercations occurred at later sessions when it was sought to put her on oath.[4] All this is not much more reassuring to the observant historian than it was to the judges. The whole effect, moreover, of Joan's answers at the trial would suggest that they are full of *suppressio veri*, and hardly deserve the implicit faith that has very generally been placed in them. Joan's elaborately woven story of the precious crown which she brought to the King, a story which she herself finally admitted to be false,[5] further indicates the dubiousness of much of her testimony. As we study it closely, we can understand why the eminent doctor of the Sorbonne, Jean Beaupère, testified, even amid the general whitewash of the Rehabilitation, that she was subtle, with all the subtlety peculiar to women.

Joan's trial judges' eighth article of accusation, based upon the

[1] *Barrett*, p. 54 (Feb. 22nd).

[2] *Ibid.*, p. 59 (Feb. 24th).

[3] *Ibid.*, p. 60 (Feb. 24th).

[4] *Ibid.*, p. 67 (Feb. 27th); p. 74 (Mar. 1st); p. 83 (Mar. 3rd); p. 93 (Mar. 10th); p. 99 (Mar. 12th).

[5] *Ibid.*, *passim*, and see especially pp. 334–8. See also, on this issue of veracity, pp. 211–17 and 220–1. Article LX of the articles of accusation, Barrett, p. 211, reads as follows: 'The said Jeanne, scornful of the precepts and sanctions of the church, many times refused to take oath to speak the truth, so exposing herself to the suspicion of having said or done certain things in questions of faith or revelation which she dare not reveal to the ecclesiastical judges, being fearful of a just punishment; this it appears she sufficiently acknowledged by the proverb "men are sometimes hanged for telling the truth", and often she said "You will not know everything" and "I would rather have my head cut off than tell you everything".' There follow supporting citations from her testimony, pp. 212–17. Article LXIII, p. 220, states: 'The said Jeanne has not been afraid to lie before the law, in violation of her oath, and affirmed successively many conflicting and contradictory things about her revelations.'

CHARLES VII^L ROY DE FRANCE

8. CHARLES VII (1403–1461). French Painting, XVth century
(*Bettman Archive*)

9. MAID OF ORLEANS, THE BURNING OF THE SAINT by J.-E. Lenepveu
From a mural painting in the Pantheon, Paris (*Bettmann Archive*)

extensive evidence which they had collected, provides a source for the statements of Monstrelet about Joan's early career. It is as follows:

'Jeanne, when she was about (fifteen), of her own will and without the leave of her said father and mother, went to the town of Neufchâteau in Lorraine and there for some time served in the house of a woman, an inn-keeper named *La Rousse*, where many young unguarded women stayed, and the lodgers were for the most part soldiers. Thus, dwelling at this inn, she would sometimes stay with the said women, sometimes would drive the sheep to the fields, and occasionally lead the horses to drink, or to the meadow, or pasture; and there she learned to ride and become acquainted with the profession of arms.'[1]

It is altogether a reasonable account, and would explain Joan's accomplished skill as a horsewoman when first she appears on the historical stage. To suppose that the sweet, home-dwelling Maid of most modern biographers is suddenly transformed into the Joan of history, is to suppose an absolute impossibility.

La Rousse is said to have been well-to-do and respectable,[2] but the above account of her inn, expressed with becoming clerical indirection, is most plausible, having regard to the customs of the time.

Monstrelet's account was followed by some writers of the Renaissance, and also by some of the thinkers of the Enlightenment, notably Voltaire and Hume. Their harsher modern critics might be well advised to reread this celebrated chronicler, upon whom they relied.

The journey of Joan and her companions from Vancouleurs to Chinon extended over at least a hundred and fifty leagues,[3] rapidly covered, mainly at night for security reasons, and it required the fording of icy, swollen rivers, in winter. These circumstances certainly suggest that Joan of Arc had not only great courage, resolution, physical strength, temperance, endurance, and power of moral suasion, but also great skill on horseback, at the very commencement of her public career. The con-

---

[1] *Barrett*, p. 147.
[2] Anatole France, *op. cit.*, I, 71.
[3] Barrett, p. 171

temporary marginal annotator of Monstrelet who wrote beside the passage we are discussing, *ne james n'avoit veu cheval, au moyns pour monter dessus* must simply have been mistaken. She 'rode horses so ill-tempered that no one would dare ride them',[1] and fine horses seem to have been the gifts of noble admirers which she most appreciated. Perceval de Boulainvilliers[2] testifies to this; and we note the horses given her by the Duke of Lorraine, Charles VII, the Duke of Alençon, the Duke of Orleans, and the Duke of Brittany.[3] Very likely she may have practised riding upon her father's farm, riding horses to water, without stirrup or bridle, riding astride and clinging to their manes, or even riding to neighbouring villages; usually romantically represented, in her own day and later, as a simple shepherdess, she herself said 'that as long as she was at home with her father, she saw to the ordinary domestic tasks; and that she did not go to the fields to look after the sheep and other animals',[4] but perhaps we need not take too literally this very feminine and domestic picture which she presented to her judges. 'I have seen (in Lorraine) with what gallantry the young farm girls ride on the backs of farm horses,' says M. Pierre Champion.[5]

As we consider the 'inn-servant' tradition of the Burgundians, we shall do well to remember that *pucelle*, the title of Joan of Arc which we translate in the phrases 'Maid of France', 'Maid of Orleans', means 'maid' in the fifteenth century in the sense of a humble kitchen-servant as well as in other senses; the word had the same variety of meanings that the word 'maid' does in contemporary English. A kitchen pump was called a *pucelle*. Clopinel's saying, *Je lègue ma pucelle à mon curé*, was considered naughty,

---

[1] T. D. Murray, p. 30.

[2] *Supra*, Chapter II, pp. 56–7, *Procès*, V, 114–21 (Boulainvilliers).

[3] Barrett, p. 95, p. 205: 'she had five chargers from the king's money, not counting the hacks, which were more than seven'.

[4] *Ibid.*, p. 54. But see also p. 147 (Article VIII of the Articles of Accusation) 'she also added that, since she was grown up and had reached understanding, she did not commonly look after the cattle, but helped to take them to the meadows and to a castle called the Island, for fear of the soldiers, but does not remember whether or not she tended them in her youth'. See also M. Siméon Luce, *Jeanne d'Arc à Domrémy* (Paris, 1887) *passim*; also the Rehabilitation testimony. The point is further considered, *infra*, Chapter VI, pp. 146–7.

[5] Barrett-Champion, p. 538.

but was applied to respectable girls. La Curne has it, quoting Deschamps:

Je laisse cent sols de deniers
À ceulx qui boivent volontiers
Et j'ay laissié à mon curé
Ma pucelle quant je mourrai.[1]

A camp follower was a *pucelle* and so was Joan, 'one of our Lord's poor'.[2]

In all ages, war-communiqués tend to exaggerate the numbers of the enemy, to overstate his losses, and to minimize those of their own side: this was notably so of the chroniclers in the period we are studying, and it was generally true of the Burgundian chroniclers, such as Monstrelet and Le Fèvre de Saint-Remy. On the other hand, Monstrelet probably exaggerated the English strength at Orleans, when he said they had sixty *bastilles*; and he certainly exaggerated their losses when he said that seven or eight thousand were killed or captured in the southern *bastilles* alone.[3] Regarding the dead and wounded in the terrible disaster of the English at Patay, the discrepancies are rather those which we should anticipate; Dunois twenty-five years later places the enemy losses, dead and wounded, at more than four thousand;[4] De Cagny, at twenty-four hundred to thirty-five hundred; while Monstrelet, in the other camp, has the low figure, eighteen hundred dead, a hundred or more wounded. Monstrelet understands well the 'expendability' of such common soldiery; after enumerating the noble victims, he says the rest of those killed at Patay were all men of small and mean estate, such as they (the English) were accustomed to bring from their own country to die in France. Observant about methods of warfare, he notes, with De Commines, that at Patay, many French knights fought on foot—a

---

[1] Jean Baptiste La Curne de Sainte-Palaye, *Dictionnaire historique de l'ancien langage françoise, ou Glossaire de la langage françoise depuis son origine*. See also Ducange, C. d. F., *Glossarium Mediae et Infimae Latinitatis:* 1688 (Niort, 1883–1887).

[2] Anatole France, *op. cit.*, I, 144.

[3] Jules Michelet, *Vie de Jeanne d'Arc, édition* Rudler (Paris, 1925), p. 32.

[4] Joseph Fabre, *Procès de Réhabil'tation de Jeanne d'Arc, raconté et traduit d'après les textes latins officials* (Paris, 1888), p. 196; hereafter cited as 'Réhabilitation'.

trick they had learned from the English. He pictures the Regent Bedford at Montepilloy, trying to lure Charles VII into an attack on a fortified camp, barricaded with ditches, wagons and an array of sharpened poles; it was the fatal and bloody device which had worked so well, for the English, at Rouvray. He gives us the significant fact that Joan was of diverse opinions, at one time wishing to attack, at another time not—she was, apparently, wavering and confused, which, if true, would tend to confute her claims to decisive and prudent generalship. It is, indeed, hard to concur with those of her historians who have sharply criticized Charles VII for not attacking at Montepilloy.

We learn much from Monstrelet about the impact of the victories attributed to Joan upon the Anglo-Burgundian camp. We see the burghers of Paris demanding that Burgundy take over their defence from the English:

Fut par les Parisiens requis au duc de Bourgogne qu'il lui plût à entreprendre le gouvernement de Paris.[1]

Monstrelet admits clearly that the large towns and strongholds of Picardy and the North—St Quentin, Corbie, Amiens, Abbeville —were ready to open their gates to Charles VII in the summer of 1429,[2] and that Charles had a strong force available to occupy them, but desisted in the hope of a 'good treaty' with Burgundy. Joan's modern historians have almost universally inferred from this that the *roi fainéant* could have swept France clear of *godons* in 1429, had he but listened to the Maid.[3] When we consider, however, the still formidable enemy in the field, under the able leadership of Bedford, and the strongly based power of Burgundy in the Low Countries and the East, Charles's attempt to follow up his coronation by detaching Burgundy from the English may appear to be statesmanlike moderation in the use of victory. Charles's objective was finally accomplished, after all, by the Treaty of Arras in 1435, thus preparing the ruin of the English position.

[1] Monstrelet, *op. cit.*, V, 264.
[2] *Procès*, IV, 391 (Monstrelet).
[3] See, e.g. Lowell, *op. cit.*, p. 171, A. B. Paine, *Joan*, I, 305, Lang, *Maid*, p. 200.

THE WITCH OF THE ARMAGNACS

Our accounts of Joan's last day in the field, before Compiègne, are confusing and contradictory, but that of Monstrelet, an eye-witness, is generally accepted as the best. He gives us a vivid presentation of the joy at her capture, which is, indirectly, a great tribute to her influence in elevating the morale of the army of Charles VII:[1]

cheulx de la partie de Bourgongne et les Angloix en furent moult joyeux, plus que d'avoir prins cincq cens combatans, car il₃ ne cremoient ne redoubtoient nul capitainne ne aultre chief de guerre, tant comme il₃ avoient tousjours fait jusques à che present jour, ycelle Pucelle.

Along with the rejoicings of the Burgundians, he describes with equal vividness the mourning and sorrowing of the Armagnacs. Monstrelet was present at the meeting of the Maid of Orleans with the Duke of Burgundy, immediately after capture—that dramatic confrontation celebrated by so many artists and playwrights, including Shakespeare and Schiller.[2] He tells us, exasperatingly, that he cannot well recall what was said upon that famous occasion.[3] So it is lost to us forever, and the imagination has free rein accordingly. Can Monstrelet really have forgotten? Was he sympathetic with Joan in this situation? Or, does he think it best to let sleeping dogs lie, and avoid embarrassing the Duke of Burgundy, who has already, when Monstrelet writes, made his peace with the monarch over whose crowning Joan waved her banner? As the Rehabilitation proceedings show, many of those concerned with Joan's affairs could remember—and forget—most conveniently, as political exigencies required, and considerations of their own security made expedient. It has been suggested, apparently without direct evidence,[4] that the Duke of Burgundy was full of hypocritical consolations for Joan. In his letter to the town of Saint Quentin, announcing the great news,

---

[1] *Procès*, IV, 402 (*Monstrelet*). See also *Chronique anonyme dit des Cordeliers*, cited in *Revue historique*, XIX, 82.

[2] For a striking pictorial representation, see Louis Maurice Boutet de Monvel's illustration for his *Joan of Arc* (New York, 1907).

[3] *Procès*, IV, 402 (Monstrelet), 'Laquelle yceluy duc a la veoir ou logis où elle estoit, et parla à elle aulcunes parolles, dont je ne suix mie bien recors, jà soit che que je y estoie present'.

[4] Blaze de Bury, *op. cit.*, p. 304.

he abounds in pious rejoicings, seeing in the event the proof of the error of all those who have trusted Joan and believed in her.

Our chronicler says a Picard archer captured Joan; and he affirms that she 'pledged her faith' and sword to her captor, Lyonnel, bastard of Vendôme (Wandonne).[1] De Cagny denies this, and Joan herself specifically denied it at her trial, and said that she felt free to escape, never having given her oath to anyone.[2] David Hume follows Monstrelet on this point; and, what is much more impressive, so does the cautious and scholarly Quicherat.[3] Incidentally, it is curious to recognize in Joan's captor, as recorded in Monstrelet, the germ, so to speak, of Lionel, the hero of Schiller's great tragedy, *Die Jungfrau von Orleans*.

Monstrelet's account virtually ends with Joan's capture; the only other information he gives is that contained in Bedford's letter to the Duke of Burgundy, which he reproduces. One cannot but feel that he is skating diplomatically over rather thin ice!

The *Chronicle of the Cordeliers*[4] appears to be the earliest of the Burgundian chronicles, though by no means the best. The only copy of it comes from the religious house of the Cordeliers in Paris. It is a typical monkish chronicle, beginning with the creation of the world, and ending with the year 1431. It is rather friendly to Joan, reflecting, we may conjecture, the relative friendliness of the religious order that produced it. Pierre Champion has proved that Monstrelet used it.[5]

The chronicle, which is apparently the work of a clerk of Picardy, supplies us with some useful bits of information, and some valuable documents on the Burgundian negotiations with Charles VII and Bedford, but it is confused as to facts and dates. Its military information is coloured by popular rumours and also by Armagnac materials.

One idea derived from this chronicle, which still crops up from time to time in modern books, is the idea that Joan let herself

---

[1] *Procès*, IV, 401–2 (Monstrelet). For the name of her captor, *cf.* Barrett, p. 27.
[2] Interrogation of Feb. 21st; see Barrett, pp. 50–51.
[3] Quicherat, *Aperçus*, p. 89
[4] *Chronique anonyme dit des Cordeliers*, no. 16f° 486 Bib. nat.
[5] Champion, *Flavy*, *op. cit.*, xi, xii.

down, by strips of cloth tied together to form a rope from the lofty tower of Beaurevoir, where she was imprisoned. Undoubtedly the chronicler did not like to accept the fact that she had committed, as charged, the deadly sin of leaping from the tower, thereby attempting suicide. But Joan admits the leap, which she had no reason to do were it not so, since it was a serious charge against her; and she admits the leap was a sin.[1] To lower herself by an improvised rope would of course have been no sin in her eyes, since she claimed the right to escape. We may, therefore, with a confidence exceptional in these discussions, reject the tale of our Picard chronicler.

We may leave him with a citation of his spirited description of Joan's entry into Compiègne the first time, riding ahead of the King, with a retinue of men-at-arms, her brother, her squire d'Aulon, her confessor Father Pasquerel, the faithful Jean de Metz, and Betrand de Poulengy, and herself *toute armée de plein harnas à estendart desployé.*

The monk, Gilles de Roye, though Burgundian, drew upon French sources also, apparently, like the chronicler of the Cordeliers. He is friendly to Joan, but does not commit himself. 'Brought to Rouen, she was, either justly or unjustly, burnt,' he says. This would seem to be a safely detached statement!

Jean de Wavrin du Forestel wrote his so-called *Chronique d'Angleterre* between 1455 and 1460.[2] The author was the natural son of Robert de Wavrin, knight, Lord of Forestel, near Lille, in the Burgundian north. Wavrin's father was slain by his son's side at Agincourt, and the son became a renowned warrior—especially valuable, therefore, as a source on the military side of our subject. His memoirs are those of an old soldier, an astute and skilful mercenary captain; they are written, for the edification of his nephew, when Wavrin must have been seventy of more, and they are largely a compilation from other historians, but with some interesting additions by himself. Monstrelet, Froissart, and Mathieu d'Escouchy are the sources upon which he chiefly

---

[1] Barrett, pp. 118, 122, 123, 180, 181, 184–6, 188–9, 262, 291, 304.
[2] See *Procès*, IV, 405–424 (*Chronique d'Angleterre*).

draws, in addition to his own recollections, and his own imagination.

This chronicler is completely sceptical regarding Joan, doubtless reproducing an opinion that was widespread in his party; he is the first to describe her as a mere political instrument.[1] As such, he admits that she was effective.[2] He sees the puppet-master who pulled the string in Robert de Baudricourt, the royal *capitaine du lieu*[3] at Vaucoulieurs, the Armagnac outpost nearest to Joan's home village of Domrémy. In this account, Baudricourt is not, as in the modern story, the rough military commander, who only after many efforts and much persuasion on Joan's part sends her on her way to the royal court at Chinon. Baudricourt here is the tutor who brings up the servant-wench for her mission, teaches her what to say and do, indoctrinates her, and instructs her how she ought to appear as the 'self-styled Pucelle inspired by divine Providence'.[4]

Wavrin knows a good deal of the war after the relief of Orleans, and he was at the battle of Patay, but he never saw Joan there, and he is acquainted with her only vaguely, by hearsay. His view of Baudricourt can hardly be accepted; if she were a puppet, she was not Baudricourt's puppet.

Baudricourt's role of rather sullen and unimaginative scepticism in this affair is pretty clearly established by the evidence at the Rehabilitation and there is no reason to doubt it. At the trial, Joan affirmed that it was only upon her third attempt to see him that Baudricourt welcomed and received her; and even the Articles of Accusation, drawn up by her judges, represent Joan as taking the initiative in the whole affair.[5] Baudricourt's words of farewell to her: 'Go, go, and come what may,'[6] are certainly

---

[1] *Procès*, IV, 406 (Wavrin).

[2] *Ibid.*, p. 418, for instance; here Wavrin informs us that the courage of the English was much changed and weakened; they saw their men enfeebled, and found them less firm in their judgement than they were wont to be.

[3] Wallon, p. 36.

[4] *Procès*, IV, 407 (Wavrin).

[5] Barrett, pp. 148–54. See also p. 70.

[6] *Ibid.*, p. 153. See, however, *Ibid.*, p. 151, Article XI, of the Articles of Accusation. (This infrequently quoted passage is obviously based upon the evidence collected for Cauchon.) It follows:

noncommittal. Her interrogator at the trial, it is true, suggested that she wore men's dress at the suggestion of Robert de Baudricourt; but this, Joan specifically denied,[1] and it seems rather improbable, considering the strength of her desire and determination, evinced at the trial, to retain her male costume.[2]

The view that Joan was essentially a puppet, an instrument of a guileful statecraft, has had a long history since Wavrin's day; it was revived at the Renaissance and in the Enlightenment, and, in the twentieth century by Anatole France, who regarded Joan as being in her own day, as in his, a political instrument manipulated by clerical personages.[3]

Jean de Wavrin was in the entourage of Sir John Fastolf at Patay, and he is a 'prime source' for that battle, so glorious for Joan of Arc. It will be recalled that Bedford stripped Sir John of his Garter after Patay, because his behaviour on that stricken field appeared cowardly; and although the Order was later restored to to him, his reputation never recovered from the blow. Remaining under a cloud, he gave Shakespeare the name, at least, for one of his most inspired creations, that celebrated figure of fun, Sir John Falstaff. Wavrin endeavours to clear Fastolf of the stigma of Patay, representing him as doing his best to rally the soldiers who were panicked. Whereas the brave Talbot was reckless (a 'fighting animal', one of Bernard Shaw's characters calls him) and fell into the French trap, Fastolf was prudent, like Quintus Fabius Maximus, and wished to await needed reinforcements before engaging the enemy. Talbot was captured, and Fastolf escaped, only to be disgraced. Was he too discreet, too

The said Jeanne, having entered into intimate relations with Robert, boasted of having told that after having dispatched and accomplished everything that had been enjoined by revelation from God, she would have three sons of which the first would be pope, the second emperor, and the third king. Hearing which, the said captain said to her: 'Now, then, I should like to give you one if they're going to be such powerful men, because I should be better off,' to which she answered: 'No, gentle Robert, no, this is not the time; the Holy Spirit will find a way!' So the said Robert, in many places, and in the presence of prelates, lawyers, and notable persons, affirmed, said and uttered.

[1] Barrett, pp. 56, 70, 103, 153–154. Joan apparently at first evaded the question as to who suggested that she wear male dress. She finally affirmed that she wore it at God' scommand.

[2] *Ibid.*, pp. 103, 120, 125, 134, 156–9, 170, 230, 272, 273, 318.

[3] See Anatole France, *op. cit., passim.*

cautious? The question is still debated.[1] It seems likely that his caution was only due military prudence, and that he was made the scapegoat for a defeat which resulted from the changed moral and political situation, following the advent of the Maid and the relief of Orleans. Incidentally, Wavrin's desire to clear the good name of Fastolf, his commander, may well explain why he is so willing to give Joan of Arc full credit as the chief factor in French success at Patay.

One of the most interesting and valuable of the Burgundian chronicles is the *Journal d'un Bourgeois de Paris*.[2] The researches of Tuetey would indicate that its author, who designates himself a clerk of the University, was Jean Chuffart, a member of the University of Paris, who kept a diary, 1400 to 1449, upon which this *Journal* is based. In this *Journal* we see the war as it appeared from inside the walls of Paris, an Anglo-Burgundian stronghold, and in the eyes of a man who sympathized intensely with the sufferings of the common people, hated war, and hated the Armagnacs as turbulent feudal disturbers of the peace which the treaty of Troyes had sought to secure. The 'Bourgeois' had strong *Cabochien* or Burgundian convictions, and the outlook of a peaceful cleric, who did not understand some of the new movements afoot among the people, and shared the political views and interests general among the members of the University. He expressed his ideas with great feeling and energy.

The romantic Michelet[3] calls the 'Bourgeois' a *barbare et grossier chroniqueur*, a great step down from the *nobles historiens du XIVᵉ siècle*. He reveals a world *misérable et bas*; his preoccupations with famine, epidemics, the cost of living, the retrogression of the devastated countryside to forest, denote in him a *pesante matérialité*. But the very qualities which Michelet deplores make this chronicler more useful to us, closer to us in

---

[1] See A. B. Paine, *Joan*, I, 217–228. Paine accuses Fastolf of 'frightening his men half to death'. (P. 227.) 'Perhaps he was not really a coward, but he leaned overmuch to discretion and inspired anything but courage in his men.' (P. 228.)

[2] *Journal d'un Bourgeois de Paris* (1405–1449). Éd. A. Tuetey (Paris, 1881); *Procès*, IV, 461 ff.

[3] Michelet, *op. cit.*, (ed. Rudler) p. 8, Introduction.

outlook. He is not merely, as he was to the Victorian Miss Tuckey, 'a gossiping and delightful writer';[1] he is an extremely illuminating one, original and observant, supplying us with the raw material for that social and economic history which we value so highly. In reading him, we are reminded of the originally popular and anti-feudal character of the Burgundian party.

The 'Bourgeois' hated Joan of Arc; he did not lie about her, but he was not always too well informed concerning her, and he drew upon hostile sources. The masters and doctors of the University of Paris were undoubtedly his main wellspring of information.

The 'Bourgeois' is one of our best sources of information on the difficult subject of the unsuccessful attack upon Paris in which Joan of Arc played a leading part. We feel in this chronicle the horror inspired by this sacrilegious assault on September 8, 1429, the feast of the Nativity of the Virgin—an assault led by that 'creature in the form of a woman . . . whom they call the Maid. Who was it? God knoweth'.[2] The 'Bourgeois', who sees war realistically, not as a romantic charade, represents Joan as bloodthirsty, threatening that, if Paris held out, all Parisians would be put to death without mercy: *veuillez ou non, et tous serez mis à mort sans mercy*.[3] The 'Bourgeois' also says that Joan called 'Surrender, in the name of Jesus' as alleged at her trial. We can sense here some of the background of the hostility desplayed toward Joan at her trial by the University of Paris, and by some of its leading lights who were among her judges.

Vividly, and doubtless accurately, too, does this writer present the revulsion against the Maid among her own forces, caused by her failure at Paris.[4] Joan's prestige, which depended

[1] Miss Janet Tuckey, *Life of Joan of Arc* (New York, 1880) p. 221.

[2] 'Estoient pleins de si grant maleur et de si malle créance. Et le dy pour une créature qui estoit en forme de femme avec eulx, que on nommoit la Pucelle. Que c'estoit, Dieu le scet.
Le jour de la Natifvité de Notre Dame, firent conjuracion, tout d'ung accord, de cellui jour assaillir Paris.' *Procès*, IV, 464 (*Journal du Bourgeois de Paris*).

[3] *Ibid.*, IV, 465.

[4] 'Et mauldisoient moult leur Pucelle, qui leur avoit promis que sans nulle faute ilz gagneroient à celluy assault la ville de Paris par force, et quelle y geyroit celle nuyt, et eulx tous, et qu'ilz seroient tous enrichis des biens de la cité, et que tous seroient mis, qui y mettroient aucune deffence, à l'espée, ou, ars en sa maison.' *Procès*, IV, 466 (*Journal*). *Cf.* Tuetey, *Journal d'un Bourgeois*, p. 246.

upon her reputation for invincibility through divine guidance, was shattered, no doubt to the gratification of her enemies at court, and probably by their design. The way was now open for the conviction to gain ground, that she was a witch. Though she herself claimed at her trial that her 'Voices' had been silent before the attack on Paris, and had not ordered it,[1] her foes inevitably claimed the contrary,[2] and thus were able to discredit her 'Voices' as well as herself.

The Burgundian view of Joan is well summed up by the Dominican Inquisitor of the Faith, and master in theology, of whose sermon at Saint-Martin-des-Champs after Joan's execution the 'Bourgeois' tells us. Her lowly birth, her wearing of men's clothes, her alleged murders, her disobedience to her parents, and her consortings and pactions with devils, are points especially dwelt upon. She is represented as calling in vain upon her familiar spirits, and admitting too late that they had deceived her—a point of which Shakespeare makes use in his *Henry VI, Part One*. Hell itself abandons her to Anglo-Burgundian 'justice'. The events of her disputed final recantation[3] form the basis of this story—or so, at least, we may conjecture.

The 'Bourgeois of Paris' is apparently, along with Monstrelet, the source of the story, which appears in a number of later writers, including Hume, that Joan of Arc was really twenty-seven years of age at the beginning of her mission, and that the Armagnacs had taken ten years off her age to make her a more romantic and interesting, not to say miraculous, figure. It is an improbable story, for, if true, it would have been likely to 'come out' at her trial. It is true that she did not know her exact age,[4] any more than she knew A from B. There is a good deal of confusion about her chronology—for instance, about the exact

---

[1] See Barrett, pp. 111, 206–8.

[2] *Ibid.*, p. 207, Article LVII of the Articles of Accusation. 'Yet many trustworthy persons have reported that these promises were uttered and published by her.'

[3] *Ibid.*, pp. 333–9.

[4] *Ibid.*, p. 61—her reply at her trial: 'Asked how old she was, she replied she thought nineteen'.

date of her stay at Neufchâteau.[1] At the same time, her trial judges, after all their preliminary inquiries, accepted her account of her age, which would seem to validate it.[2]

With all his realism, the 'Bourgeois' provides us with some miracles of his own. It is from this source that Michelet derives his story of birds coming at the call of the youthful Joan of Arc to be fed.[3] The 'Bourgeois' adds, however, to this story of her communion with the birds *in veritate apocryphum est*, a phrase which Michelet incautiously ignores, so anxious is he for a pretty tale. If this were the only apocryphal detail in Joan's story, the path of the historian would indeed be easier! The 'Bourgeois' himself has others, such as the story of the Maid's prophecy of doom to Glasdale, the English captain who was drowned in the storming of the Tourelles at Orleans.

The 'Bourgeois' gives us a vivid picture of Burgundy's manoeuvres in Paris, after Patay, and of life within the threatened city, where the Armagnacs were expected almost daily; Bedford had withdrawn to Vincennes.[4] The people of Paris were attached to Burgundy rather than to the English, with whom there were constant petty frictions. The English even 'hedged' against the loss of their Burgundian alliance. The invaders, of course, were 'draining' France, as the Germans have done in our own day; the 'Bourgeois' saw this clearly, and he speaks of Bedford as always enriching his own country with the spoils of France, and never bringing anything from England, upon his return, but a load of taxation. We learn from this chronicle that even the factious spirits of Paris, despite their hatred of the dauphin and his Armagnacs, nevertheless thought

[1] *Cf.* Mrs Florence Caddy, *op. cit.*, p. 27. The Abbé Bourgaut, curé of Domrémy, stated local tradition placed her age at the time of the stay at Neufchâteua at ten years. On the other hand, Wallon, p. 33, states that she was then sixteen years of age. Barrett, p. 147, says 'about (fifteen)' etc., etc.

[2] Note Barrett, Article IV of the Articles of Accusation (p. 143). It states 'that she was brought up in her youth until the age of 18 or thereabouts, in the village of Domrémy on the Meuse'. Article VII of the Twelve Articles drawn from Jeanne's own sayings (p. 231) places the beginning of her mission 'in or about her seventeenth year'.

[3] Michelet, *op. cit.*, (éd. Rudler), p. 21—citing *Journal du Bourgeois*, XV, 387, 1827 edition.

[4] *Journal d'un Bourgeois* (éd. Tuetey), p. 248.

it cruel and shameful to become subjects of the English.

Behind all his discussion of politics there loom the ever present spectres of famine and pestilence—of the grinding miseries of the people.

Le povre peuple souffroit tant de pouvreté, de fain, de froit et de toute autre meschance, que nul ne le scet que Dieu de paradis. Car quant le tueur de chiens avoit tué des chiens, les pouvres gens le suyvoient aux champ pour avoir la char ou les trippes pour leur manger.[1]

Georges Chastellain (1420–1474) was justiciar and official historiographer of the Duke of Burgundy. Widely read and travelled, he was, in his day, the most highly esteemed of French stylists, and he reflects the taste of a period when most people still thought Latin the only literary language. In his discussion of Joan, in his *Chronique* (1460),[2] he made great use of Monstrelet and Le Fèvre de Saint-Remy,[3] with whom he actually corresponded; but he also introduced new and more friendly material, presenting a more living, moving, picture of the Maid. In fact, Chastellain admired Joan greatly, and he decorated her tale with literary flourishes. He thought, however, that she was misled by the Devil, and justly condemned. He criticizes the credulity of the Armagnacs: 'misled by her prophecies of which some came true, the French believed her'.

For a courtier, Chastellain had exceptional knowledge of the popular mind, and he well expressed the late mediaeval taste for the wonderful. His poem on the wonders of his time[4] is dominated through all its tinkling verses by the struggle between God and Satan, who is the challenger. Here is the style of his speech concerning the Maid:

---

[1] *Journal d'un Bourgeois* (éd. Tuetey), p. 153. *Cf.* Lanéry d'Arc, *Le Livre d'Or de Jeanne d'Arc, op. cit.*, No. 47.

[2] *Ouevres de Georges Chastellain pub. par M. le baron Kervyn de Lettenhove*, 8 vol. *in*-4 (tome ii)—*Académie royale de Belgique* (Brussels, 1863). See also *Procès*, IV, 440–8.

[3] *Cf. Jeanne d'Arc et ses récents historiens. Étude critique des dix-huit principaux ouvrages historiques relatifs à la Pucelle, publiés dans les dernières années* (Paris, n.d.) p. 154.

[4] *Recolleccion des marveilleuses avenues en nostre temps*, completed and edited by Jean Molinet, pub. 1531. See *Procès*, V, 90.

En France la très belle
Fleur de crestienté
Je veis une Pucelle
Sourdre en auctorité,
Qui fit lever le siège
D'Orléans en ses mains,
Puis le roy par prodiege
Mena sacrer à Reins.

Saincte fut aorée
Par les oeuvres que fit;
Mais puis fut rencontrée
Et prise sans prouffit;
Arse à Rouen en cendres
Au grand dur des François,
Donnons depuis entendre
Son revivre aultre fois.[1]

Quicherat sees in these last verses an allusion to the celebrated false Pucelle, Jeanne des Armoises—the pretender who posed after Joan's death as the real Joan, miraculously snatched like a brand from the burning. Marius Sepet, too, thinks that the false Joan, confounded with the real, influenced Chastellain's somewhat masculine interpretation of Joan's character,[2] as that of a chivalrous virago, rather than an humble and sweet peasant maid. However this may be, Chastellain certainly expresses the general folk-belief of his day that Joan, *la bonne Lorraine*, would come back in time of need. Like Charlemagne, like Frederick Barbarossa asleep with all his knights in the mountain called Kaiserstuhl, Joan had joined the select company of those folk heroes who never really die. The legend was forming, the legend that still lives; for centuries to come, Joan was to be the embodiment of the desire of her people for salvation from the sufferings of war and invasion. Her memory was embedded in their very souls, and when they were hard beset, and princes and captains had failed, they would turn to her for rescue.

Huizinga[3] expresses surprise that Chastellain omits Joan from

---

[1] *Procès*, V, 90 (Chastellain).
[2] H. A. Wallon, p. 433 (article by Marius Sepet).
[3] J. Huizinga, *Herbst des Mittelalters* (Munich, 1924), p. 90.

his *Mystery on the Death of Charles VII*, where he deals with the great captains; but, as Jan points out,[1] she found her place in a very special category of popular marvels.

Chastellain dwells on her pride:[2] *et se contenoit en son harnas et en ses mannières, comme eust fait un capitaine meneur d'ung grant ost*. He is careful to explain, however, that her state was necessary in order to impress the multitude of men-at-arms. He blames her for the death of Franquet d'Arras and for the undue influence of that agent of Charles VII, charlatan and heretical impostor, Brother Richard, upon her mission. He tells us, in corroboration of Monstrelet, that upon her capture, she 'gave her faith' to an archer after asking if he were noble.

Chastellain cannot, however, though he alleges this surrender which she denied, withhold his tribute to Joan's magnificent courage, 'passing the nature of woman'; he describes her heroic efforts at the time of her capture to save her company from loss, staying behind them like a captain, and like the bravest of the troop.[3] No wonder that, upon her capture, the Bastard of Wandonne was *plus joyeux que s'il eust eu un roy entre ses mains*.

While Chastellain repeats stories of marvels of all sorts, he is not taken in by them, and preserves a sceptical judgment. As regards Joan, he tells us that there were certain ones on both sides who perceived that she did not greatly differ from other women, but these were folk who believed in nothing, and that sort of person is always outside public opinion.[4]

The notary of the Parlement of Paris, Clément de Fauquembergue, set down news of the Maid between his recordings of official notices and enactments of the *parlement*.[5] He was much interested in her, and, though a Burgundian, he was rather neutral in attitude. On the margin of his *Register* for the tenth of May, 1429, when he had just received news of the raising of the

---

[1] Eduard von Jan, *Beihefte für Zeitschrift für Romanische Philologie* (Halle, 1928), LXXVI, 23.

[2] *Procès*, IV, 445 (Chastellain).

[3] *Ibid.*, IV, 446 (Chastellain).

[4] Georges Chastellain, *Oeuvres, op. cit.*, ii, 49.

[5] *Journal de Clément de Fauquembergue* [éd. Tuetey] (Paris, 1903–1915).

IO. JOAN OF ARC'S HOUSE AT DOMREMY

11. JOAN OF ARC AT THE CORONATION OF CHARLES VII IN THE CATHEDRAL
AT RHEIMS by J.-E. Lenepveu
From a mural painting in the Pantheon, Paris (*Bettmann Archive*)

siege of Orleans, he sketched an imaginary figure of her, with rather full breasts, long hair, and long neck. He had not seen her, but like all else that he had to say, this is strictly contemporary, and the only surely contemporary representation.[1]

Fauquembergue's *Register* is one of the most valuable 'sources' on the ill-fated Armagnac attack on Paris in the summer campaign of 1429—the attack which is so much a bone of contention among the Maid's biographers. He indicates[2] that there was a commotion within the city coinciding with the assault without, and that the latter was almost perfunctory. Apparently the Armagnacs, who had their own party within the city, were counting on a 'fifth column' enterprise that failed. This may explain the mysterious hints in some of Joan's letters of a good fortune of which she may not speak. It will be recalled that she stated at her trial that she wished to exchange Franquet d'Arras for the landlord of the Bear Inn, an Armagnac leader within Paris, who had been imprisoned; and she gave up this plan only when she learned he had been executed.[3]

Fauquembergue makes it clear that four times as many men as the King had under his command could not have taken the city, once the internal uprising which was attempted had failed; the city was well provisioned, and most of the inhabitants were loyal to Burgundy. (We must recall the strong Burgundian influence of the clergy and the University of Paris; it would appear that a section of the commonalty was Armagnac.) Moreover, the besiegers were not adequately equipped. In view of ths situation in Paris, King Charles was perhaps justified in withholding his person from so dubious a venture, and in frustrating the plans of Joan and the war chiefs for renewed assault on the city—though this opinion runs counter to the well-nigh unanimous conclusion of Joan's biographers.[4] They all

---

[1] The original is in the National Archives in Paris. See Plate 7, facing p. 49.

[2] On the siege see *Procès*, IV, 456–8 (*Register of Clément de Fauquembergue*).

[3] Barrett, pp. 117, 183.

[4] See, e.g. Andrew Lang, *Maid, op. cit.*, Appendix B. We must agree with Lang's refutation of M. Anatole France's opinion that the assault was a serious one, as proved by the siege material lost.

agree with the Maid, who, carried off the field wounded, exclaimed, according to De Cagny, 'By my staff, the place would have been taken!'[1]

We have already seen that Chastellain derived much of his material from Jean le Férre, seigneur de Saint-Remy, who also wrote his memoirs on his own account (1460).[2] Saint-Remy, a gentleman of Picardy, had grown old as a servitor of the Dukes of Burgundy; he was their herald-at-arms, under the honoured title of King-at-arms of the Golden Fleece, and was a most respected counsellor, entrusted with important confidential missions.[3] He draws heavily on Monstrelet in his *Chronique*,[4] but he also gives first-hand evidence on many important events, especially military ones. He was apparently at Agincourt as a Burgundian agent with Henry V;[5] he may have been at Compiègne when Joan was captured, and he may have formed from observation his opinion that she was a brave girl, whose claim to a mission, however, was confuted by the failure of her promises. Le Fèvre certainly gives us the best account of the Pont l'Evêque engagement, where Joan, he informs us, was *chef de guerre* for the King.

Pierre Cochon's *Chronique normande*,[6] very hostile to the Orleans party, is not of great value, though there are occasional interesting details. Cochon was at Rouen, apparently, during Joan's trial; but we must dismiss with laughter the contention of Bouton, who, invoking the authority of the genealogist Hozier, tries to identify Cochon with Peter Cauchon, the presiding judge.[7] It has been plausibly suggested that fear of the English explains why Cochon ceases to concern himself with Joan after she appears in Rouen.

There are other minor Burgundian chronicles, such as the

[1] *Procès*, IV, 27 (*De Cagny*).

[2] Le Fèvre died in 1468. For his work see *Chronique de Jean le Fèvre, transcrite d'un manuscrit appartenant à la bibliothèque de Boulogne-Sur-Mer et publié par F. Morand*, 2 Vol., 8°. (Paris, 1876–1881). *Société de l'Histoire de France (Publications)* v. 178, 204.

[3] See Le Fèvre, *op. cit., prologue*, vii, 258. *Procès*, IV, 429.

[4] See Mlle Dupont, *Bulletin de la Société de l'Histoire de France*, iii, 1.

[5] Jules Michelet, *Jeanne d'Arc* (éd Nelson, Paris, 1934), pp. 32–5.

[6] *Chronique normande*, in *Bibliothèque de l'école des chartes*, 2°série, iii, 116.

[7] Albert Sarrazin, *Pierre Cauchon, juge de Jeanne d'Arc; Reims, Paris, Beauvais, Rouen, Lisieux* (Paris, 1901), p. 253.

chronicle of Edmund de Dynther. Several Belgian chronicles were published after Quicherat's great work, and were not known to him.[1] Jean Germain, bishop of Nevers and Châlons, chancellor of the Order of the Golden Fleece, counsellor to the duke of Burgundy, has a strange and interesting tale of Joan's capture, which is ignored by most of her biographers. He tells us that she sought to conceal herself in the crowd when she saw that she could not escape, and that she endeavoured to pass herself off as a man. Her armour had to be removed to expose the imposture:[2]

> *nam prelo armorum constrictae mammae laxatae ad ventrum fluunt; turgidae nates ad nenias matrum aptissimum consignat; gesticulatione tamen atque procaci verborum audacia se virum mentitur.*

There seems no reason why the eminent cleric's testimony should be so wilfully disregarded by modern students, lay or clerical; his anatomical observations are confirmed by other evidence, and they bear all the marks of careful observation. The worthy gentleman's attitude toward Joan is but the general Anglo-Burgundian attitude, that she is a species of monster.[3] Joan was too good a warrior not to know the meaning of a *ruse de guerre* when in the hands of the enemy. We cannot agree with M. Alexandre Sorel's shocked dismissal, more creditable to his patriotic sentiments than to his historical judgment:

> *Or, à qui fer-t-on jamais croire que Jeanne d'Arc, elle si pure, si sincère, si chevaleresque, si éminement Française, ait songé un seul instant à récourir, même au prix de son existence, à de pareils artifices?*[4]

Another Belgian source, the *Livre des Trahisons*, tells us that throughout France fools and simple folk called her the Angelic.[5] The same work describes Bedford's English soldiers' banner, on

---

[1] *Chroniques relatives à l'histoire de la Belgique sous la domination des ducs de Bourgogne.* Latin texts published by M. le Baron Kervyn de Lettenhove, *membre de la commission royal d'histoire* (Brussels, 1876).

[2] *Ibid.,* p. 28.

[3] Barrett, pp. 19, 31, 33, 152, 154, 158 ff.

[4] Alexandre Sorel, *La Prise de Jeanne d'Arc devant Compiègne et l'histoire des sièges de la même ville sous Charles VI et Charles VII d'après des documents inédits avec vues et plans* (Paris, 1889), p. 206.

[5] *Chron: Belg. inéd.,* ii, 197.

which were blazoned a distaff and spindle, with hanks of yarn, and the motto[1] 'Come on, my pretty girl'.

The *Mémoire sur Guillaume de Flavy* echoes the frequent Burgundian assertion that Joan gave her faith to her captor, who dragged her from her horse by her long cloak.[2]

The Burgundian chroniclers, because of their superior amplitude, clarity, and relatively rationalistic approach, long dominated the views of historians of the France of the fifteenth century, except for their attitudes toward Joan of Arc. History, Michelet said, *parle bourguignon*. But, from the early nineteenth century, the influence of the Burgundian point of view rapidly declined. In the past century, the Burgundian 'sources' have not been as much considered, since they did not at all appeal to French nationalists, to Anglo-Saxon romantics, or to those who were bent on canonization proceedings for Joan of Arc. Intellectual fashions change, and perhaps—who knows?—their time may come again.[3]

---

[1] *Chron: Belg. inéd.*, ii, 198.

[2] *Procès*, V, 177 (*Mémoire*); also, V, 368–73.

[3] See Jacques d'Avout, *La Querelle des Armagnacs et des Bourguignons* (Paris, 1943), for an excellent recent work, written largely from Burgundian sources and a Burgundian point of view, by a descendant of loyal servitors of Jean sans Peur and other Dukes of Burgundy.

IV

A SIMPLE SHEPHERDESS

The fame of Joan of Arc in her own lifetime rang throughout Europe. Already a legend, continental in the range of its interest, began to form about her, as all Christendom—in so many ways more a unity then, than now—responded with eager interest to her marvellous story.

The age was fond of miraculous occurrences, and Joan generally received full credit, after the patron saints of the city, for the relief of Orleans. There were many who agreed with Guillaume Girault, the former magistrate, who said that the taking of the Tourelles under the Maid's leadership was the most obvious miracle since the Passion.[1]

There were, moreover, wonderful prophecies about Joan. A letter written from Germany predicted that before St John the Baptist's day, in 1429, there would be not one Englishman, howsoever strong and valiant, to be seen throughout France, either in battle or in the open field.[2] Joan herself, at the same time, was promising Lord Guy Laval, 'I will shortly give you to drink at Paris'. Everywhere, Joan was expected to lead crusades to exterminate heretics and infidels. Bonne Visconti, hoping for her help in recovering Milan, addressed a pressing appeal—*A très honorée et très devote Pucelle, Jeanne, envoyée du roy des cieux pour la réparation et extirpation des Anglois tyrannisans la France.* Bertrandon de la Broquière, *premier écuyer-tranchant du duc de Bourgogne*, tells us that, upon voyaging to Constantinople in the year

---

[1] *Procès*, IV, 282.
[2] *Ibid.*, V, 351. Joan was said to have guaranteed this; Joan's promise, *ibid.*, V, 107.

1433, he was asked whether it was true that the Pucelle had been taken, for it seemed to the Greeks *que c'estoit une chose impossible.*[1] There is truth in Anatole France's comment upon certain of the foreign chronicles:

> Thus, we learn from these good merchants that at no period of her existence was Jeanne known otherwise than by fables, and that if she moved multitudes it was by the spreading abroad of countless legends which sprang up wherever she passed and made way before her. And indeed, there is much food for thought in that dazzling obscurity which from the very first enwrapped the Maid, in those radiant clouds of myth, which, while concealing her, rendered her all the more imposing.[2]

The view of Joan's judges, in 1431, that her mission was not authenticated by miracle,[3] was certainly not an opinion generally held.

Certainly the Italian and German newsletters dealing with the Maid, like the dispatches of foreign correspondents today, are often full of false gossip; this is true even of foreign diplomatic dispatches, memoirs, the jottings of diarists. Yet from time to time we learn interesting things from these sources, as when a number of them, German and Italian, tell us that the Maid asked the dauphin to be clement, to live by God's will, to be a good lord to rich and poor, friend and enemy. She thought, so she admitted at the trial, that the misfortunes of France were a punishment for the sins of her people.[4] How natural, then, that she should have considered that the vices of the sovereign might also be visited upon the people!

'It is the mind that argues, but the heart that decides'; and since the hearts of Germans and Italians were not so violently involved in the Joan affair as were the French, we should expect to find more philosophic doubt, more rational suspension of judgement, among them than on the part of Joan's countrymen. This is, indeed, the case. Foreign opinion on the whole reserved judgement upon what must appear to it an incident,

---

[1] *Procès,* IV, 532. For Visconti's letter, *ibid.,* V, 253.

[2] Anatole France, *op. cit.,* I, xxii, comment on Windecke and Morosini.

[3] Barrett, pp. 239, 249, 252, 259, 292-3 (judgement of the University of Paris).

[4] *Ibid.,* pp. 126, 179.

although a major one, in a French party struggle.

The most important of the German chronicles of Joan's career is to be found in the long reference of Eberhard von Windecke (1380–1442), although this work is largely based on the *Chronique de Tournay*. Windecke was treasurer of the Holy Roman Emperor, Sigismund, whose deeds he chronicles in the account from which his reference to Joan is drawn, and Quicherat thought his chronicle based on official correspondence to which he had access. Beckmann, however, in 1872, was successful in exploding this theory.[1] Lefèvre-Pontalis has further considered it critically.[2] Actually, Windecke is full of improbable marvels and sentimentalities.

It is, therefore, hard to credit Jeanné's conjecture[3] that we have in Windecke a faithful echo of the lost Book of Poitiers, to which Joan repeatedly referred at her trial.[4] Jeanné assumes Windecke gives us extracts from an official résumé of the proceedings of Joan's vindication at Poitiers, sent from France to the Emperor Sigismund. Actually, we do not have, in reading Windecke, any such sensation of nearness to events as this would imply.[5]

Johann Nider was in his day a famous theologian. Born in Alsace, Doctor of Theology of the University of Vienna, where he resided for a long period, he was later Prior of the Dominican Cloisters in Nuremberg and in Basel.[6] This 'very zealous discoverer of witches', as Trithemius calls him, wrote his *Formicarium*[7] in order to direct pious inquisitors in the search for heresy, sorcery and magic. His book is full of stories about divination, sorcery, phantoms, 'haunts', incubi and succubi. It is

---

[1] Beckmann, *op. cit.*

[2] Germain Lefèvre-Pontalis éd., *Les Sources allemands de l'histoire de Jeanne d'Arc* (Paris, 1903), includes *Chronique*, Eberhard von Windecke.

[3] *Jeanné, op. cit.*, p. 90.

[4] *Procès*, III, 391; IV, 487; V, 472–3.

[5] For Windecke, see also *Eberhard Windeckes Denkwürdigkeiten zur Geschichte des Zeitalters Kaiser Sigmunds* (Berlin, 1893), pp. 245–60; 518–22; *Procès*, V, 487 ff.

[6] Barrett-Champion, p. 448.

[7] Johann Nider, *Formicarium, seu dialogus ad vitam Christianam exemplo conditionum formicae imitativus*, in 4° (Paris, 1519). See also, *Tractatus de visionibus et revelationibus* (Strasbourg, 1517). *Procès*, IV, 502 ff, gives the text of Nider's discussion of Joan.

in this book that he discusses Joan, in a tone which is circumspect, but hostile. He had derived from his friend Lami, a former rector of the University of Paris, his information concerning her, and also concerning the woman condemned at Paris, who said that Joan came from God. Regarding Joan, he had expressly learned from his friend

> *se habere familiarem Dei angelum, qui iudicio litteratissimorum virorum judicatus est esse malignus spiritus ex multis conjecturis et probationibus.*

Yet, with detached scholastic wisdom, Nider refrains from coming to any final conclusion as to whether Joan's inspiration was diabolical or divine:

> *Dubitant exinde saeculares et ecclesiastici, regulares et monastici quo spiritu regeretur diabolico an divino.*

Heinrich von Gorckum's work is very similar to that of Nider. Gorckum was also a German theologian, a professor and vice-chancellor of the University of Cologne.[1] The town of Gorckum, from which he came, is in what is now Holland, then part of the Holy Roman Empire of the German nation. In June, 1429, he wrote a treatise on Joan of Arc, based largely on rumour. In this treatise he advances six reasons for and six reasons against the acceptance of her mission, good or bad.[2] He reaches no conclusion; and it is interesting to contrast the cautious open-mindedness of this scholarly neutral contemporary with the blind dogmatism of some leading authorities of more recent centuries.

The *Sibylla Francica*[3] is a Latin dissertation, in two parts, written by an anonymous author, an erudite and mystical German clerk of the diocese of Spire, June–September, 1429, and it thus affords us a strictly contemporary impression. It is one of several treatises, some of them even written by subjects of the Duke of Burgundy, which were published soon after the relief of Orleans, and reveal clearly the impression made by that tremendous event. We can see in it how strange, not to say

[1] See Trithemius, *Catalogue of Illustrious Men*, cited by Ayroles, *La Pucelle devant l'Eglise, op. cit.*, p. 60.
[2] See *Procès*, III, 411–21; V, 474–5.
[3] *Ibid.*, III, 422–68; V, 475–6.

unnatural, appeared the phenomenon of Joan in the eyes of people in her own day. The clerk of Spire is perhaps rather favourable than otherwise to the French prophetess, but he weighs the arguments pro and con judiciously. He compares Joan to the ancient sibyls, both Biblical and classical, and seems to think she possessed knowledge of astrology and other occult sciences, by means of which she was able to foretell the future; it is this aspect of her career which interests him above all. He finds that Joan made prophecies both of predestination and of commination, though her predictions were only in the service of her country.[1] The troubled times were full of prophets, but where most were vague, she was precise. He tells us that he talked, on September 9th, with a doctor of laws, recently come by sea from the English kingdom, who had spoken of the 'French sibyl' and had stated that her deeds were much detested in England, and rightly so. She was especially reproached with wearing men's clothes, which led many to think that she accomplished her prodigies only with the aid of magic arts and diabolical suggestions. The clerk of Spire, who remarks that 'the French nation, which shines by its intelligence, has not accepted her without examination', advances defences for Joan, quoting St Thomas to show that the wearing of men's clothes by a woman can be justified in case of necessity, or where reasonable cause exists. He also defends her against the charge of diabolic inspiration. He attributes to Joan two predictions which were not destined to be fulfilled, and the reality of which a modern theological champion is therefore anxious to discount.[2] These predictions were that Charles VII would reign for twenty years (actually he reigned for thirty years) and that his son (the later Louis XI, penny-pinching and hunchbacked) would be the most glorious ruler since Charlemagne.

The *Sibylla Francica* is, indeed, confused and badly written, a medley of controversial literature; but it is the most often cited of the theological treatises. Its author is certainly not too well informed; even in September, 1429, for instance, he is still not

---

[1] *Procès*, III, 435 (*De Sibylla Francica, Rotulus* I). See also Quicherat, *Aperçus*, p. 74.
[2] J. B. J. Ayroles, *La Pucelle devant l'Église*, p. 74.

sure that the dauphin has been crowned!

Hermann Koerner, or Cornerius, another German contemporary of the Maid, was the author of a Universal History very favourable in its allusions to her.

There were, of course, Italians who hailed Joan as 'the Messenger of Heaven'; but generally speaking, contemporary Italian comment reflects the cool and sceptical spirit of the Renaissance, already well advanced in Italy.

Cardinal Aeneas Sylvius Piccolomini (Pope Pius II, deceased 1464) the subtle Italian ecclesiastical diplomatist, poet, historian, theologian, mediator of the Peace of Arras in 1435 between France and Burgundy, gives us a long and perhaps fairly accurate account of Joan in the sixth book of his *Commentaries*[1] on the memorable events of his century up to the year 1463. He confesses an inability to decide what spirit moved Joan; his judgement is tactfully and diplomatically balanced between the Armagnac and Burgundian accounts of her, as he had mingled much with both parties, and had sought in his politic way to conciliate both and to hold the scales more or less even between them; he does not know whether she was inspired by good or evil spirits, whether she was hallucinated or manipulated by clever statesmen, but his own narrative seems to indicate that, on the whole, he is inclined to give her the benefit of the doubt. Perhaps he is influenced by the traditional tie between the Pope and the King of France, 'the eldest son of the Church', often the supporter of the Papacy in its struggles with the Emperors. He gives an emphatic account of Joan's vindication at Poitiers, pays tribute to her purity, modesty, courage, energy, boldness, cleverness; and he acknowledges her great services. He admits that he had heard among the Burgundians that she had been manipulated by clever politicians trying to mediate the jealousies of the nobles, and he is not sure whether to see in her career the hand of God or the hand of man.[2] Concluding that the true

---

[1] *Commentarii rerum memorabilium quae temporibus suis contingerunt.* See *Pii Secundi commentarii* (1614 edition). Book VI, Ch. XLIII; *Procès*, IV, 508 ff.

[2] *'Divinum opus an humanum inventum fuerit difficile affirmaverim.'* (*Procès*, IV, 518.)

history of Joan will find in posterity more admiration than belief,[1] His Eminence can find nothing reprehensible in her, save her wearing of men's clothing; but he gives a very incomplete picture of her trial, which probably embarrassed his ecclesiastical conscience. He admits that the English may have sought to kill her because they dreaded the influence of her prestige upon the popular mind, or feared the possibility of her escape. When we consider Piccolomini's calm, his philosophical detachment, and his subtlety we can well understand and concur in Quicherat's favourable verdict upon him, recognizing him as the best fifteenth-century commentator upon Joan of Arc from outside her own country.[2]

Another Italian chronicle which gives an account of Joan is that of Giovanni Sabadino degli Ariente of Bologna.[3] Written in 1483, it was printed only in 1888. It contains many glaring errors; for instance, he has Joan leading the army of Charles VII for eight years. He has an inaccurate description of the Rehabilitation, and a totally false story of the great vengeance visited by Charles upon all those responsible for Joan's death. His story of the secret which Joan told the King represents an interesting stage in the evolution of that strange legend. According to him, when the King hesitated to trust her upon their first meeting, Joan sought a secret conference. 'The King then took her by the hand and led her into a private room. What she said no one knew. The King having heard her and, perhaps, having made some objections, remained thoughtful and surprised at the will of heaven, and at once made her general of his army—without opposition of his barons.'

[1] '*Digna res quae memoriae mandaretur. quamvis apud posteros plus admirationis sit habitura quam fidei.*' (*Loc. cit.*)

[2] See *Procès*, IV, 507. Quicherat says: 'Comme récit et comme appréciation, ce morceau peut passer pour ce qui a été écrit de meilleur à l'étranger au XVᵉ siècle. L'esprit scolastique ne s'y montre nulle part. L'opinion est celle d'un homme habitué aux affaires, qui admet la diversité des sentiments sur un fait si extraordinaire, mais qui montre combien ceux qui voudraient le réduire aux proportions d'une intrigue, sont réfutés par la grandeur des résultats.'

[3] For this writer, see M. le Comte de Puymaigre, 'Jeanne d'Arc, Sa Vie par un Italien du XVᵉ siècle (Sabadino degli Ariente),' *Revue des Questions Historiques*, April 1, 1889.

THE JUDGEMENTS OF JOAN

Philip of Bergamo (Giacomo Filippo Foresti of Bergamo), an Augustinian friar, wrote many pages concerning Joan of Arc, very friendly in point of view, both in his *Universal History*, and in his *De claris eclectisque mulieribus*, a work of considerable literary charm, published at Ferrara in 1497.[1] His work bears some resemblance to that of Sabadino, and also to Antoine Dufour's *Livre des femme célèbres*[1] composed in Brittany, at the request of Queen Anne, by a confessor to Louis XII.[2] It is the source of the legend of the special solicitude of Louis XI for the reputation of Joan of Arc, 'la Pucelle française', a legend which passed, through Hordal[3] and Villaret[4] to Lenglet-Dufresnoy, later to be exploded by l'Averdy. Philip of Bergamo transposes the Rehabilitation to Louis XI's reign, in a fantastic recital filled with popular errors. He describes the burning alive of two 'disloyal judges' who had served at the original trial, the burning of the bones of others, and the general confiscation of their goods in order to set up a foundation for the saying of perpetual masses for the repose of the soul of Joan of Arc. We may contrast this story with the true picture, that, for instance, of Thomas de Courcelles, one of the leaders among Joan's judges, preaching the funeral oration over the body of Charles VII, the object of distinguished consideration on the part of Louis XI, and dying in peace, full of years and honours, in 1469.

To Philip of Bergamo, however, we owe one of our best

---

[1] See *Procès*, IV, 521 ff; Clément-François de l'Averdy, *Notices et Extraits des Manuscrits de la Bibliothèque du roi*, etc. (Paris, 1790), iii, 548–9; Guy Endore, *The Sword of God* (New York, 1931), p. 340; Joseph Fabre, *Libératrice*, p. 265, and *Réhabilitation*, II, 272; Gower, *op. cit.*, p. 289; Marius Sepet, *op. cit.*, p. 529. M. l'Abbé Lenglet-Dufresnoy discusses Philip of Bergamo in the last part of his work *Vierge, Héroïne, et Martyre d'État, suscité par la Providence pour rétablir la Monarchie Française, tirée des Procès et autres pièces originales du temps* (Paris, 1753); 2 Vols. Here he gives a favourable verdict, contrasting with the later writers cited above, who find Bergamo's account rather fantastic, 'a work where in legend almost eclipses history'.

[2] See Champion, *Flavy, op. cit.*, p. 285.

[3] Jean Hordal: *Heroinae nobilissimae Joannae d'Arc, Lotharingae, vulgo Aurelianensis Puellae, historia ex variis gravissimae incorruptissimae que fidei scriptoribus excerpta, ejus que innocentia, a calumniis vindicata: auctore Johanne Hordal, J.U. doctore et professore in alma civitate Ponte Mussana, Ducis a Lotharingia consiliario*, in 4to, Ponti Mussi (Pont-à-Mousson, 1612).

[4] Villaret, *op. cit.*

descriptions of Joan's physical aspect; he derives it from Guillaume Guasche, an Italian gentleman at the court of King Charles VII.[1] It is a description which conforms to the probabilities, and is confirmed by other evidences. The reference to her black tresses reminds us of the black hair in the seal which, until it was stolen, adorned her letter in the archives at Riom,[2] and the letter of Guy de Laval bears confirmation also to this testimony as to her 'sufficiently feminine' voice. Her whole career displays her strength, and we can hardly doubt, despite the illusions which countless painters have sought to create, that her visage was rustic. As for her alleged *petite taille*, Lebrun des Charmettes and Wallon both truly remark that she might be quite tall for a woman, and yet appear short in men's clothes. It is interesting to note that friar Philip bears witness to Joan's early acquisition of equestrian prowess.[3]

From Guillaume Guasche, Philip of Bergamo derives his story of Joan, at the age of sixteen, falling asleep in a chapel where she had sought refuge from the rain while guarding her flocks. As she slept, she had a dream which she believed sent from God, ordering her to go to the aid of King Charles, and this was the decided intimation of her great mission. The story, which shows the influence of Renaissance rationalism, was probably current at the French court. It has been generally discredited because it contradicts Joan's own evidence at her trial, but it is in itself more plausible than her own wonderful story of the 'Voices' taking her quite by surprise in her father's garden, at the age of thirteen. Mrs Caddy[4] has suggested that the chapel where the dream occurred was the one on the hill of the *Bois-chesnu*, rebuilt by Etienne Hordal, destroyed by the Swedes, and

---

[1] *De claris eclectisque mulieribus, cap. CLVII* 'Erat brevi quidem statura, rusticanaque facie et nigro capillo, sed toto corpore praevalida. Ejus sermo satis, et more feminarum illius patriae lenis erat.' (*Procès*, IV, 523.)

[2] See also the *greffier de l'hôtel de ville de la Rochelle, op. cit.*, who says her hair was black and cut round: *capillos quos in rotundum tonsos*, as the Trial Record describes it. (I, 220.)

[3] 'A principio aetatis suae . . . pascendo pecora . . . saepius cursum exercebat; et modo huc atque illuc illi frequens cursus erat; et aliquando currendo hastam ut fortis eques manu capiebat, et arborum truncos . . . percutiebat.' (*Procès*, IV, 523.)

[4] Mrs Florence Caddy, *op. cit.*, p. 43.

in modern times replaced by a white temple.

Cosmo di Raimondi of Cremona was a Franciscan friar who was sent from Milan to inquire about the news of Joan of Arc, concerning which a good deal of doubt was felt by interested parties. We have his letter, of the year 1431.[1] Cosmo Raimondi finds his doubts assuaged by recollection of the shepherd boy, David, and of Jacob, and by the predictions of astrology; but, though assuaged, they are not dispelled.

Saint Antoninus, Archbishop of Florence, was essentially a sceptical cleric of the Renaissance. As he died in 1459, we may assume that he wrote before Joan's rehabilitation. In any case, he was doubtful concerning the spirit which animated Joan,[2] though her works made him believe it was the spirit of God. He devoted to her only a short page in his *Chronicle*.

Guarneri Berni's *Chronicon Eugubinum* has a paragraph on Joan, and there is a page in Lorenzo Buonincontro, both in substance favourable, and not inaccurate, though adding little to our knowledge. Regarding her magic sword—*una spada antichissima*, as the *Morosini Chronicle* calls it—Berni gives us the valuable information that it was one of those which had been deposited in the tombs of knights and nobles, a detail which renders more intelligible the strange tale of the finding of the sword in the Church of St Katherine of Fierbois.

In 1892, Adele Butti introduced to the world the *Morosini Chronicle*,[3] a collection of histories and letters gathered by the Morosini family of Venice, not hitherto examined by scholars, and throwing a new if at times rather flickering and uncertain light upon many aspects of Joan of Arc's brief and sensational career.

Whatever their defects, the Morosini records are probably the most important source-materials dealing with Joan which have

---

[1] *Lettera su Giovanna d'Arco* (1431), *MS. Biblioteca classense* of Ravenna, reported by M. Germain Lefèvre-Pontalis, in an appendix to his edition of the Morosini Chronicle—*Chronique d'Antonio Morosini*, 4 vols., with introduction and commentary, text established by Léon Dorez, (Paris, 1901–1902).

[2] See *Procès*, IV, 506: *quo autem spiritu ducta, vix sciebatur;* it seems strange indeed that Lenglet-Dufresnoy failed to detect the scepticism of Antoninus.

[3] Lefévre-Pontalis edition. (*Procès*, V, 505, 519, for Berni and Buonincontro.)

come to hand since Jules Quicherat's monumental collection published a century ago.[1] They have been too much neglected by French historians,[2] and by those of other countries, who generally follow the French lead. The letters of Pancrazio Justiniani from Bruges in Flanders to his own son in Italy give an account of the Joan story full of wild rumour, of errors and contradictions, of legend mingled with history, but relatively detached, reflecting faithfully the impact of Joan upon her time, and supplementary to certain other accounts. Morosini's correspondents are Venetian men of business, thoughtful, sceptical, subtle, influenced by the spirit of the Italian Renaissance—yet, in their writings, the Maid appears as a figure of white and blazing purity, against a setting of the blackest and most devilish villainy.

These letters reveal how there were being circulated throughout Christendom a whole multitude of fictitious stories, imitated some from the Romances of Chivalry, others from the Golden Legend, concerning that *Demoiselle* as she is called, at once famous and unknown.[3]

The Morosini correspondents are in no doubt of Joan's divine inspiration; they know what magnificent consequences resulted for France from her high deeds.[4] Her origins are incredibly humble: she was 'a simple shepherdess', 'a maiden guarding her flocks, born beside Lorraine', a 'most pious damsel'.[5] Actually, Joan was not, usually at least, a shepherdess, and she was of higher social status than this description would suggest.[6] David Hume may have been right when he said she was represented as a shepherdess in order to render her more 'interesting', and, we may add, more romantic, more miraculous.[7]

[1] *Procès.*

[2] Dunand rejects them completely. See Dunand, l'abbé Philippe Hector, *Études critiques d'après les textes sur l'histoire de Jeanne d'Arc*, 5 vol., (Paris, Toulouse, 1903–1909).

[3] Anatole France, *op. cit.*, xxi.

[4] 'Dio la sa grandisime cose eser séguido de la Francia per i fati de la dita damixela, per la virtù divina operada in ela.'

[5] 'Una simpla bergereta: una poncela varderesa de piegora, nasudo varso la Rena; donzela pientisima,' Marino Sanuto *Vita de' Duchi* gives a similar picture.

[6] Barrett, pp. 54, 64. Siméon Luce, *Jeanne d'Arc à Domrémy, recherches critiques sur les origines de la mission de la Pucelle*, Paris, 1886.

[7] David Hume, *The History of England from the Invasion of Julius Caesar to the Revolution in 1688* (new ed., Boston, 1868). *Infra*, Chapter VII.

A Morosini letter from Avignon does not hesitate to compare Joan to the Virgin Mary.[1] We have a graphic picture of the collapse of the English after their failure at Orleans; their prestige shattered, their defences are reduced to a cheesy consistency, so to speak; they fly without a fight as never before.[2] In the whole coronation campaign, Joan is in the van.[3]

Incidentally, the Morosini Chronicle fortifies Quicherat's effective refutation[4] of the traditional notion that Joan's mission was complete at the zenith of her career, the coronation of Charles VII at Rheims[5]—a notion originally derived from the Rehabilitation, it would seem, in an effort to account for her later failures. 'For she said to all,' we read in the Morosini record, 'that she would chase the English from France.'[6] This accords well with her own tone at her trial.[7]

Perhaps the most important feature of the Morosini Chronicle is the evidence it affords of Charles VII's attempt to ransom Joan of Arc, after her capture. This has been much doubted by historians, but it is corroborated by certain passages in the Trial Record itself.[8] One may with some confidence assert that it compels a revision, which historians have been reluctant indeed to make, in the universal modern portrayal of Charles VII as one of the most slothful and ungrateful wretches in history, deserting his benefactress, the woman who had brought about his coronation, in a most base and craven manner. After all, the traditional portrait was always, one may be permitted to think, more dramatic than plausible; the trial of Joan was a blow aimed above all at the reputation of Charles. Enlightened self-interest, if nothing else, would have impelled him to block, if he could, the

---

[1] 'Et voyez comme Dieu l'a secouru (le Royaume de France) de même que par une femme, Notre Dame Sainte Marie, il a sauvé le genre humain, ainsi par cette jeune fille pure et nette, il a sauvé le chef-d'oeuvre de la chrétienté et c'est bien un grand exemple de notre foi.'

[2] 'Voltase y le spale senze far defexa: de che non fo (fu) mai aldido (udito).'

[3] 'La dita damixela li va davanti chontinuamente per spacio di una giornada o cercha.'

[4] Jules Quicherat, Aperçus.

[5] Supra, Chapter II, Chronique de la Pucelle, pp. 46–9.

[6] 'La quale i dixe el tutto la cacera Ingelexi de Francia.'

[7] Barrett, pp. 80, 126, 159, 165 (her letter to the English), 166, 179, 230.

[8] See Barrett, pp. 23–5.

12. PIERRE CAUCHON, BISHOP OF BEAUVAIS. From his tomb, formerly
in the Cathedral of Beauvais

13. PORTRAIT OF THE DUKE OF BEDFORD. From a miniature in the British Museum

attempt to show that he was crowned with the aid of a heretic and a witch. It is significant that he brought about the subversion of the hostile verdict, the official clerical rehabilitation of Joan's reputation, just as soon as he was powerful enough to bring adequate pressure to bear to secure the desired end.

It may be said—and, indeed, it has been said times without number—that we have no direct documentary evidence of a ransom offer by Charles; but one may be sure that a ransom offer on Charles's part, whose existence is suggested in the Trial Record, would be made very discreetly, because of the heresy issue which had been raised; and documentary evidence of it would later, in all probability, be suppressed, in order to minimize the monarch's inevitably compromising involvement in Joan's conviction.

The Morosini Chronicle reflects faithfully the close interaction, political, religious and cultural, of France and Italy in the time of Joan of Arc. There was much Italian sympathy with the House of France; the Dukes of Milan, bound to it by ties of blood, provided silver, arms and troops to aid Charles VII against the English. Not only Italian soldiers of fortune, but regular, well-trained Italian troops followed Joan, and constituted almost her entire force in her last campaign.[1] The Hundred Years' War was really a European War, in its ramifications and its implications; Scotland and Castile, Aragon and Germany, Milan and Flanders, Emperor and Pope, all were involved in it, or affected by it, directly or indirectly. That is why the 'simple shepherdess', Joan of Arc, rose so promptly into a fame that was as European in breadth as it was lofty in dimension.

---

[1] General S. Visconti-Prasca, *Giovanna d'Arco*, Milano, translated from Italian to French by Jean Godfrin, Preface by General Weygand (Paris, 1938), p. 17, *et passim*.

V

ASHES IN THE SEINE

The career of Joan of Arc has traditionally been regarded by historians as the turning-point in the Hundred Years' War. It has also been assumed that her execution was one of those crimes which are worse than crimes, since they are also blunders; that it left the sainted Maid a martyr, enshrined in popular memory and more potent in death even than she had been in her lifetime. The English, it has been thought, were impaled upon the horns of a dilemma; they could not release her without confessing her spotlessness, and they could not bring her to her death without glorifying her. Guizot saw two nations hanging breathless upon her fate:

> During the trial of Joan of Arc, the war between France and England, without being discontinued, had been somewhat slack; the curiosity and the passions of men were concentrated upon the scenes at Rouen.[1]

One is reminded of that 'pathetic fallacy', dear to some of the poets, which makes the affairs of nature depend upon the doings of men! England, says Guizot again, was 'already half beaten by the divine inspiration, the triumph, the martyrdom of Joan of Arc'.[2] Even Francis Lowell,[3] that hard-headed Puritan, so fond of sifting out superstitious notions, believed that the auto-de-fé, never a popular spectacle in Normandy, produced a reaction in Joan's favour.

[1] Guizot, *France*, translated by Robert Black, 8 vols. ('Nations of the World Series'), II, 281.
[2] *Ibid.*, II, 308.
[3] Lowell, *op. cit.*

Familiar also is the old idea, still echoing in twentieth century literature, that Joan's judges came to a bad end.

> All had to undergo public contempt and the reproaches of their own conscience; Cauchon died overwhelmed with remorse. The people dug up his body in order to throw it into a sewer. The promoter of the trial, Jean d'Estivet, died in the gutter.[1]

The reality, it would seem, was utterly different from that suggested by these stories. All the great personages and events in her age are now quite usually, as we have seen, looked at and judged only in terms of their relationship to the peasant girl from Lorraine; but following her death she was almost forgotten, especially by the great and powerful, even of her own party. The news of her fate was received in a kind of stunned silence, succeeded by oblivion. In 1433, at Blois, Jean Jouvenel des Ursins, in an assembly of the three estates of the realm, celebrating the glories of the reign of Charles VII, thanks God for the King's miraculous successes and marvels that 'a small number of valiant heroes to whom God had given courage to undertake the cause, sufficed for such an enterprise';[2] but he says not a word of the Maid. She had become, apparently, a compromising circumstance in the life of Charles VII, to be forgotten as soon as conveniently possible; doubts concerning her mission had been deepened into negative certitudes by the trial at Rouen.

She perished on a flaming pyre, her soul shattered, her guiding faith and hope gone, for her dust no winding sheet, save the silver waters of the Seine, and with no hope of posthumous fame to brighten the tragic ending of her life; the fickle and sheeplike multitude which had admired her was equally quick to forget her. She had failed. She might well have said: 'My God, my God, why hast thou forsaken me?'

Joan, herself, before her death, was well aware that she could not count upon her own party. It is to be noted that she refused, at her trial, to refer her story of the crown brought to the King to the

---

[1] Léon Denis, *The Mystery of Joan of Arc*, translated by Arthur Conan Doyle, p. 115. In the Rehabilitation testimony, Boisguillaume speaks of the shameful fates of the judges (T. D. Murray, pp. 284–285). Here, no doubt, is the origin of these tales.

[2] Baron Henri Blaze de Bury, *Jeanne d'Arc* (Paris, 1890), p. 477.

arbitrament of the Archbishop of Rheims, or of divers notables and warriors drawn from her own camp, specifically named.[1] She refused to submit her claims to the judgement of 'three or four clergy of her own party' who might come, under a safe-conduct, to attend the trial.[2] When she was asked to submit to the church of Poitiers, where had been held the original hearing which had vindicated her, she replied, 'Do you think you will catch me in that way and draw me to you so?'

The lost Book of Poitiers, recording the hearings which led to Joan's cautiously worded vindication by a tribunal of ecclesiastics at Poitiers at the very beginning of her public career, has disappeared completely; and this is probably because her public trial at Rouen, so much more impressive than has been realized, discredited her so completely that the Book of Poitiers became a compromising document for those who had signed it. Their views, broadcast, with what limited facilities the time afforded, throughout France and Europe, had furnished a weapon of propaganda warfare for the Armagnacs; the Trial Record of

[1] *Procès*, I, 396, 401; Barrett, p. 277.
[2] *Ibid.*, p. 278.
[3] *Ibid.*, p. 278; *Procès*, I, 397. Joan's judges have been criticized for their failure to present at her trial the favourable testimony of Poitiers. Bishop Cauchon is said to have been irritated at the time by this criticism from Jean Lohier and Nicolas de Houppeville (*Ibid.*, II, 11; III, 171). Cauchon could, however, argue that even the Armagnac clergy had become convinced of its error, as proved by the absence of favourable communications from it, regarding Joan (see Quicherat, *Aperçus*, pp. 113 ff.) and by her unwillingness to appeal to it, save for her request at the beginning of the trial that equal members of clergy of both parties be summoned (Barrett, p. 48). In this connection, we note, also Joan's own admission of the initial hostility of the clergy of her party (Barrett, pp. 96–7): 'Asked what reverence she showed the sign when it came to her king, and whether it came from God, she answered that she thanked Our Lord for her deliverance from the trouble arising from the opposition of the clergy of her party. . . . She said the clergy ceased opposing her when they had recognized the sign.' Later (*Ibid.*, p. 336), she admitted that the 'sign', a crown, was pure fiction and she herself was the 'angel' whom she had mentioned as bringing a sign to the King. This whole theme is significant, but has been neglected by scholars.

In regard to it, we observe a reference in the solemn admonition at Joan's trial: 'V. Many doctors and notable ecclesiastics have considered and examined with diligence the statements of the said Jeanne concerning her revelations and apparitions, and in view of the manifest falsehoods regarding the crown brought to Charles, and the coming of the angels, which she had invented, falsehoods and imaginations which have been recognized as such, both by those who afterwards were of our party, and by others . . .' (Barrett, p. 273).

Rouen was a far more potent weapon for the Anglo-Burgundians,[1] and the letter, written in the name of the English King, Henry VI, announcing the Rouen verdict to the courts and principalities of Europe, was an effective counterstroke in the battle of propaganda.

We do hear of one champion of Joan immediately after her trial; Pierre Bosquier, a friar of the Order of Preaching Brothers, was sentenced to almost a year's imprisonment by Joan's judges, Bishop Pierre Cauchon and Jean Le Maistre, after an abject recantation, because he had impugned the justice of the court that tried Joan; but it would appear that he was under the influence of liquor when he committed his indiscretion![2]

The riots at the time of Joan's execution, introduced by Carl Dreyer into his great film, *The Passion of Joan of Arc* (1928), are entirely fictional, so far as we know.

M. Pierre Champion has summed up this matter:

> Save in Orleans, where the worship of Jeanne persisted, associated as she was so inextricably with the memory of the city's deliverance, the Trial Record put public opinion to sleep. She who had been worshipped in her lifetime, before whom candles had been burned and prayers said, whose ring had been kissed and clothing touched as a sacrament, she who had heard her legend run from one end of Europe to the other, was forgotten. The great *procès*, the record in all ways regular, was there; the University of Paris and authority had spoken. She was doubted. See how the testimony became uncertain on the subject of Jeanne; we can find the only opinion favourable to Jeanne in a book of controversy, *Le Champion des Dames* by Martin Le Franc in 1440; and even there, the pro and con is given.[3]

We must remember that the tribunal which condemned Joan was a tremendously impressive array of the leading ecclesiastical talents and reputations of the time—almost a synod of the church.

---

[1] It is significant that Séguin de Séguin was the only examiner present at Poitiers called at the Rehabilitation. M. Siméon Luce (see *Jeanne d'Arc à Domrémy*, p. 274, Note 1) thinks, however, that the Book of Poitiers was destroyed about 1443 because it contained evidence of the treason of the Comte de Vaudemont and others whom the king intended to pardon. See *Procès*, III, 391–2; V, 471–3.

[2] Barrett, pp. 347–8.

[3] Barrett-Champion, p. 481.

THE JUDGEMENTS OF JOAN

No trial of that time—save that of Jean, duc d'Alençon, tried by his peers—was conducted in so impressive and stately a manner.[1]

It is small wonder that Gilles, Lord Abbot of Sainte Trinité de Fécamp, said of the trial judges and consultants:

such men, in so great numbers, cannot be found in the whole world.[2]

As that leading authority, Quicherat, puts it;

on réunit tout ce qui avait qualité pour prononcer en matière de foi.[3]

One need not be surprised that the verdict of such a tribunal dealt Joan's reputation a shattering blow. The trial at Rouen was commenced very deliberately and with great publicity; and yet, even seven months after the plan for trial had been announced, there was no public intervention from Charles VII, from the Archbishop of Rheims or from Rome.[4] From other sources we gather that the Archbishop of Rheims, the leading French cleric, chancellor of France, and presiding officer at Poitiers, was not ill pleased with the proceedings at Rouen; he was frankly critical of the Maid as having 'sinned through pride', in a letter reassuring the good people of Rheims at the time of her trial.

The outcome of the Rouen trial was certainly pleasing to the English. The importance of it to them was apparent from the appearance of Henry VI and the Cardinal of Winchester in Rouen during its continuance. The trial was financed by their authority; and a letter of guarantee from the royal government given to Cauchon, June 12, 1431, promised to pay all expenses involved

---

[1] Barrett-Champion p. 480. See also Charles de Beaurepaire, *Notes sur les juges et les assesseurs du procès de condamnation de Jeanne d'Arc.*

[2] Barrett, p. 240.

[3] Quicherat, *Aperçus*, p. 102.

[4] *Ibid.*, p. 114 ff. In the first article of the Articles of Accusation against Joan of Arc, Promoter d'Estivet affirmed the competence, 'according to divine as well as canon and civil law'. (Barrett, pp. 140–1), of Joan's two judges to act on Joan's case, 'the one as ordinary judge, the other as Inquisitor of the faith'. No higher tribunal challenged this competence at the time. The Faculty of Theology of the University of Paris, in submitting its extremely influential 'deliberations and conclusions' regarding the Maid, affirmed its submission (*Ibid.*, p. 289) to 'the judgement of Our Holy Father, the Pope and the Holy General Council.' Neither of these authorities contested the view of the Theological Faculty of the great University for many years, though the Council of Basel convened in the year of Joan's trial (1431). *Procès*, V, 168–9 (Archbishop's letter).

if any of the judges were attacked before the Pope, a general council or the deputies of one or the other.

Yet it is noted[1] that the idea of a Church trial of Joan originated, not with the English, but with the University of Paris. It seems difficult, despite the almost universal execration to which Joan's judges have been subjected in modern times, to read the Trial Record without feeling the deep sincerity of the ecclesiastics in their quarrel with Joan—their shock, for instance at her male dress![2] We note the letters from 'Our Mother, the University of Paris' addressed 'to the most illustrious lord Duke of Burgundy',[3] 'to the noble and puissant lord Jean de Luxembourg,'[4] and to Cauchon, reproaching him for dilatoriness (!) and urging that the trial be held in Paris, which[5] was quite contrary to English intentions. There is even a letter of reproach for his alleged delay in bringing Joan to trial, addressed to 'our Lord the King of France and England',[6] Henry VI. The University was sincerely Burgundian and Anglophile in sympathy, of course, and it pursued Joan with conviction; it found that she had disseminated a poison which had infected almost the whole Western world.[7] It stood behind the tribunal which tried her, and which (despite later attempts at evasion on the part of some of its members)[8] unanimously found her to be a heretic, a sorceress, schismatic and apostate. In a letter to Henry VI, the University of Paris, his 'most humble daughter', states 'it appeared to us that in this women's trial extreme gravity and a holy and just procedure had been observed, which must be pleasing to all men'.[9] The University praises the zeal, in this letter, of its representatives at the trial,

---

[1] *Procès*, I, 9.
[2] E.g. Barrett, p. 22. It is to be observed, even today, how often religious representations of Joan show her wearing some sort of skirt!
[3] *Ibid.*, p. 22.
[4] *Ibid.*, p. 24.
[5] This was for security reasons, primarily. The English had a much firmer grip on Rouen than upon Paris, Rouen being the seat of their power in France, the point, therefore, at which their influence was at its maximum.
[6] *Ibid.*, p. 30.
[7] *Procès*, I, 409.
[8] At the Rehabilitation proceedings. *Vide infra*, Chapter VI.
[9] Barrett, p. 284.

'unsparing of their efforts, their persons, and their faculties, and careless of the great and threatening dangers, particularly on the roads'. Again, the University set its seal of approval upon the trial:

We approved of this celebrated trial, and of its form, and considered it to be according to the holy canons and to emanate from the most eloquent and experienced minds.[1]

However unintelligible these sentiments may be to modern French patriots, there can be little doubt of their sincerity and good faith, and equally little of their immense moral authority throughout Christendom; for the University of Paris was then at the very height of its immense mediaeval fame and influence as a theological authority, having gained in weight from the Great Schism and the conciliar movement, which temporarily weakened the power of the Pope. The great University occupied a highly privileged and independent position.[2] Given its tremendous ascendancy, its opinion had a crushing effect, even upon the clergy of the Armagnac party; they had no such instrument of influence upon their opponents. Even Gerson, the leading Armagnac theologian, had called the University of Paris the 'eldest daughter of Kings, this beautiful bright sun'. We may note in Joan's trial the eagerness of canons of Rouen, like Robert Le Barbier and Jean Alespée, to escape responsibility by deferring to the judgement of the University of Paris.[3]

It is clear, therefore, that in the two decades following Joan's death it appeared that her name had been branded, presumably forever, throughout Christendom, in a sentence which did not appear to be English, but Gallican and Catholic, for the University of Paris was Gallican in sentiment. The Vice-Inquisitor, Jean le Maistre, was a timid and feeble individual, but his signature upon the chief legal instruments of the trial was invaluable throughout all Europe, for it directly implicated the papal power. To say that he had committed a wrong would be to 'undermine

[1] Barrett, p. 286.
[2] Quicherat, *Aperçus*, p. 96.
[3] Barrett, pp. 244-5.

all human authority'. Bishop Cauchon[1] apparently feared the nullification of the trial for lack of adequate powers in the court, and would have preferred, it would seem, the attendance in person of the lord Inquisitor of Heretical Error for the Kingdom of France. Failing that, he wished a vicar armed with 'more extensive and particular powers'. Jean le Maistre, the vicar of the lord Inquisitor, at first cautiously avoided attendance at the trial; he was unwilling to act unless especially authorized to do so by his superior, although his commission included the city and diocese of Rouen, and was deemed adequate by learned authorities.[2] In order to hasten the trial, Le Maistre consented that Cauchon proceed with it pending more adequate authorization, which was finally forthcoming,[3] and gave to the trial an authority which could hardly be challenged.

In the last analysis, however, the mainspring of the whole procedure was that redoubtable personage, Pierre Cauchon, bishop of Beauvais. No one, in his own time or later, could challenge Cauchon's claim to great ability, or to thorough legal and theological training; he was one of the brightest lights of the University of Paris, in which he had occupied the position of Rector, and had been protector or conservator of its privileges.[4] He was a strong, energetic, zealous man, the sort of man whom it is good to have on one's side in a fight; he was the right-hand man of the Anglo-Burgundian government, and had held many of the highest offices of Church and state, and performed many of the most delicate missions. We know what his Alma Mater, the University of Paris, thought of him; its letter to him described him as 'animated by an immense fervour of most singular charity'

---

[1] Bishop Cauchon's own claim of power and authority to act in the case was based on the fact that Joan had been captured in his diocese of Beauvais, therefore within his episcopal jurisdiction (Barrett, p. 2). A letter from the chapter of the Cathedral of Rouen accepted Cauchon's jurisdiction, and granted him territory, during the vacancy of the archiepiscopal see, for the conduct of the trial of Joan (Barrett, pp. 33–5). Cauchon's jurisdiction was challenged at the Rehabilitation, but it would seem that the denial is not easily sustained.

[2] *Ibid.*, pp. 42–3.

[3] *Ibid.*, pp. 97–9.

[4] Quicherat, *Aperçus*, p. 98.

and is studded with phrases like 'most firm righteousness', 'stable and constant industry', 'pious concern for the public safety', 'virile and famous martial spirit of your most sincere fervour', 'valiant and forceful probity', 'vigilant solicitude', 'true pastor'. 'Thus when the Prince of shepherds shall appear,' it concludes, 'he will grant to the pastoral fervour of your reverence a crown of eternal glory.'[1] King Henry VI (or rather, one of his advisers, acting in his name) writes to Cauchon in much the same ardent terms; the Duke of Burgundy, even the Pope, also place themselves on record. It was in 1432, after the trial, that Pope Eugenius IV, confirming the choice of Martin V, transferred Peter Cauchon to the diocese of Lisieux from that of Beauvais, which, captured by the forces of Charles VII, was no longer tenable by such an eminent champion of the Anglo-Burgundian cause.[2]

Cauchon's letters, inserted at the beginning of the record of the trial proceedings, reveal him to be an able man of business and of large affairs—precise, direct, authoritative. He was determined that 'we should proceed in such a way that by God's help the matter should be conducted to the praise of Our Lord and to the exaltation of the faith, so that our trial might be without flaw'.[3] He was no brute; he showed both humanity and good judgement in opposing the use of legally permissible torture upon Joan, upon the ground that it was 'neither necessary nor expedient';[4] he judged it would accomplish nothing, and might weaken the author- of the trial; besides, the evidence was already sufficient. Pierre Cauchon, then, was much trusted, and much esteemed in his own time by many outstanding and influential people.

We can understand the confidence he inspired when we look

---

[1] Barrett, pp. 285–7.

[2] Denifle, P. H., *Auctarium Chartul*: Univers. Paris. T.I., p. 935. Cauchon did not obtain the archiepiscopal see of Rouen, which he had administered both spiritually and temporally. He narrowly escaped being taken prisoner when Paris fell in 1436; he made several visits to England, in pursuance of peace negotiations. Dying in 1442, rich and full of years and honours, he was buried in the magnificent Chapel of the Virgin at Lisieux, which he had rebuilt and decorated at his own expense.

[3] Barrett, p. 133. Manchon (T. D. Murray, p. 183) gives an indication of his firm discipline at the trial.

[4] *Procès*, I, 402.

at his firm and intelligent face, whose outlines, at least, are preserved for us by the image on his black marble tomb, formerly in
the Cathedral of Lisieux.[1] It is one of the ironies of history that
this man should have gone down alike in popular and in literary
tradition as one of the blackest villains of all recorded time,
worthy of comparison only with Pontius Pilate, because of his
leading part in the trial of the peasant maid from Lorraine, whom,
we must believe, he regarded sincerely as a heretic and a witch, a
poisoned sheep which it was a matter of Christian duty to remove
before it tainted the whole flock. Nothing could illustrate better
than the fate of Cauchon's reputation, the fickleness of fortune
and popular favour, the vanity of human ambition, But, in any
case, we must recall Cauchon's weight and repute in the eyes of
his contemporaries in order to understand clearly the prestige of
the trial he conducted, its legal rigour, and its great impact upon
his time.

The record of the *Procès* was edited some time after the death of
Joan,[2] probably not before 1435, and was translated into Latin
from the French of the original Minutes—one part of which, as
Quicherat proved, is preserved to us in the so-called *MS
D'Urfé*. We may believe that the Trial Record was edited because
Charles VII's cause was looking up, Joan's reputation was
beginning to revive, and the record was needed as a vindication
and an instrument of partisan propaganda warfare. It was also,
as M. Pierre Champion has pointed out, the judges' apology to
posterity. Thomas Courcelles,[3] who carried through the actual
redaction, suppressed his name in some compromising places,

[1] See Plate 12, facing p. 96.

[2] *Procès*, III, 196, deposition of N. Taquel, notary and secretary to the Vice-Inquisitor
at the trial of Joan: 'Dicit quod hujusmodi processus fuit redactus in forma in qua est, per
magnum temporis spatium post mortem ipsius Johannae.'

[3] A distinguished Latinist, he was called 'the light of the Council of Basel and the
second Gerson'. See *Procès*, I, 30, note 3, for the tribute of Aeneas Sylvius Piccolomini to
his capacity, amiability and modesty, 'so modest that he was always looking at the
ground, like one who would fain pass unnoticed'; a tribute generally accepted in his own
time as deserved. He refused a cardinalate, and he died simply Dean of the Chapter at
Paris—a strong Gallican leader, of wide influence. See also Pierre Champion, *Procès de
Condamnation*, II, 343–4; Joseph Calmette, *Jeanne d'Arc* (hereafter cited as 'Calmette';
Paris, 1946), p. 129.

such as the record of his vote for torture. Reading the signs of the times, he was preparing already, no doubt, for his later transformation from Burgundian to Armagnac. No wonder he was evasive at the Rehabilitation in 1456, and suffered from curious attacks of amnesia, though not of repentance.

So great was the effect of Joan's trial that it is acknowledged today by writers of all schools of thought. Thus Monahan:

A strange silence followed the death of Jeanne d'Arc, a silence universal, absolute, as far as we may gather. The English government communicated a report of the affair to other governments, and its accomplice, the University of Paris, reported to the Pope.[1]

One of the most distinguished of contemporary French writers, Georges Bernanos, says:

Until the beginning of the Process of Rehabilitation—that is, until the day when the King of France made his power sufficiently felt—it is impossible to discover a single written testimony, or even the record of a single verbal witness, in favour of the little saint who had been dishonoured, convicted of witchcraft, and branded with the terrible sign.[2]

In spite of all this, however ,there exists a good deal of evidence that Joan was not completely forgotten. The upper classes, many of whom in her lifetime had viewed her claims with jealousy, scepticism, suspicion or fear, were glad to forget her; but the common people, who had acclaimed her in life, did not forget her so readily, and many of them continued to love her after her death. They felt instinctively that she was one of them, that she was sent for their succour and consolation, and had been their champion, incurring enmity therefor; they found faith easier than did their betters. Marvellous stories of her exploits continued to circulate, as we have seen and shall see.[3]

It is in the atmosphere thus created that we have the strange and rather mysterious episode of the 'false Joan of Arc'—or 'false Joans of Arc', for we cannot be quite sure now whether there were one or several. It was a curious resurrection, which

[1] Monahan, *op. cit.*, p. 273.
[2] George Bernanos, *Sanctity Will Out* (New York, 1947), p. 14.
[3] *Supra*, Chapter II; *infra*, Chapter VI, pp. 140–1.

can be paralleled, as we have seen,[1] in the case of a number of other historical characters. The careers of those martial Maids, the 'false Joans', showed that Joan's popular cult, which had so flourished during her lifetime,[2] was already growing; her achievement had been sufficient to assure that men would not quite let her die; perhaps it showed, also, that some of the influential and official personages who had found her useful during life still found her memory useful and her successors convenient. The career of the 'false Joan' was in a way a kind of anticipation of the Rehabilitation, except that it did not have the sanction of the Church—was, in fact, very far from having such sanction.

Men, we may conjecture, did not quite believe in the 'false Joan'; they merely wanted to believe in her. This must be the explanation of the fact that in Orleans, where Joan was so well known, men fêted Jeanne des Armoises, the pretender, and at the same time continued to say masses for the repose of the soul of Joan of Arc. Joan's mother never acknowledged any would-be impersonator of her daughter; it is curious that Joan's brothers did so, but no doubt they found the 'false Joan' a useful connection, a useful ally in their military and official careers. After all, were they to challenge someone who must have had powerful and authoritative support? Moreover, the acceptance of the 'false Joan' was a kind of rehabilitation of their sister in the court of public opinion. In 1452, apparently, a second 'false Joan', the Maid of Sarmaize, visited Joan's cousins and was received by them; she finally married and 'settled down'![3]

It is certainly true that the 'false Pucelle', with her feats of extraordinary valour in France, Germany and Italy,[4] reawakened the memories of Joan of Arc in the minds of the people. The exploits of the false and of the true Joan were confounded, and the tradition of the *egregia bellatrix* was formed—the tradition in which the Pucelle, like the heroes of the Carolingian romances,

---

[1] *Supra*, Chapter III (Chastellain), pp. 78–80.
[2] Barrett, pp. 87, 88, 142, 202, 203.
[3] Anatole France, *op. cit.*, II, 393.
[4] See, e.g. *Procès*, V, 321–61; Quicherat, *Aperçus*, p. 156, assumes there was *one* 'false Joan', who affected, after Joan's death, to be the Maid.

absorbed herself in military glory all of her time.[1] One element in Joan's career, the element of religious respect and devotion, was not restored for the 'false Pucelle'. The great trial had made that impossible. The 'false Pucelle' approximated more closely to the pagan and Renaissance image of the Amazon.

There had been mourning for the death of the Maid at Metz and Compiègne, but there was one place, above all others, where Joan was always and most sincerely mourned—her ever loyal city of Orleans, which never forgot she had saved it from the English. In addition to the annual May 8th fête of liberation, the anniversary of Joan's martyrdom was observed with a service in the church of St Sauxon; tapers, adorned with the shields of her arms, were burned, and great flambeaux of wax, while eight monks of four mendicant orders sang masses for the repose of her soul. Orleans pensioned Joan's mother, Isabelle de Vouthon, who came there in 1440, although très forte malade; and Joan's younger brother, Pierre du Lys, was the recipient, also, of the bounty of Duke Charles of Orleans. Isabelle lived with Pierre in a house on the rue des Africains at the time of the Rehabilitation.[2]

It would appear that both of Joan's brothers were ambitious, and fully aware of the prestige and opportunity which her career had opened to them; thanks to her, they were now of the noble family of du Lis.[3] Jean, the older brother, was provost of Vaucouleurs for many years, succeeding Baudricourt, who played such a notable part in his sister's career; he was given a sum of money when finally relieved of his command in 1468. He was also Bailly of Vermandois, and Captain of Chartres. Both he and Pierre left living descendants of the family of du Lis. Joan's father had

---

[1] See, e.g. Procès, IV, 329, the 'Chronique de Lorraine' published by Dom Calmet. For this, vide supra, Chapter II, pp. 55–6.

[2] See Chapter VI. In Orleans, a tablet over a factory entrance has marked, in recent times, the home of Joan's brother, Pierre d'Arc du Lys; it states he lived there 1452–1509, which would make him almost, if not quite, at the time of his death, a hundred years old! In the late fifteenth century, Jean du Lys, son of Pierre, and seigneur of l'Ile-aux Boeufs, came every year to appear at the head of the annual May 8 procession in Orléans, in memory of the Maid; he carried before him a great white candle, lighted, and bearing upon its face a painted picture of the Pucelle (Sepet, op. cit., p. 588).

[3] Also du Lys, Dulys. For Orléans tradition, Procès, V, 212–15, 274–6, 279–81, 285–320.

died in Domrémy, soon after Joan's death; a rather improbable sentimental tradition relates that he died of grief as a result of her execution.[1]

Joan, then, was pretty thoroughly discredited for many years by her trial, as far as the upper classes were concerned, and her soul did not go marching on, except in the chivalrous exploits of the 'false Pucelle', who was accepted by the common people, and in the memory of her ever faithful city of Orleans. The English were, it is true, driven out 'at the point of the lance' as Joan had desired,[2] but this was accomplished by detaching Burgundy from their cause by the Treaty of Arras (1435)—the successful conclusion of the Burgundian negotiation which made her so impatient in the summer of 1429.[3] The Treaty of Arras consummated the reconciliation of the French parties and provinces—that 'French friendship' of which Napoleon emphasized the importance in the entry which he made upon the municipal register of Orleans.[4] The prelates and the lawyers had consolidated the great victory which the soldiers had prepared. Bedford's attempt to bluff his way to peace at Arras upon favourable terms failed miserably; and the withdrawal of the English from the peace congress left the way open for the French to compose their differences there.

The death of Bedford's wife, Burgundy's sister, in 1432, had weakened the Anglo-Burgundian alliance; the return to political power at Charles VII's court of Burgundy's brother-in-law, the Constable de Richemont, also had contributed to a change of

---

[1] Dom Calmet, *Histoire de Lorraine*, and other early writers thought the house of Joan of Arc which stands in Domrémy the original family home, but Nicolas Villiaumé, *Histoire de Jeanne d'Arc et réfutation des erreurs publiées jusqu'aujourd'hui* (Paris, 1874), p. 49n., challenges this on the basis of du Lis family traditions and examination of the evidence, and contends that the house was reconstructed about 1480, on order of Louis XI, 'pleine de vénération et d'enthousiasme pour la mémoire de l'héroïne'. Villiaumé claimed a linkage with the du Lis family through his mother.

The reconstruction of the simple d'Arc cottage, and the placing over its door of the royal coat of arms and the coats of arms of du Lys and Thiesselin, may be taken as symbolic, it would seem, of the final acceptance of Joan, after the Rehabilitation, by Crown, Church and nobility.

[2] Barrett, pp. 90, 160, 179.

[3] See her letter to the good people of of Rheims, 1429; see also Barrett, p. 90.

[4] *Vide infra*, Chapter VII, p. 158. *Procès*, V, 243-4.

diplomatic partners; growing competition of the English-made cloth with that of the Low Countries weakened the former economic interdependence of England and Flanders,[1] and the growth of French nationalism, which was both cause and effect of the career of Joan of Arc, undoubtedly made itself felt in some of the Burgundian provinces. Burgundy had never really wished to help the English consolidate their power. There were, moreover, personal tensions; Burgundy's archives contained letters of Gloucester and Bedford discussing his arrest or death.[2] Burgundy made good terms with Charles VII; he did no homage, kept his gains, and the King asked his pardon and made excuse for the tragic slaying of the previous duke, John the Fearless (Jean sans Peur), on the bridge at Montereau.

A strong France was often important to the mediaeval papacy as a makeweight against the Holy Roman Emperors of the German Nation; the King of France was 'eldest son of the Church'. We must recall, too, the close trade ties between France and many of the Italian cities. The special understanding between the papacy and the kings of the Franks goes back to the earliest Carolingians, or even beyond, to Clovis. The popes owed their temporal power to a Frankish alliance, as the Carolingians owed to the same tie their consecration for royal and imperial power. We are not surprised, therefore, in view of this long standing connection, to find the legates of Pope Eugenius IV active at the peace congress at Arras, endeavouring to make peace between Charles and Burgundy, and trying to restore the unity of the French kingdom; free of the incubus of struggle with England, that kingdom would be able to play an independent role in European politics once more. The papal intervention gave the Congress of Arras essentially a European character, as was fitting, since the Hundred Years' War was essentially a European war. No doubt an Anglo-France consolidated under Lancastrian rule

[1] In 1428, 1446, 1464 and 1494, the importation of English cloth into Flanders was forbidden, in order to protect Flemish production against the growing competition from a former source of raw materials. Michelet, éd. Nelson, p. 340.

[2] Ibid., p. 332, citing 'Archives de Lille, chambre des comptes, inventaire,' V. VIII, 1424.

14. JOAN OF ARC AT DOMREMY. Sculpture by H. M. A. Chapu, in the Luxembourg Gallery, Paris

15. JOAN OF ARC MONUMENT by Princess Marie of Orleans, erected at Orleans
(*Bettmann Archive*)

would have been too powerful for comfort from the point of view of the papacy—a threat to the European balance. A France indefinitely divided and paralysed was also inconvenient, so we may surmise; but Charles VII, one may suggest, could not be acceptable until he took, in Richemont, a chief minister of impeccable orthodoxy and loyalty to the Church, an inveterate enemy of witches, and dropped the dubious friends upon whom he had had to depend in his day of adversity.

By 1435, the way was prepared; Charles, ably served, was already strong enough to serve as a rallying point for a united nation. He and the Pope could move toward an ultimate *rapprochement*. The papal legate offered to release Burgundy from his oath of vengeance, and the doctors of Bologna who had come with the legates impugned the authority of the Treaty of Troyes.[1] Burgundy found an excuse for abandoning the English by suggesting papal mediation between the English and French dynasties; when the English refused to accept this, he declared himself released from all obligation to them.

In view of Burgundy's role in the tragic fate of Joan of Arc, the Treaty of Arras could hardly be expected immediately to improve the prospects of the Maid's rehabilitation, even though it did prepare the way for her triumph, and that of France, in the long run.

In any case, the English remained quite strong. It is true that their numbers were always small; only in Normandy did they have any roots. Bedford, in view of the increasingly wavering attitude of Burgundy, had been forced, prior to the Treaty of Arras, to fall back on Henry V's original plan of holding Normandy, which the English were to do for another twenty years. Court was held at Rouen for a year, and a university was maintained at Caen.

The death of Bedford, however, left England impoverished and with a weakened and divided leadership, a clash of feudal and popular elements which foreshadowed the later quarrel of

---

[1] Michelet, *éd.* Nelson, p. 339. See also *Cambridge Mediaeval History*, VIII, 252 (Joseph Calmette).

Lancaster and York; and, following the Treaty of Arras, England's decline in France was slow, but steady. The English had taken advantage of French divisions, and in view of French superiority in wealth and strength, they could not hope to maintain themselves, as these divisions disappeared, and as, under pressure of necessity, reforms were effected in the French military and fiscal systems. French political stability brought economic recovery, strengthening the third estate, the main support of the Crown. The organization of a rather modern-style regular army and a more efficient tax-collecting bureaucracy by Charles VII's government, after the truce with England in 1444,[1] made possible the final eviction of the English from Normandy, their stronghold. All the English attempts to mediate a peace—through the release of the Duke of Orleans in 1440, for instance, and through the marriage of Henry VI and Margaret of Anjou, in 1445—ended in failure.

Discontent grew, even in Normandy, as the occupying power failed to maintain really effective law and order. Guerrilla warfare continued. In 1449, Rouen was lost, and on April 15, 1450, the English made their last stand in Normandy at Formigny, on a lonely roadside far on the way to Cherbourg, near the very spot where the liberating Anglo-Americans were to return in 1944. In 1453, Talbot, the 'English Achilles', fell at Castillon, and the English lost Guienne and Bordeaux, which they had held since the twelfth century. Calais alone remained, English on sufferance. England had hammered France into unity—had made her the most compact and harmonious state in Europe.

Chanoine Dunand[2] argues that Joan could not be rehabilitated until her mission was fulfilled by this complete liberation of France: 'Entre autres témoins à entendre il y avait la Providence.' Rather defensively, he insists that the Pope was not officially informed, or asked to intervene by England or France in the trial, though he admits Rome was informed of its outcome by the

---

[1] See the *Ordonnances*, providing military and financial reforms. *Cambridge Mediaeval History*, VIII: 254 ff. (Joseph Calmette summarizes them.)

[2] Philippe-Hector Dunand, *Chanoine théologal du Chapitre de Toulouse, éd. Histoire de la Pucelle d'Orléans par Edmond Richer, Docteur de Sorbonne, Syndic de la Faculté de Théologie de Paris.* (Paris, 1912) II, 149.

University of Paris.[1] He considers it possible, rather strangely, that the Vatican did not know of the trial when it was going on. He finds, in this culpable lack of official information from the powers concerned, an explanation for the Pope's not intervening, as Clement V did under Philip the Fair in the trial of the Templars, or Leo X did in the trial of the German humanist, Reuchlin. Even Anatole France, whose outlook in so many ways is a polar opposite to that of Chanoine Dunand, raises the question as to whether Charles VII could not have influenced Joan's fate by an appeal to Rome; by an intervention of Cauchon's metropolitan, the Archbishop of Rheims; by the transmission to the trial seat of the Book of Poitiers; or by other such means.

There seems, however, little enough reason to believe that an appeal by Charles would have done any good. The newly-elected Pope, Eugenius IV, not too securely seated in a Europe in which the Schism was just past, and the conciliar movement at high tide, was not likely to offend the University of Paris and the powerful Anglo-Burgundian interest in order to please the weak and insecurely seated Charles VII, who, moreover, was not too friendly to him. The English, who had opposed the French-supported Avignon popes, were bound to back the papacy, now that its unity had been restored by the Council of Constance, and it has been re-established in Rome. The Burgundians, also, supported the papacy under Clement VII and his successors; Charles VII leaned toward the Council of Basel, which was pro-French and anti-papal, and, in 1438, we find him proclaiming, through Pragmatic Sanction of Bourges, the autonomy of the Gallican church. Just at the time Joan's fate was decided, the Pope charged Cardinal Albergati de Sainte-Croix[2] to effect a *rapprochement* between France and England;[3] there could be no question, then,

---

[1] Barrett, pp. 348–52, Copy of the letters addressed by the University of Paris to our Holy Father the Pope, to the Emperor, and the College of Cardinals.

[2] See Richer (Dunand) II, 149.

[3] Pope Martin V had no cause for friendship to Joan of Arc, especially as her letter to the Count of Armagnac, read at her trial (Barrett, pp. 167–70), had implied doubt as to the Pope's powers, and had assumed a right of arbitrament concerning them, between him, the anti-pope backed by the King of Aragon, and another, more obscure, anti-pope. Had he considered her, she was bound to seem to the Pope an incredibly arrogant

we may confidently suggest, of mortally offending England in order to please Charles VII in the affair of the Maid. We have seen that the Archbishop of Rheims was hostile to Joan; she had very powerful enemies among Charles's own court and clergy,[1] and we have cited evidence that she knew this very well. Charles VII knew equally well, must have known, since he was certainly intelligent, that the trial of the woman who had been so prominent at his crowning in Rheims cathedral was a direct blow at him, an attempt to compromise that great event, the turning-point in his rise to power, with the taint of heresy and witchcraft, and thus to destroy its effect upon the popular mind, and to turn it from a legitimation of his power into a definite liability. But Charles knew, also, that any more he made to help Joan, other than secret attempts to ransom her,[2] would do her no good, and would only serve to compromise the monarch completely, and alienate utterly the Church of France, thus bringing about the complete ruin of the Armagnac cause. M. France's republican venom and Chanoine Dunand's desire for a scapegoat led them both alike to ignore the actual situation of Charles VII—as historians very generally have done.

There can be no doubt that the Rehabilitation was delayed by English insinuations to the Pope that Charles had made use of sinister forces.[3] It would appear that the bulk of the French Church, and certainly its most powerful elements, such as the University of Paris, leaned to the Anglo-Burgundian side, just as many of the same forces in our own day supported Marshal Pétain and Vichy. The Armagnac cause was, perhaps, somewhat suspect from a clerical point of view; we must recall that the south of France, the Armagnac region, had been the nursery of the Albigensian heresy. Modern nationalist notions were alien to the international-minded clergy, loyal citizens of the *Respublica*

upstart. One cannot but suspect that in writing the letter she had fallen into a trap set by intriguers in her own camp.

[1] M. Champion thinks Regnault de Chartres, Archbishop of Rheims, was primarily responsible for the delay in the rehabilitation. See his *Procès de condamnation*, II, 354.

[2] *Supra*, Chapter IV, pp. 96–7.

[3] Lucien Fabre, *Jeanne d'Arc* (Paris, 1948), p. 535.

Christiana, and Henry V had astutely favoured the clergy, in England and France alike, much more than had his Armagnac opponent. Charles, but for his lack of strong clerical support, and the desperate weakness of his position, would not have had to resort to such informal theological devices as the use of brother Richard, of Catherine de la Rochelle,[1] of the shepherd of Gevaudan, and of the Maid of Orleans. Only when his position was very greatly strengthened could Charles come to terms with the Church, and thus finally open the way to something more than a mere popular and informal rehabilitation of Joan of Arc, tacitly countenanced by officialdom.

---

[1] Barrett, pp. 89–90, 205–6; Article LVI of the Articles of Accusation.

VI

WITCH UNWITCHED

Charles VII did not abandon the goal of 'rehabilitating' Joan of
Arc formally and officially; on the contrary, he pursued that goal
with characteristic tenacity.[1] There was popular pressure involved,
above all from Orleans, 'truly worthy to be called the city of Joan
of Arc,' which advanced her tardy rehabilitation by its annual
celebration; more important, there was the King's own interest.
Charles pushed through the Rehabilitation, on the ground that
the judgement of Cauchon dishonoured him,[2] despite the fact that
the original trial is, regarding him, a 'masterpiece of reserve'. In
spite of that reserve, it would seem, Quicherat's view to the contrary notwithstanding, that the dishonour was real enough, and
no mere pretext.

Guillaume Bouillé, who ought to have known, clearly pro-
claims the motive. It was not only the glory of God, but also
'the exaltation of the King of the French, that is, the House of
France, which has never been reported to have favoured heretics
or to have adhered to them in any way'. Joan, he saw as the

---

[1] For the Rehabilitation see *Procès*, Vols. II and III; Quicherat, *Aperçus*, pp. 149 ff;
Fabre, *Réhabilitation*, Vol. I, especially *Préface*, see also Vol. II; Lowell, *op. cit.*, pp.
350–1; Thomas Lawrason Riggs, *Saving Angel. The Truth about Joan of Arc and the
Church* (Milwaukee, 1943), pp. 8, 58 ff., 83–90; Régine Pernoud, *Vie et Mort de Jeanne
d'Arc; les témoignages du procès de réhabilitation 1450–1456* (Paris, 1953); Shaw, *op. cit.*,
pp. x–xi; Lang, *op. cit.*, pp. ix, xii, xiii, 277; Paine, *Joan*, *op. cit.*, II, 319; Blaze de Bury,
op. cit., pp. 366, 494, 501–6; Calmette, pp. 90–111, 126–31; France, *op. cit.*, I, xx–xxx,
II, 385, 445–52; Edward Garnett, *The Trial of Jeanne d'Arc*, *an historical play in five acts*
(London, 1931) ix; Dr Jules Dumas, 'Psychologie de Jeanne d'Arc, *Annales Médico-
Psychologiques*, sér. 8 (1904) 19: 375. For the rehabilitation decree of Calixtus III, see
J. B. J. Ayroles, s. j., *La Pucelle devant l'Église, op. cit.*, pp. 603–5.

[2] This point is made, *Procès*, II, 316, Article 26 of the Questionnaire presented to the
witnesses of 1452; also Article 25, in 1456, tended to establish the same point.

restorer of the kingdom, the inspiration of the troops. We may also note the letter of the Archbishop of Rheims to d'Aulon, April 20, 1456, inviting testimony at the rehabilitation proceedings:

> By the sentence pronounced against Joan the English wish it to be believed that the Maid was a sorceress, a heretic and in league with the devil, and therefore that the King had received his kingdom by those means, and thus they hold as heretics the King and those that have served him.

Similarly, Inquisitor Jean Bréhal writes to a learned Dominican friar, Brother Léonard:

> the process of rehabilitation particularly interests the very Christian king, who considers that the honour of His Majesty has been enormously injured by his enemies of the English party, when they persecuted in a matter of faith this simple virgin who, obedient to divine inspiration, as seems proved by irresistible evidence, so fortunately conducted the war in his service . . .[1]

What shame in the future if enemies could declare that a King of France had retained a heretical woman, and one in communication with demons, in the ranks of his army! It was a work of 'public security' to proclaim her innocence. Clearly, it was the rehabilitation of the Crown of France, rather than of the memory of Joan, that was mainly involved. It was also the trial of the enemies of Joan—of those who had condemned her, not of those who had abandoned her. As always, Joan was a piece on a complex political chessboard. Her career, and the career of her reputation afterward, supply the best examples in the fifteenth century of the use of 'psychological warfare'. Charles VII wished to crown his victory by removing the slur which his enemies had cast upon his triumphant coronation in the cathedral at Rheims. It is not without reason that Mr George Bernard Shaw, in his play *Saint Joan* has the King say:

> provided they can no longer say that I was crowned by a witch and a heretic I shall not fuss about how the trick has been done.[2]

---

[1] Joseph Fabre, *Réhabilitation*, II, 188–9. See also Marie-Joseph Belon and François Balme, *Jean Bréhal, grand Inquisiteur de France, et la réhabilitation de Jeanne d'Arc* (Paris, 1893); contains texts of his *Summarium* and *Recollectio*.
[2] Shaw, *op. cit.*, p. 142.

We may be reasonably certain that Joan, like other noble-hearted persons convicted of heresy, would have been left to the verdict of Time and History, the stigma upon her never formally erased, had not political considerations dictated her rehabilitation.

As the Abbé Rabbe puts it; 'le procés de réhabilitation fut surtout l'apothéose politique de Charles VII.'[1]

The Church Universal yielded, with apparent reluctance, to the political exigencies of the King of France; as, in canonizing Joan, it yielded, again with the evidence of a good deal of resistance behind the scenes, to the urgings of French nationalism, and of the Church of France. There was an English pressure against her in the fifteenth century, as there was a German pressure in the twentieth. To all men, Joan was to become the symbol of France.

Mediaeval authority had passed a final moral judgement on Joan; but a quarter of a century later, by action on a higher level, it contradicted itself. The Rehabilitation not only removed a blot from Charles VII's reputation; it placed the Church squarely behind his title to the throne, and tied him to it more firmly. Charles had 'arrived'. The Church now took over the popular commemoration of Joan; as a matter of fact, there is some reason to believe that the May 8th festival in Orleans gives new meaning to a far older pagan celebration. For Joan, the Rehabilitation meant a revival of faith in her, the culmination of a process of what Arnold Toynbee would perhaps call 'withdrawal and return'. The gamine de France had withdrawn from the world, and ultimately she returned invested with the aureole of a saint— the 'Sainte de la patrie'.

Charles's peace with the Church was the fruit of his victories, and of his victorious peace with the English. The Church rallied to established authority, much as, in our time, the hierarchy rallied to De Gaulle after the Liberation, although some of its members had given countenance, in varying degrees, to Pétain. A victorious ruler had every reason to come to terms with established ecclesiastical authority and to reject dubious allies of doubtful orthodoxy, such as were to be found in the old Armagnac party—just as

[1] L'abbé Rabbe, *Jeanne d'Arc en Angleterre* (Paris, 1891), v.

De Gaulle in due course dropped the Communists, with whom he had had a temporary *mariage de convenance* in the course of his struggle with Vichy.

By 1450, Charles VII had Rouen, the record of the Trial Proceedings, and many of those who had taken part in the trial, in his grip, so it was possible to proceed toward the rehabilitation of Joan.

It was on February 15, 1450, near Rouen, that Charles commissioned Guillaume Bouillé to inquire into the whole affair of Joan of Arc, with full power to summon people and documents. Bouillé, Doctor of Theology, former Rector of the University of Paris, *doyen* of its theological faculty, *doyen* of Noyon Cathedral, member of the Great Council, sometime ambassador to Rome, was a distinguished man, and he displayed great zeal in the cause of Joan of Arc.[1] Bouillé heard some seven witnesses in the next month, and prepared a *Mémoire* favourable to Joan, the first in time, after Gerson's, to be included in the final Rehabilitation. Bouillé's proceedings, of course, had no canonical standing, and the evidence which he collected is not included in the final record of the Rehabilitation; it is neglected as of no value. Only papal authority could reverse the conviction of Joan; and Bouillé served the King, and reported to him, not to the Pope. His favourable opinion was intended to move the Pope to grant a new trial of Joan, and it was, in fact, the initial step in the whole process.

It is uncertain whether an attempt was made to secure the aid of Pope Martin V for the project of rehabilitation in 1450; if made, the attempt was premature, and it failed; the English were still too strong. The complete defeat of the English was required to overcome clerical reluctance and pave the way for the Rehabilitation, as in our own day the complete defeat of Germany in World War I was required to overcome a similar reluctance and pave the way for Joan's canonization.

---

[1] Albert Héduin, 'Rôle prépondérant de Guillaume Bouillé ... au procès de réhabilitation de Jeanne d'Arc,' in *Société des Antiquaires de Picardie, Bull.* (Amiens, 1939), attributes to him the chief part in the Process of Rehabilitation; but Calmette, p. 127, calls Bréhal 'l'âme de toute la procédure'. For Bréhal, see Belon et Balme, *op. cit.* Both undoubtedly played major parts, Bouillé initially, Bréhal later.

Cardinal Guillaume d'Estouteville, Bishop of Digne, was sent to France in 1451 as papal legate, to promote negotiations for peace between England and France, with a view to uniting them for a crusade against the Turks, who threatened Constantinople. D'Estouteville was of a noble Norman house, a relative of Charles VII, French in sentiment, an energetic reformer of the University of Paris; he had been sent in the hope of ironing out some frictions between the Pope and Charles, and increasing papal authority over the French clergy. To accomplish anything, it was necessary to humour the King, and of course the mere hearing of evidence about Joan committed the Pope to nothing; so agreement to do this was readily secured.

It was in 1452 that d'Estouteville and Inquisitor Bréhal[1] issued a new commission for the taking of evidence, this time with canonical authority. More than twenty witnesses were examined at Rouen, and their evidence is included in the final report of the Rehabilitation Proceedings along with the memoirs of French and Italian theologians, which were assembled at this time. The new inquiry took cognizance of the earlier inquest. It is significant that the King financed it, and received its report, which was without formal issue—fortunately, since otherwise we should not have the volume of evidence collected later. Bréhal's *Summarium*, summing up the findings of this commission, is a basic document in the whole procedure. Cardinal d'Estouteville, because of his other duties, had had to be represented by a delegate, Philippe de la Rose, treasurer of the chapter of Rouen; though, after d'Estouteville became Archbishop of Rouen, he was able to keep more closely in touch with proceedings.

Negotiations dragged on for three years. Jean Bréhal, the Inquisitor, being a strong 'King's man', altogether under Charles's influence, made a series of appeals and visits to Rome, gathered elaborate written opinions of Roman and French ecclesiastics favourable to Joan, and submitted them, along with the proceed-

---

[1] A Norman and a Dominican Professor of Sacred Theology, and one of the two Inquisitors-General of the Heretical Error for the Realm of France. He was also Prior of the Convent of the Jacobins at Paris.

ings of the first trial, and evidence gathered in 1450 and 1452. It was apparently Bréhal who carried to Rome in 1454 Joan's mother's appeal for a new trial. Up to that time, all his efforts had seemed to be of no effect.

D'Estouteville, however, was just the man to push through the Rehabilitation, and Charles VII, by implicating him in the proceedings, virtually forced the hand of the Pope. The fall of Constantinople, a distracting disaster, and the death of Martin V, March, 1455, without his having taken any steps toward the Rehabilitation, delayed it; the new Pope, Calixtus III (Alphonsus Borgia) was a devout Spaniard, of firm and uncompromising character, though advanced in years (aged seventy-seven). He was so anxious to draw Charles VII, now the leading monarch in Europe, into a new crusade, that he was willing to humour him in the Joan affair, despite his fear of offending England and damaging the prestige of the Inquisition and of the Church courts.

The thing was not easy; as Quicherat says

Il s'agissait de faire déjuger l'Église par elle-même.[1]

It was a proceeding which might well seem calculated to shake men's confidence in all authority, for the Inquisition was an international institution, deemed well-nigh infallible and impregnable. However, to avoid undue offence to England, or a royal challenge to the Holy Office and the University of Paris, and to minimize the seriousness of the affair, and its political implications, resort was had to an ingenious expedient. What would be the competent tribunal, in any case, if the King made appeal? Someone, apparently Jean de Montigny, Doctor of Canon Law at the University of Paris,[2] conceived the happy idea of having the d'Arc family bring suit against the chief religious officials of the diocese of Beauvais, acting upon the express invitation of the King, for the removal of the stigma on the family name by appointment of a commission with authority to annul the

---

[1] Quicherat, *Aperçus*, p. 150.
[2] Riggs, *op. cit.*, p. 62.

verdict of 1431. In this way, the process was made relatively easy, despite its inherent difficulties.

Finally, on June 11, 1455, Calixtus III designated in a papal bull a tribunal to reopen Joan's case, and arrive at a just decision, which it should cause to be observed without appeal. The judges were given full power to act, separately or together. It would not be unfair to say that a decision contrary to the original decision was strongly indicated. The judges were all men upon whom the King of France could count—Jean Juvenal des Ursins, Archbishop of Rheims, Guillaume Chartier, Bishop of Paris, and Richard de Longueil, Bishop of Coutances. The apostolic rescript directed that the judges were to add to their number a representative of the Inquisition; quite naturally, they chose Bréhal. The opening session of the court was held at Notre Dame cathedral in Paris, November 7, 1455. After hearing the appeal of Joan's mother, Isabelle Rommée, the judges stated that it was not easy to grant what she asked, as there was grave presumption of her daughter's guilt, but they promised to inquire into the matter carefully. Ten days later, they had another public session, in the episcopal palace of Paris, at which Isabelle Rommée's counsel delivered a panegyric about Joan; this may have been intended to influence public opinion in Paris, which had been very hostile to the heroine in the past.[1] There followed an exhaustive inquiry, with sources of witnesses summoned. The process moved to its foreordained outcome, July 7, 1456.

Sainte-Beuve has well summed it up:

Aussi, dans le procès de réhabilitation qui se fit depuis, ne trouva-t-on pas Rome aussi empressée, aussi bien disposée qu'on aurait pu croire. Le roi dut forcer la main au pape, et Jeanne, qui avait tant de vertus et de qualités requises pour etre canonisée sainte comme on l'entendait en ces âges, ne fut jamais que la Sainte du peuple et de la France, la Sainte de la patrie.[2]

In the next century, the Church in due course removed the ground of Sainte-Beuve's complaint.

The Rehabilitation of Joan of Arc might perhaps be described

---

[1] See *Journal d'un Bourgeois de Paris, op. cit., passim.*
[2] Sainte-Beuve, *Causeries, op. cit.,* p. 327.

as the death blow of the Inquisition in France, despite the efforts of the judges of the Rehabilitation to spare that institution insofar as possible, and to suggest that Jean le Maistre was coerced and overawed, a most reluctant accomplice of Cauchon. Lenglet-Dufresnoy justly remarks that the Rehabilitation sentence of 1456 'est des plus solonnelles que l'on ait jamais rendu en pareil cas'.[1] The effect of the Rehabilitation was to place, whether justly so or not, the brand of cruelty and injustice upon the brow of the inquisitorial system, and also to stigmatize this international institution as somehow against the interest of the French monarchy and people; it was the consequence, presumably, which had been foreseen and feared at Rome.

The Rehabilitation judges 'ne virent pas sans effroi quels abus pouvait enfanter un droit ai contraire au droit naturel'.[2] In 1461, the same group, named commissioners in the case of the Vaudois of Arras, rejected the prosecution's contentions, and rehabilitated the numerous victims who were already dead.[3] Their rehabilitation involved civil actions, and the summoning of the Holy Office, through its agents, before the *parlement*. Again, the stable door was locked after some, at least, of the horses were stolen; but it was locked in good time to prevent any further thefts.

In the sixteenth and seventeenth centuries, the writ of the Inquisition does not run in France as it does in Spain and Italy; the Holy Office falls in discredit in France just as it is gaining strength and authority elsewhere in Europe. From this point of view, we may perhaps suggest, paradoxically enough, that the Rehabilitation has the flavour of the triumph of a kind of middle-class and legal anticlericalism, strongly nationalistic in tone—the triumph of a movement antecedent to the Enlightenment, and one with which the monarchy was identified. This force was stronger in France than in most other European

[1] Cited in Calmette, p. 131.
[2] Quicherat, *Aperçus*, p. 154. They used the old Stoic and Scholastic concept of natural law, that is, as a basis for a critique of inquisitorial law.
[3] *Mémoires of Jacques du Clerc liv.* IV, CXXVII (*édition du Panthéon littéraire*), cited Quicherat, *ibid.*

countries; France lay athwart the main trade routes, and was not the centre of the Roman traditions. It is curious that the later development of this new movement of opinion, culminating in the Enlightenment, was to discard that very image of Joan which the Rehabilitation had elaborated.[1]

There has been much sentimentalizing of the role of Joan's family in the Rehabilitation—a sentimentality which arises from the failure to grasp, even partially, the political factors involved. It is rather surprising that a contemporary writer, at times very realistic, Victoria Sackville-West, finds 'astounding'[2] the part played by Joan's mother, Isabelle Rommée de Vouthon. We cannot know that she was, as suggested, a woman proud in spirit; her role was little more than nominal. *Décrépite par l'âge* (she was apparently, sixty-seven years of age at the beginning of the proceedings) she asked to be excused from attending the sittings. She was, of course, present with her sons,[3] some kinsfolk and a number of notables of Orleans at the opening, on her formal initiative and that of her family, of the Rehabilitation process beneath the spacious vaults of Notre Came Cathedral in Paris, November 7, 1455. It was, apparently, an occasion for emotional overflow;[4] Joan's mother was in tears as she recited her plea, and so were many of its auditors. The tumult was such that the judges withdrew to the sacristy of the cathedral.

Surely this must have been one of the most moving of the many historic scenes which the great cathedral has witnessed, vying in historical interest with the *Te Deum* in celebration of Joan's capture, the worship of the Goddess of Reason, the coronation of Napoleon, or the *Te Deum* in honour of the triumph of General

---

[1] *Infra*, Chapter VII, pp. 156–7.

[2] Victoria Sackville-West, *Saint Joan of Arc* (New York, 1936), p. 29.

[3] It seems probable that Pierre and Jean du Lys were both present. The *MS.* D'Urfé, the earliest manuscript, joins the two brothers in the initiation of the Rehabilitation, though the final manuscript names only Pierre. The earliest manuscript names the two together several times after the first mention (Fabre, *Réhabilitation*, p. 21). We know that Jean d'Arc as provost of Vaucouleurs worked for the rehabilitation of his sister, formed a commission to collect evidence from their native district, and produce witnesses. (Barrett-Champion, p. 396).

[4] Fabre, *Réhabilitation*, p. 23.

de Gaulle—all in the same place! Indeed, this popular demonstration at the beginning was the first and the true rehabilitation of Joan, a moral if not a legal rehabilitation, a rehabilitation in the eyes of the public.

Jean, Joan's brother, was also present at the final and ceremonial erasure of the stain, July 7, 1456, when a document setting forth the Articles of Accusation was formally destroyed; the long sentence was solemnly delivered by the Archbishop in the great hall of the archiepiscopal palace at Rouen, in the presence of a vast concourse of people, among them the Bishops of Paris and Coutances. A procession and sermon at the Place St Ouen, the site of the alleged abjuration, immediately followed. It was decreed that a cross of honour (*crux honesta*) be erected next day, to the accompaniment of solemn ceremonial and sermon on the site of the burning.[1]

The D'Arc family was present at the great fête at Orleans, July 21, 1456,[2] to celebrate the decision which had restored Joan's reputation. Perhaps the *Mystère du Siege d'Orléans* was played then; at any rate, a bronze cross on the bridge was dedicated, with an image of the Virgin, and the figures of Charles and Joan kneeling at her feet, all armoured, save for their helmets, and Joan, most unrealistically, with hair sweeping modestly to her shoulders. The monument was erected at the expense of the young girls and women of St Aignan's city of Orleans; thus early, Joan was already the object of a feminine cult.

If it unnecessary to sentimentalize too much the motives of Joan's family, it is also unnecessary to attribute to them purely mercenary motives for supporting the Rehabilitation, or for previously accepting the 'false Joan', as does Dr Margaret Alice Murray.[3] Dr Murray suggests that the motive force in the Rehabilitation was the desire of Joan's family to annul the sentences of excommunication in order to inherit her considerable

---

[1] This cross has long ago disappeared, but crosses were erected in various places after the Rehabilitation, and one was still, in 1893, extant in the forest of Compiègne. *Cf.* Lord Gower, *op. cit.*, p. 286. It was said to have been erected by Dunois himself.

[2] Calmette, p. 131.

[3] Margaret Alice Murray, *God of the Witches, op. cit.*, p. 384.

property, which she had left to them.[1] But surely, as the old English judge said, 'The devil himself knoweth not a man's motive'; motives are hard to prove. In any case, Dr Murray's contention is partially negated by the fact that, as we have seen, the Rehabilitation was a matter of high politics. There is no reason, surely, to doubt the sincerity of Joan's mother in seeking to clear the stain from her daughter's memory, which, after all, affected the reputation of the dead girl's relatives.

It is impossible here to consider the Rehabilitation Process or its technique in full detail. We shall confine ourselves to a limited number of observations. One is that nothing could demonstrate more clearly than the Rehabilitation the flexible variety of late mediaeval doctrine, before the hardening and defining process set in, which was incidental to the Catholic Reformation and the struggle with Protestantism. In order to sanction the claims of Joan's conscience, and find special dispensation for her, her judges go to antinomian extremes which would seem to leave little enough room for later Protestant agitations for the right of private judgement. Some of the views expressed by Joan's 'rehabilitators' are almost suggestive of Tolstoyan Christian philosophical anarchism. Even Bréhal, the Grand Inquisitor, is prepared to find that, 'If you are led by the Spirit you are no longer under the law'. 'The Church does not judge concerning hidden things.' It is all very different from the atmosphere of Joan's trial, or of many other such procedures in an authoritarian age.

The Rehabilitation is marked by an earnest search for formal legal defects in the trial.[2] To break a sentence 'pour vice de forme' was a favourite mediaeval device; note, for instance, as a parallel to Joan's case, the breaking on appeal, by three cardinals, in 1416, of the sentence passed upon Jean sans Peur, Duke of Burgundy. It is, of course, a moot point whether the defects of form detected in Joan's trial are real, or, largely imaginary, as thought the great scholar Quicherat, who wrote a

---

[1] See Jehanne d'Orliac, *Joan of Arc and Her Companions* (London, 1934), p. 296.
[2] See *Procès*, II, 56–67, for alleged defects in law of Joan's conviction.

masterly analysis of the trial and Rehabilitation.[1] Isambard de la Pierre, an obscure Dominican of Rouen, and perhaps the most upright person near Joan during her trial, said, in his Rehabilitation evidence:

Satis observabant judices ordinem juris.[2]

It would be remarkable indeed if a man of Cauchon's intelligence and legal training had allowed his *beau procès*[3] to be marred by the kind of obvious legal flaw which the Rehabilitation attempted to find. No mediaeval heresy trial, one may be sure, could have stood up under such a raking as was given this one.

Joan's abjuration was denounced by the Rehabilitation as obtained by fear and duress, the presence of the torturer and the threat of fire; the whole of the proceedings was null and void:

Dolum, calumniam, iniquitatem, repugnantiam, iurisque et facti errorem continentes manifestum.[4]

The interrogatories were attacked, and the exhortations were declared full of lies, subtleties, artfulness and confused prolixity. Bréhal even went so far as to attack the English nobles present at the abjuration scene for not resenting the preacher's attacks on the French King, a relative of their own King! This is rather an extreme specimen of an attack over a wide front!

We cannot take entirely seriously much of the Rehabilitation evidence of fear of the English and pressure from them at the original trial.[5] Such a powerful and authoritative body of churchmen carried too much weight in the fifteenth century to submit tamely to outright coercion. Several of the more reputable witnesses at the Rehabilitation solemnly declared that the court which condemned Joan was not coerced.[6] Nicholas Taquel,

---

[1] See his *Aperçus.*

[2] *Aperçus,* p. 147. Isambard's testimony that the trial was conducted in due legal form is the more important, as the Rehabilitation judges, backed by royal authority, were seeking to prove the contrary, and it would certainly have been the line of least resistance to humour them by confirming their views.

[3] For his use of this phrase, see Manchon's evidence (T. D. Murray, p. 184).

[4] *Procès,* III, 361.

[5] See, e.g. T. D. Murray, p. 172 (Manchon); p. 174 (Erard, Massieu); pp. 188, 190 (Ysambard de la Pierre); p. 193 (Ladvenu).

[6] 'I never perceived any kind of fear, nor did I know of prohibitions or coercion by the

assistant notary at the trial, stated he saw no English in the court during the examination of Joan, except her guards. Guillaume Manchon stated on oath on two several occasions, in the Rehabilitation Proceedings, that, when Joan complained of the conduct of her guards, the Earl of Warwick was furious with the men and removed them, giving Joan other guards who behaved themselves.[1]

Even the Rehabilitation testimony made it clear that Cauchon was, in fact, no tool of the English, notwithstanding the all-but-universal execration to which he has been subjected, and notwithstanding his undoubted Anglo-Burgundian sympathies, and possible expectations for promotion to the vacant archiepiscopal see of Rouen—expectations which, if they existed, were not destined to be fulfilled. When, as the law of the Church required, Cauchon admitted Joan to penance after her abjuration, the English who had assembled to see her burned were furious, and some of them not only insulted Joan, but also hurled stones at Cauchon and threatened him with swords, saying he had ill earned the money spent on him;[2] but he defied them in a gesture

English.' Master Nicolas Taquel, Rector of Basqueville, T. D. Murray, *op. cit.*, p. 194. 'As to the question of fear and pressure, I do not believe it, so far as it affected the judges.' Houppeville, *ibid.*, p. 198.

[1] See T. D. Murray, p. 180. Joan was placed in the custody of a squire of the royal bodyguard, John Grey, sworn on oath to protect her. She was left in chains because of her previous attempts to escape and her refusal to promise not to renew them. Barrett, pp. 51-2, 119, 225.

[2] Barrett-Champion, p. 507. See evidence of Beaupère, *Procès*, II, 21, concerning the dissatisfaction of the English with Cauchon and the delegates from Paris, and concerning the threatening attitude of the English later when Cauchon sent Midi and Beaupère to Joan to advise her not to relapse, and bring her back to her senses, when she resumed man's dress. The English threatened to throw them into the river, and drove them away. André Marguerie had the same experience (*Procès*, III, 184); and so did Manchon (*ibid.*, II, 19); both indicate the violent hostility of the English, as does Grouchet. The Rehabilitation here unintentionally cleanses Cauchon and Joan's judges of some of the mud thrown at them, and goes far to vindicate their good faith, in its effort to show the reality of English pressure on the court. We can certainly credit such testimony, so strongly prejudiced against him, when it tells in Cauchon's favour. For evidence of Cauchon's altercation with the churchmen attached to the Bishop of Winchester, who charged him with favouring Joan; see Du Desert, Lebouchier, De Mailly, Migiet, De Fave, Marcel, Marguerie. Cauchon, insulted at the stone-throwing, stated: 'I will not proceed until I have been satisfied' (Massieu). De Mailly tells us the Bishop of Winchester had to intervene; Lebouchier tells us that Cauchon threw his papers in anger upon the ground, and refused

of which the significance has generally been ignored. Cauchon turned on the English ecclesiastic who accused him of traitorously favouring Joan, with the lofty words:

> You lie. It is my duty and profession to seek the salvation of her soul and body.[1]

Here we see the proud prelate adhering faithfully to his official line of religious duty, as he understood it.

Nor is there reason to withhold our confidence from the Trial Record, as did the promoter of the Rehabilitation in 1452, and the lawyers of the D'Arc family in 1455. Even at the Rehabilitation, the notaries, Manchon, Taquel, Bois-guillaume, who compiled the *Procès-verbal* and attested it,[2] bore witness to its authenticity, and an analysis of the manuscript D'Urfé, which Quicherat proved to be a fragment of the original French minute of the trial, bears the notaries out. The few discrepancies, such as the omission of *qu'elle eust une femme* from the Latin version of Joan's conditions for submission,[3] seem trivial, despite the efforts of Henri Martin and others to make much of them. The repute of the judges should itself be a guarantee.

More significant still is a line of reasoning which has generally

---

to continue. Contradictory rumours ran through the crowd (De Lenozoles). People said that it was all pure trickery (*pure trufferie*) and that Joan was laughing at them.

[1] Barrett, Introduction, p. 14. See T. D. Murray, p. 186 (evidence of Manchon); p. 187 (evidence of Migiet); p. 205 (evidence of Du Desert). A slightly different version is given by Margerie (*ibid.*, p. 206): 'I can well believe that some of the English acted from hate and fear, but of the more notable ecclesiastics I do not think this. A chaplain of the Cardinal of England, present at the first preaching, said to the Bishop of Beauvais, that he was showing too much favour to Jeanne; but the Bishop said to him, "You lie! For in such a case I would show favour to no one." The Cardinal of England reproved his chaplain and told him to be silent.' Other references to English insults in Murray's translation are: Massieu (*ibid.*, pp. 176, 200); Beaupère (*ibid.*, p. 178); Manchon (*ibid.*, p. 183); Taquel (*ibid.*, p. 195); Lebouchier (*ibid.*, p. 197); Grouchet (*ibid.*, p. 206).

[2] Boisguillaume put his seal at the bottom of each page, and all three signed the statements at the end. Barrett, pp.331–2. See, for their oaths, *ibid.*, pp. 40, 111–12. Brother Migier, Prior of Longueville, affirmed at the Rehabilitation: 'I think the notaries were truthful, and that they wrote with fidelity' (T. D. Murray, *op. cit.*, p. 187). Similar testimony is given by Maître Richard Grouchet, Master of Arts, Bachelor of Theology, Canon of the Cathedral Church of La Saussaye in the diocese of Evreux (*ibid.*, p. 206). For Manchon's testimony, see *ibid.*, pp. 170, 181. For Boisguillaume, see *ibid.*, p. 283: 'For nothing in the world would we have failed in anything that should have been done.'

[3] *Procès*, I, 456.

been neglected. Annexed to the trial is a document, a so-called 'Posthumous Information', unattested by the notaries, described in its text as:

Information given after the execution on many things said by her at her end and *in articulo mortis*.[1]

This document contains important statements which Joan is alleged to have made on the morning of her execution, concerning her 'Voices', etc., and purporting to set forth a final recantation by Joan; its authenticity has been much disputed. It consists of sworn depositions made to Joan's judges a week after her death, by seven assessors. We incline to accept it, if only because of the Rehabilitation evidence (Guillaume Manchon, Massieu, Martin Ladvenu) confirming the fact that Joan was visited by the bishop and several canons, and received the sacrament at the end, which, since she was excommunicate, would only legally have been possible in the event of a second and final recantation and admission to penance.[2]

As Quicherat[3] points out, Cauchon was too shrewd to disfigure his trial with a forgery. Courcelles accepts the final deposition, at the Rehabilitation, and so does Théodore de Leliis.[4] It is significant that the document was not challenged then. Out of forty-two assessors, thirty-nine had voted that it would be well that the terms of her recantation should be recalled to the accused; and we may assume that Cauchon did this on the morning of her execution.[5] Joan's statements (e.g. that her apparitions appeared in the guise of minute things)[6] have the ring of authenticity. In any case, the point to note here is that the

---

[1] Barrett, pp. 333–9; see also *Procès*, I, 478–84.

[2] Note, the conclusion of the final sentence, Barrett, p. 331. See also *Sextus decretalium lib.* V, *tit.* I, *c.* IV, cited in Quicherat, *Aperçus*, p. 144. Cauchon's act in according her the sacrament was legal in view of her repentance, but was an evidence of magnanimity on his part, not of bad conscience, as suggested at the Rehabilitation (*Procès*, II, 254 and 315). For Massieu's evidence that the sacrament was administered, see T.D. Murray, *op cit.*, p. 176.

[3] *Aperçus*, p. 138 ff.

[4] *Procès*, V, 427, *Sommaire de la cause*, and *ibid.*, II, 26, *Consultatio*.

[5] See deposition of greffier Nicolas Taquel (*Procès*, II, 320), who mentions being at an interrogation the morning of the martyrdom.

[6] 'Quantitate minima, sub specie quarumdam rerum minimarum, minibus rebus.'

notaries did not attest these final and most important proceedings because they were not present[1]—a fact which strongly suggests, in the opinion of the writer, that they were uncoerced, free to sign or not to sign as they pleased. If—as usually suggested, on the basis of certain evidence at the Rehabilitation—they were harried from pillar to post, as it were, they would certainly have been coerced into signing this final document. Clearly, the notaries were conscientious, and were free agents. Their failure to sign the 'Posthumous Information' strengthens the authority of the trial as a whole, more than it weakens the authority of its concluding document.

We learn from the Trial Record that Joan herself accepted its accuracy at the time:

> Finally, after the contents of the register had been read to her the said Jeanne confessed that she believed she had spoken well according to what had been written in the register and read to her, and she did not contradict any other saying from the register.[2]

From the Rehabilitation comes the story, contradicted at the time, but generally accepted, of the omission of a secular sentence for Joan, presumably because the English were in such indecent haste to consummate the burning. Any such dubious irregularity is directly contradicted by the letter written by his advisers in the name of King Henry VI of France and England to the Emperor, kings, dukes and other princes of all Christendom. The document states that:

> she was given up to the judgement of the secular power, which decided that her body was to be burned.[3]

This letter was written immediately after the execution, and is prior evidence, as compared with that of twenty-five years later, especially in view of the inherent improbability of a process so

---

[1] *Procès*, II, 14, Deposition of Guillaume Manchon: 'Il ne fut point à quelque certain examen de gens qui parlerent à elle à part, comme personnes privées; néantmoins monseigneur de Beauvais le voulut contraindre à ce signer; laquelle chose ne voulut faire.'

[2] Barrett, p. 133.

[3] *Ibid.*, p. 342; *Procès*, I, 488. See also, letters from Henry VI, King of France and England, to the dignitaries of France, prelates, dukes, counts, other nobles and cities. Barrett, pp. 342 ff.

deliberate, and so solemn and important, culminating in a shocking irregularity such as that suggested. However, it is impossible not to be impressed by the evidence given at the Rehabilitation by Laurence Guesdon, who acted at the execution as the deputy of the *Bailli* of Rouen, the civil authority to whom the office of passing civil sentence belonged.[1] Guesdon denied that there was a civil sentence of Joan. Guesdon's evidence, corroborated by others, must leave the matter in doubt.

Certainly, in attacking the trial presided over by Cauchon, the judges of the Rehabilitation essayed a difficult task. As Pierre Champion, the leading contemporary Joan of Arc scholar, puts it:

It took almost twenty-five years to destroy, piece by piece—and after endless formalities—this imposing machine that is the *Procès de Condamnation*.[2]

The Rehabilitation judges took the opinions of two eminent counsellors of the papal *curia*, Paul Pontano (Pontanus) and Théodore de Leliis. Their consultations, drafted in the form of treatises on the canon law bearing on the matter in hand, are not in the dossier of the proceedings, but the existence of these documents permitted the French canonists to feel more confidence in the opinions which they tendered. Pontano laid down nineteen disputed points, solution of which would seem to settle the matter.

There were three transcripts of the Rehabilitation Process, one with nine theological memoirs attached, one with one memoir, that of Gerson, and a third with five memoirs, conclusively identified by M. Pierre Champion among the manuscripts in the British Museum.[3] The memoirs, like the 101 articles of the revision process, attack the trial at every possible and impossible point; many of their contentions, as in the case

---

[1] T. D. Murray, p. 286. *Ibid.*, p. 166 (Ladvenu), p. 181 (Manchon).

[2] Barrett-Champion, p.481.

[3] See *Procès*, Vol. II, and Lanéry d'Arc, *Mémoires et Consultations en faveur de Jeanne d'Arc par les juges de Procès de Réhabilitation d'après les manuscrits authentiques* (Paris, 1889). Lanéry d'Arc reprints a number of these theological memoirs, which Quicherat did not consider worth including in the *Procès*.

of the articles, have been disproved by Quicherat[1] by means of a careful examination of inquisitorial procedure as set forth in Eymeric.[2]

It is hard not to be impressed, then, by the cogency of the evidence which Quicherat presents for the view that the trial of Joan of Arc was indeed *un beau procès*, conducted by a great lawyer, and sound in canon law, regardless of the Rehabilitation's strictures. This view in no way passes a verdict on the trial from the point of view of ideal justice, as conceived in a later age; a legal system, of course, reflects the reigning ideals of its own age. Perhaps the truth is that man's concepts of justice were changing in the fifteenth century, and the Rehabilitation is really a condemnation of the old inquisitorial order in the light of new and more humane ideals of justice which were coming into being. There is no doubt of the ability, learning, and sincerity of the Rehabilitation judges, as there is, to our mind, little doubt of the ability and sincerity of the original trial judges whom the Rehabilitation so much maligned. The human mind is easily self-deceived. It seems reasonably clear to us that in response to royal and popular pressure, the Rehabilitation judges convinced themselves that Cauchon and his associates were grievously at fault alike in character and in method; their imagined faults concealed the very real faults of the inquisitorial procedure, as viewed from the standpoint of the age which was coming into

[1] In *Aperçus*. As an example of the more extreme arguments of the memoirs, we may cite the denial by Thomas Basin, Bishop of Lisieux (whom we have already encountered, *supra*, Chapter II) of Cauchon's jurisdiction over Joan, even though she were captured in his own diocese of Beauvais (Lanéry d'Arc, *opi cit.*, p. 192: 'Concludo ex incompetentia judicum et fore, processum et sententiam contra Johannam habitos corruire et nullos de jure existere.') One cannot doubt that Cauchon, a great jurist and canonist, if confronted with this opinion, would have replied, as he did to Joan, with a statement of an elementary fact of the law of the Church—the fact, namely, that: 'the ordinaries were each in his own diocese competent judges' (Barrett, p. 312; *Procès*, I, 445). Moreover, in the trial of Joan, his authority was reinforced by the sweeping powers, direct from Rome, of Jean Graverent, 'the lord Inquisitor of Heretical Error by apostolic authority in the kingdom of France', who had deputed Jean le Maistre to act on his behalf as his vicar, with full powers 'up to and including the final sentence' (Barrett, pp. 98–9).

[2] Eymeric, Nicolas, *Directorium Inquisitorum* with Pegrra's Commentary (Rome, 1578). That oracle of the inquisition stated (*quaest.* 85) that the bishop and the judge of the Inquisition acting jointly, possessed authority sufficient to interpret the law. See *Aperçus*, p.109.

being. In other words, Cauchon and the other judges were the scapegoats for the institution which they served, and have remained so ever since. To dispose of collective feelings of guilt by loading them on a sacrificial victim is a very primitive human ritual; and we can trace a parallel 'will to believe' in human devils and personal scapegoats even in our own time—in war-crimes trials, for instance.

The condemnation of Joan's original judges in part took the form, however, of finding legal flaws in Joan's trial under the old rules, even where those legal flaws did not exist. In that way, a direct challenge to the old order was avoided and a necessary tribute was paid to the innate conservatism of mankind. All history shows that men accept new things most readily when they present themselves in traditional guise. All the great revolutions, Protestant, English, French, American, even Russian, affect to be going back to some lost excellence.

The Rehabilitation was conducted in such a manner as to minimize the opening of old sores, the reawakening of old controversies. There was no general indictment of those who conducted Joan's trial; a number of them, in fact, testified at the Rehabilitation and showed as much zeal in 1456 as they had in 1431. Only certain scapegoats were selected, and those all safely dead and beyond the reach of judicial recriminations. It was really they who were placed on trial in the Rehabilitation.

The University of Paris, which had condemned Joan in its exceedingly influential advice to the judges at Joan's trial, was considered by Bouillé to have been 'deceived' by the fraudulent indictment of the Twelve Articles extracted from Joan's evidence by the judges for its information. The articles were attacked in a manner for which the text of Joan's trial offers little enough justification.[1] Bréhal, the Inquisitor of the Faith, professed his respect for the University, and suggested that its professors involved in the trial were few in number! Obviously he, himself a member of the Order of Preaching Friars, did not want the

---

[1] The Twelve Articles are called 'corrupte, dolose, calumniose, fraudulenten et malitiose ex ipsis practensis processu et confessione dictae defunctae extractos'. *Procès*, III, 359.

Rehabilitation to become involved in the University's quarrel with the mendicant orders. Isabelle Rommée de Vouthon's lawyer, Pierre Maugier, when he read the papal order for an inquiry at the opening session in Notre Dame, said that the commission would not question the guilt or innocence of those who had only the Twelve Articles as a basis upon which to form a judgement.

Pierre Cauchon, Bishop of Beauvais, was dead, as were most of the judges; the Promoter, Jean d'Estivet, a personage of the second rank, was also deceased; and the Vice-Inquisitor, Jean le Maistre, could not be found. These men were saddled with the whole responsibility for the assumed miscarriage of justice in the case of Joan of Arc; and influential living ecclesiastics, such as Courcelles, were thus protected. No informers or accusers came forward to testify against them; none, certainly, were desired. The heritors of D'Estivet and Le Maistre could not be found. Cauchon's heirs, through an advocate, denied liability for his alleged misdeeds, and did not protest the proceedings, nor defend his memory; they pleaded the amnesty which was proclaimed when Normandy was reconquered.[1] Nobody appeared to defend the accused judges. Nobody, therefore, had any reason to fear or hinder the commission of inquiry; in fact, quite the contrary. Men such as Courcelles had convenient memories, and could forget a good deal in testifying about their parts in the trial; others remembered the most remarkable things! Joan's judges and assessors had been unanimous in their verdict; but the Rehabilitation Record contains evidence of sympathy and support for Joan which is not at all apparent in the original Trial Record. No doubt time, and changing political circumstances, mellowed Joan's judges' memories. One judge even denied participation in Joan's trial, although his name figured in its *procès-verbaux*, and in the registers of the indemnities paid to the judges!

The Pope, Calixtus III, apparently would have liked to protect that devout servitor of the Church, Pierre Cauchon,

[1] *Procès*, II, 194.

from infamy. Representing him as having been duped by the false reports of d'Estivet, he called him a bishop of good memory.[1] It proved impossible, however, to rehabilitate Joan while at the same time salvaging the reputation of Cauchon. He appears in the Rehabilitation Proceedings as an inhuman brute, with an aspect in utter contrast to that which he bore in his lifetime. When Warwick says, 'The King is ill-served, since Joan has escaped us', Cauchon's reply, as alleged, is, 'Be of good cheer, we shall catch her yet'.[2] Ladvenu tells us that Cauchon would not keep Joan in an ecclesiastical prison for fear of displeasing the English,[3] and Ysambard de la Pierre says that Cauchon said to the English, after her final sentence, 'Farewell! it is done; be of good cheer'.[4]

Obviously, many of those who were present at Joan's trial, who took part in her final unanimous excommunication,[5] and who testified in the later proceedings, were eager to exculpate themselves by incriminating those who were not present to defend their own deeds. One is reminded of the similar eagerness in France after World War II to clear oneself of the charge of collaborating with the Germans during the occupation of France. The charge of collaboration with the English was just as damning in 1456; and, unfortunately for Cauchon, he had fought hard on what proved to be the losing side.

Joan's second judgement was really the judgement of her

[1] See *Procès*, II, 96, 'Bonae memoriae Petro, episcopo Belvacensi'. See also Joseph Fabre, *Les Bourreaux de Jeanne d'Arc et sa Fête Nationale* (Paris, 1915). p. 51. The passage leaves open the possibility that the reply may have been made on Cauchon's behalf by a member of his staff who accompanied him.

[2] Cf. *Procès*, II, 376, evidence of Jean Fave 'Domine non curetis; bene rehabebimus eam'.

[3] See also *Procès*, II, 14 (Manchon). The truth is, as Henry VI's letter to Cauchon makes very clear (Barrett, pp. 32–3), that the English had no intention of letting their valuable and dangerous prisoner, Joan, out of their custody for a moment; they agreed merely to make her available for trial, with the announced intention to 'retake and regain possession' of her, whatever the outcome! 'C'est nostre entencion de ravoir et reprendre pardevers nous icelle Jehanne, se ainsi estoit qu'elle ne fust, convaincue ou actainte des cas dessusdiz.' (*Procès*, I, 19.)

[4] *Procès*, II, 5. Surely Cauchon was too much a stickler for the legal and religious properties ever to have said this; and it does not fit other evidences of his attitude, cited above.

[5] *Ibid.*, I, 468; see Barrett, pp. 322–5.

judges. A judicious modern writer says

> And so it is Jeanne's judges that we, in our turn, shall judge; posterity makes a bill of accusation of their apologia.

He calls the trial a 'masterpiece of partiality under the appearance of the most regular of procedures'.[1]

Witnesses charged the original trial with bias and pressure, and many historians have ignored the bias and pressure in a contrary direction in the later hearing. Francis Lowell, himself a judge, and of notably judicial temper, is surely right when he says of the Rehabilitation:

> All the judges were strong supporters of Charles, and it is doing them no injustice to say that their decision was predetermined like that of Cauchon.[2]

The English appear, in the Rehabilitation, impatient to get on with the burning, fearful that the delays of the wretched priests will cause them to miss their dinners. On the other hand, there is the record of the English lord who said during the trial;

> My God, a glorious woman! Why wasn't she born English?

Bedford, the able and devout statesman who captained the English cause in France in 1431, is, as befits his prominence at the time, let off very easily in the Rehabilitation, appearing only once, though not in a very edifying role—namely, as 'peeping Tom', during the examination of Joan by the Duchess of Bedford and her ladies—the examination which vindicated Joan's claim to virginity.[3] Some English writers have doubted the authenticity of this information about Bedford. At least, however, it testifies to his attention to detail!

As for Joan, she is presented as spotless, humble, devout, rather solitary, chaste, ascetic, a true prophetess, like those in the Scriptures, whose victories are a 'sign' from Heaven.[4]

---

[1] Barrett-Champion, p. 480.

[2] Lowell, *op. cit.*, p. 351.

[3] *Procès*, III, 163; evidence of G. Colles: 'Deponit . . . quod ipsa Johanna fuerat visitata per matronas . . . et quod dux Bethfordiae erat in quodam loco secreto, ubi videbat eamdem Johannam visitari'.

[4] See, e.g. *Procès*, II, 389–90, deposition of Jean Morel; p. 413, Perrin le drapier; p. 420, Jean Waterin; p. 430, Mengette Joyart; p. 439, Michel Lebuin; III, 87, dame Régnier de Bouligny, Joan's hostess at Bourges. See also Gaucourt: 'No one could be more chaste . . . she had always at night a woman in her room.' (T. D. Murray, p. 236.)

Bréhal and the Rehabilitation judges lay great stress on that touching figure, the simple shepherdess who knew neither 'A' nor 'B', and who could not understand the entangling subtleties of the theologians.[1] Here we have that idyllic picture, with its background of flocks and herds, church bells, oak forest, ladies' tree and well of the thorn, which so charmed the romantic poets. It is a concept which stands in ironic contrast to the frequent nineteenth-century conception[2] of the polymorphous genius, the military commander of almost incredible courage and strategic insight, who is worthy of comparison with Napoleon. The germs of this concept, too, however, may be found in the Rehabilitation.[3]

It is interesting to note that the Church avoided pronouncing on the divine inspiration of Joan's 'Voices', in the Process of Rehabilitation. This touchy question was left over for the controversies of future generations.

In general, the Rehabilitation Proceedings are very sparing of miracles, and more than one theological quagmire is deftly skirted. Dunois and Pasquerel are the only witnesses who give us miracles, the change of wind on the Loire, the sudden drowning of the man who blasphemously insulted Joan, the miraculous prediction of the arrow wound.[4] The clairvoyant prediction of Rouvray, the strange affair of the finding of the sword,[5] the birth miracles recorded by Boulainvilliers,[6] etc., are not touched upon. No doubt the judges did not wish to ask of

[1] Many avowals along this line were elicited. 'C'estoit une pauvre femme assez simple, qui à grant peine savoit *Pater noster* et *Ave Maria*.' Deposition of her confessor, Martin Ladvenu, *Procès*, II, 8, 364–5, also III, 166, 'Erat multum simplex'; *ibid.*, III, 20, Garivel 'Ipsa puella erat una simplex filia'; *ibid.*, III, 87, La Touroulde, 'Ipsa Johanna erat multum simplex et ignorans'. 'The effort was made,' says M. Anatole France, 'to prove that Jeanne was destitute of intelligence, to show that the Holy Spirit was more manifest in her.' Mr Andrew Lang, *Maid of France*, Chap. XI, comments, not without reason, that M. France himself really thinks much the same of her intelligence and *esprit*, despite the evidence of her ability. See Chapter VII, *infra*, pp. 167–8.

[2] It is also encountered in our century; see e.g. M. Burke, 'Generalship of Joan of Arc', *Contemporary Review* (Sept. 1950), 174–9.

[3] Note, e.g. d'Alençon's evidence, *Procès*, III, 100, that she was apt at wielding a lance, at ranging an army, at ordering battle and preparing artillery—old captains marvelled at her skill in placing cannon. See also Marguerite la Touroulde, *Procès*, III, 85.

[4] See Barrett, pp. 74, 174. See also T. D. Murray, p. 229.

[5] Barrett, pp. 71–2, 161–2.

[6] *Supra*, Chapter II.

the Pope any more than they could help, fearing reluctance and opposition; they made the minimum claim upon a pontiff in an Italy in which Renaissance scepticism was already at high tide. Some of the wonderful stories which enshroud Joan's memory had not yet had time to form. A cogent objection, we may conjecture, to such stories as that of the magic sword with the five crosses, and some of the clairvoyant predictions, is that they had about them a certain flavour of sorcery, and might hinder the Rehabilitation more than they helped it.

The Rehabilitation Record, is, of course, the source of the touching and beautiful stories of Joan's edifying end, on a pyre so elevated that death must come slowly. We learn of the tears of her judges, of those, at least, who could bear to witness the spectacle; we hear of John Tressart, secretary to the King of England, who exclaimed; 'We are lost; we have burnt a saint!'[1] We are informed of the word 'Jesus' in letters of flame at the burning, and of the white dove which flew away from the flames toward France;[2] it was seen by the English soldier who came to add a faggot to the pile but who fell on his knees when he heard the cry 'Jesus' from the midst of the flames. We hear of the executioner who feared that the fact that Joan's heart was not consumed meant that his victim was a saint; we are told of Joan's final affirmation that her 'Voices' had not deceived her. We learn that she died embracing a cross and with her eyes fixed upon another cross held before her by a sympathetic priest.[3]

We are spared here the horrid realism of the 'Bourgeois of Paris', who tells us that after the burning the ashes were pushed aside to expose the body, so that all might see that it was indeed that of a woman; and no doubt, also, so that all might see that the witch of the Armagnacs had not escaped by aid of the Devil, or of wicked and abandoned men.[4]

[1] *Procès*, II, 347, Deposition of Pierre Cusquel.
[2] *Ibid.*, II, 372, Deposition of Thomas Marie.
[3] T. D. Murray, p. 177 (Deposition of Massieu).
[4] *Ibid.*, p. 287 (Deposition of Jean Ricquier): 'And after she was dead, because the English feared that people would say she had escaped, they ordered the executioner to part the flames a little, in order that those present might see she was dead.' (*Procès*, IV, 471.)

In sum, what is the value of the Rehabilitation as historical evidence? That its value is considerable can be doubted by no one. It is immense in size; it fills two large volumes[1] of Quicherat's great edition of the evidence about Joan, and even so, he omitted, as we have seen, much material, the 'Mémoires et Consultations' with which Lanery d'Arc was later to supply us.[2] All of the original trial is in one volume, the first, of Quicherat's edition in five volumes of the 'sources' for students of Joan. The bulk of the Rehabilitation process consists of evidence attested on oath, as the original trial proceedings are attested by the notaries. Historians generally would give priority over the chronicles to this attested evidence, along with Joan's letters, the accounts of Orleans, and other such direct contemporary material; the chronicles, of course, as we have seen, are of varying merits. The real problems arise as to the trial and the Rehabilitation. Which are we to follow, where the two differ? They do, at many points, clash; the trial and Rehabilitation are, in fact, a Hegelian thesis and antithesis; from various permutations and combinations of them, all the later syntheses flow. The case against Joan at the trial, the case for her at the Rehabilitation; these are the primary sources of two main traditions. The Rehabilitation also has its interior clashes. There is conflict within it over the reliability of the Trial Record, the extent of English pressure, the abjuration, the relapse; Cauchon's character appears in a very different light in the two Records, Trial and Rehabilitation, and so does Joan's. To which are we to give priority, the Trial Record or the Rehabilitation Proceedings? Here we find a wide spectrum-band of opinion among scholars, to whom both records have been freely accessible. In general, the more a writer approaches the clerical school of opinion the more he accepts the Rehabilitation completely, and gives it priority as evidence, using it as a touchstone to test other sources. The more closely, on the other hand, a writer approaches to the sceptical or rationalist position, the more he treats the Rehabilitation with reserve and scepticism,

---

[1] Vols. II and III.
[2] Lanéry d'Arc, *op. cit.*

tending rather to use the Trial Record as a touchstone. In short, his attitude to the Rehabilitation and to the trial is likely to furnish us with a master key to any writer's general philosophy as well as to his attitude toward Joan of Arc, in particular. From his view of the Rehabilitation flows his interpretation of the Maid. The basic question about Joan cannot be settled merely by looking at the evidence; for those of varying faiths, of differing philosophical preconceptions, will evaluate the evidence differently, and will approach it with varying types and degrees of the 'will to believe'. In some cases, indeed the will to believe approaches the point of *credo quia impossibile!*

Be that as it may, the Rehabilitation was conducted under the official sanction of the highest authority in the Church, and is sealed with its seal. In the eyes of believers, its decision and its procedures are stamped with the highest possible sanction, and automatically supersede those of Cauchon's tribunal.

Even a modern historian so cautious and authoritative as Joseph Calmette[1] has to admit that the pontifical power was present at Joan's trial by the intermediation of the delegate who had been commissioned by the absent Grand Inquisitor to represent him at the trial; but, on the other hand, the Rehabilitation was directly sponsored and approved by papal authority. The pure image, ineffable in its whiteness, which it presents, has inevitably formed the basis of official clerical attitudes ever since. After all, it is evidence on oath; and as General Canonge says:

Les principaux des cent vingt témoins entendus en 1456 n'avaient pas encore atteint l'âge où le souvenir, surtout de faits anciens aussi étonnants, peut être sérieusement altéré.[2]

It has been remarked that the absence of all contradictions in the Rehabilitation evidence would be really suspicious, and would strongly suggest coaching; there is corroboration, but not complete corroboration. Certainly, there is variety in the testimony; the 143 depositions by 123 witnesses represent

---

[1] Calmette, p. 103.
[2] Le Général Canonge, cited by Philippe-Hector Dunand, *éd.* Richer, *opi cit.*, II, 472, note.

people in all walks of life, and the evidence was diligently gathered all along Joan's pathway—at Domrémy, at Vancouleurs, at Toul, at Orleans, at Paris, at Rouen—and even at Lyon, where Joan never was, d'Aulon's testimony was taken.

It is true, of course, that there are gaps which Joan's biographers may regret; but then, the Rehabilitation was not concerned to prepare a historical 'source', or to write a biography of Joan; it was simply concerned to shatter a judgement. Most of the evidence, which was overwhelmingly favourable, was eagerly given, though some of her judges were less eager; nevertheless, twenty or more of the assessors at her trial testified at the Rehabilitation, and all three of the notaries. Two or three who had participated in the first trial refused to condemn it or to praise Joan, apparently without evil consequences to themselves so far as we know. All witnesses answered the same questions, and answered them fully and freely. Marguerie, as we have seen, said that some notable men at the first trial acted from proper motives, and he denied that Joan submitted to the Church. Beaupère, too, conducted himself with dignity and self-respect at the Rehabilitation, and refused to curry any favour with the court.

As we have indicated, there can be no question of the competence and repute of the Rehabilitation judges,[1] and equally no question of their industry. Both the trial and the Rehabilitation were marked by the most careful and extensive weighing of evidence; after all, the title to a kingdom lay in the balance. We have already sampled the difficult problems with which the judges had to deal. Their inquiries were certainly meticulous and prolonged.

There is no doubt, then, of the value of the Rehabilitation as an historical 'source'—a mine of curious information upon all phases of Joan's career. The great contemporary French Roman Catholic writer, Jacques Maritain, has deeply regretted the oblivion in which many historians have left it.

---

[1] Quicherat admits their uprightness, though he may have thought it was combined with a considerable capacity for self-deception: 'Les juges de la réhabilitation étient la probité même', *Aperçus*, p. 150.

Jean's Bréhal's *Recollectio* . . . is an admirable piece, both historical and theological, without which the significance of Jeanne's story and ordeal cannot be understood.[1]

Francis Lowell has noted the freshness of the recollection of witnesses, especially when they recalled Joan's phrases, full of her personality, which are often left in their original French.

Even when the witnesses' recollection of her words is translated into Latin, her quaint terseness can often be recognized.[2]

If the Rehabilitation is used with care, every part of Joan's career is illuminated by it. Thus, from the evidence of la Touroulde, we learn that Joan's companions on the way to Chinon had the idea of throwing her into a ditch, thinking her mad, but at length resolved to obey her in everything. We learn many fascinating details of the battle for the Tourelles, and of the siege of Orleans in general, from the depositions of Dunois, the Bastard of Orleans; of Joan's squire, d'Aulon; of her confessor, Pasquerel; and of her page, Louis de Contes. This part of the Rehabilitation evidence is fullest and most reliable, without the evasions of the testimony of the later period. Thibaut d'Armagnac tells us of Joan's assurances of victory with slight losses, at Patay. Manchon, Massieu and others give us behind-the-scenes glimpses, more or less reliable, of the original trial itself.

At times, the Rehabilitation enables us to correct Joan's statements at the trial. Thus, several Rehabilitation witnesses testified to Joan's having repeated, with application to herself, the prophecy of the maid from the *nemus canutum* (*le Bois-chesnu*).[3] Yet Joan at the trial denied taking any stock in it,[4] doubtless because of its flavour of magic and witchcraft. Here

---

[1] See letter to Riggs, cited by Riggs, *op.*, *cit.*

[2] Francis Lowell, *op. cit.*, p. 354.

[3] See, e.g. T. D. Murray, p. 223 (Deposition of Catherine, wife of Leroyer).

[4] Barrett, p. 65. 'Further, she says, when she came to the king several people asked her if there were not in her part of the country a wood called the oak-wood; for there was a prophecy which said that out of this wood would come a maid who should work miracles; but Jeanne said that she put no faith in that.' See also Article VI of the Articles of Accusation, *ibid.*, p. 146.

again we see, as we have already seen,[1] that she told her judges no more than was good for them.

The English had called Joan a cowherd, which would place her very low in the social scale, and would imply a doubtful reputation. This presumably, made her so angry that at her trial she denied having had anything to do with cows,[2] sheep or any other animals, and represented herself as having worked in the house with her mother, though there can be little doubt that she took her turn in looking after her father's animals. There may be something in M. Louis Bertrand's suggestion[3] that she was eager to disclaim any activities as a shepherdess because 'the games played by shepherds and shepherdesses in the fields were not always entirely innocent'. Certainly, the Rehabilitation witnesses were all in agreement that she took her share in tending the flocks, following the usual custom. Miss Sackville-West, reluctant to face the obvious inference, thinks the old witnesses' memories failed then,[4] and that she evaded duties as herd, preferring solitude! The witnesses were ready enough in their replies, and it seems rather unlikely that so strange a circumstance would have escaped the minds of all of them, even of her godparents. The *Chronique de la Pucelle*, significantly, has her saying after the coronation at Rheims that she wished to return to her father and mother, to keep the sheep and cattle, and do what she was accustomed to do.[5] Joan's own mother, in

---

[1] *Supra*, Chapter III, pp. 63–4.

[2] *Procès*, I, 51. 'Addens ulterius quod, dum esset in domo patris, vacabat circa negotia familiaria domus, nec ibat ad campos cum ovibus et aliis animalibus.' But see also *Procès*, I, 66. Here Joan rather qualified her earlier statement. She said that she had answered elsewhere; and that since she had grown up, and had reached understanding, she did not generally look after the beasts, but helped to take them to the meadows and to a castle called the Island, for fear of the soldiers; but she does not recall whether or not she tended them in her youth. See also Barrett, pp. 54–64; Waldman, *op. cit.*, pp. 101–2. *Vide supra*, Chapter III (Monstrelet), pp. 65–6.

[3] Louis Bertrand, 'Jeanne d'Arc en Lorraine' in *Pays Lorrain* (Nancy, 1928), *Année* 20, pp. 529–42.

[4] Sackville-West, *op. cit.*, pp. 47, 50. For the evidence of the Rehabilitation witnesses, see T. D. Murray, p. 212 (Beatrix), 213 (Jeannette), 215 (Perrin le Drapier), p. 217 (Isabellette), p. 290 (Séguin de Séguin). According to the last witness, Joan at Poitiers testified that her 'Voice' came while she was minding the cattle.

[5] *Chronique de la Pucelle*, *éd.* Vallet de Viriville (Paris, 1859), Chapter 59, p. 285, 'et garder leur brebis et bestail, et faire ce que je soulois faire'.

pleading for the revision of the verdict upon her, said that she was raised 'according to her circumstance, which required her to be of the meadows and of the fields'. One of Joan's godmothers called the D'Arc family 'Simple labourers, honest in their poverty for they were of small means'.[1] It is no doubt true that, though the humility of Joan's station was formerly exaggerated, on the basis of such statements, some recent writers, influenced by the evidence cited by M. Siméon Luce,[2] have swung to the other extreme. Joan's rather confined and ladylike character, as indicated at her trial, would serve to make her later hard-riding career appeal all the more a miracle of God.

We have been considering the merits of the Rehabilitation, as historical evidence; and even its severest critics must concede that, in the voluminous and rather carelessly edited document, many things which are exceedingly illuminating and suggestive are bound to slip through, whether or not one is in accord with its general tone. Nevertheless, from the rationalistic camp, the Rehabilitation has been subjected to stern and perhaps increasingly severe criticism in recent times. No one has yet gone quite so far as to suggest that the real perversion of clerical justice under political pressure is not the trial, but the Rehabilitation; but, as we have seen, the attack of the latter upon the procedure at the original trial has been subjected to a withering criticism. The guns levelled at the trial in 1456 may equally well be turned about and directed against the later procedure. If Henry VI financed the trial from interested motives, so equally did Charles VII finance the Rehabilitation from motives at least equally interested. If time-serving theologians found it to their advantage to convict Joan in 1431, did they not find it even more advantageous to clear her in 1456? Even more, because in 1431 the outcome of the war was more than doubtful, with the victory, thanks largely to Joan, inclining to Charles VII, and prudent men might well be reluctant to offend him; but by 1456, Charles

---

[1] Rehabilitation evidence of Jeannette, widow of Thiesselin de Viteau, see *Procès*, II, 403.
[2] Siméon Luce, *Jeanne d'Arc à Domrémy, op. cit., passim*; for this subject, see also A. B. Paine, *Joan*, I, 6.

had won a complete victory, and there was no longer any reason for ambitious Frenchmen to worry about what the English court thought. If the court of 1456 was eminent, that of 1431 was at least equally so, in ability and reputation for probity; in fact, many of the same men, as we have seen, took part in both proceedings, cheerfully contradicting themselves at every turn. There is certainly no more reason, and perhaps there is considerably less, to suspect tacit pressure, royal or clerical, in 1431, than in 1456. The Rehabilitation was conducted after the lapse of a quarter of a century; the examination and questioning of witnesses was highly selective. Only certain questions in a fixed schedule were asked, and certain answers were expected, which most witnesses were polite or circumspect enough to give. If they would not, we may assume that, in most cases, they were not called; this may explain some otherwise unexplained omissions from the list of witnesses. After all, a vital matter was involved—the honour of a crown, the validity of a King's title to this throne, upon which depended, especially in that age, the stability of a state. Most of the witnesses seem to have engaged in a competition to see who could contribute most to the good cause. As Parton says:

In 1456, the period of her 'rehabilitation' that man was accounted happy who had something pleasing or glorious to tell of the Maid whom France then revered as a deliverer.[1]

As Monod says:

dans vingt-cinq ans, les souvenirs ont le temps de se brouiller, de subir toutes les cristallisations, les superpositions, et les déformations possibles.[2]

There is, moreover, much hearsay in the Rehabilitation: 'It is common report', 'It was generally believed', 'I heard it said'. Some spoke of her bearing at the trial, and then acknowledged that they had not been present. The executioner's evidence was given entirely at second hand. Joan's family's neighbours would naturally put the best face upon her youth, when that was expected by authority, at a formal inquest, with the honour of a prominent local family at stake. Always, there is the political

[1] James Parton, *The Trial of Jeanne Darc* (New York, 1881), p. 109.
[2] Cited Richer, *éd.* Dunand, *op. cit.*, II, 471.

motive, which crops out so clearly in Massieu's report of Maître Guillaume Erard's sermon preceding the abjuration, in which Charles and his clergy are denounced as heretic and schismatic because they endorsed, or did not rebuke, the words and deeds of a useless, infamous, and dishonoured woman. Considering the tact with which Charles and his clergy were handled at the trial, one may doubt that they were thus described, and Joan may or may not have called him 'the most noble of all Christians'.[1]

It is significant to note the way in which some of the Rehabilitation witnesses contradict themselves, perhaps as they are more carefully dovetailed into the picture which it is desired to present. Thus, Ladvenu says in 1456 that violence to Joan did not occur, though in 1450 he said that it did. Massieu, in 1456, altering his earlier evidence, says that Joan's abjuration was only some eight lines long.

When we turn to the leading modern historical authorities on Joan of Arc in the Anglo-Saxon world, we find that, in general, they treat the Rehabilitation with considerable circumspection. This is especially true of the cool-blooded, unromantic, and unsentimental Francis Cabot Lowell III of the Boston, or Brahmin, Lowells.[2] Lowell even discounts the pretty stories of Joan's farewells to her village, as told in the Rehabilitation.[3] Indeed, considering the known intensity of her father's opposition, her leaving must have been rather secret!

The warm-hearted, romantic, and in some ways rather feudal-minded Scot, Andrew Lang, criticizes Anatole France's criticism of the Rehabilitation, as he does just about everything else that France wrote about the Maid.[4] Lang does point out that *secular* trials, even a hundred and forty years later—e.g. the trial of Bothwell's accomplices in Darnley's murder—often displayed the same weaknesses, mechanically identical evidence, and the

[1] See *Procès*, II, 17, Deposition of Jean Massieu. See T. D. Murray, p. 172 (Manchon), p. 174 (Massieu).

[2] He was, in fact, a cousin and law partner of the late Abbot Lawrence Lowell, President of Harvard University. See Ferris Greenslet, *The Lowells and their Seven Worlds* (Boston, 1946), pp. 329–331.

[3] *Lowell, op. cit.*, p. 38.

[4] Lang, *op. cit.*, pp. x–xii.

like, which we see in the Rehabilitation. But he does agree that the memories of the Rehabilitation witnesses 'were probably malleable and plastic'.

On one point, Lang is sharply critical of the Rehabilitation. He finds 'most unsatisfactory' its silence on the whole later phase of Joan's military career—a silence which leaves us with but meagre information upon many interesting points. The judges in 1431 had especially impugned this phase of Joan's conduct; but the judges of 1450–1456 asked nothing regarding what she did at Paris, La Charité, Lagny, Melun and Compiègne. There were no questions regarding her leap from the tower, or her attempted escape from the fortress at Beaurevoir.[1] It is, says Lang, 'a singular fact' that only two witnesses testified to any event between her failure at Paris, September, 1429, and her capture in May, 1430. No questions were put to her confessor, Pasquerel, or her equerry, d'Aulon, about this period.[2] Quicherat had previously pointed out that it was significant that no hearings were held at Compiègne, Senlis, Lagny, where Joan's misdeeds were chiefly alleged to have occurred.[3] Certainly, this makes it clear that the judges were concerned with making a showing, with achieving a politico-religious effect, rather than with getting to the bottom of their problem.

Why the reticence in the Rehabilitation about Joan's later career? What was being covered up? Was the motive, as Lang thought, a desire to spare the feelings of Charles VII by leaving in oblivion a period 'full of tormenting memories'? Was it a desire to spare the feelings of his former enemies, now reconciled? Was it rather, as Lang also suggested, that they did not wish to show the Maid promising victory in the name of her Saints, and not achieving it?[4] Was it, as Fabre supposed,[5] merely that the judges were concerned above all with deeds committed before

---

[1] *Ibid.*, p. ix.

[2] See *Procès*, III, 217, for one mention.

[3] See Quicherat, *Aperçus*, p. 152. France, *op. cit.*, I, xxx, suggested that Pasquerel's evidence was cut short following the assault upon Paris. May this not be one of the 'elisions' of which Quicherat spoke, and of whose existence Lang finds no proof?

[4] Lang, *op. cit.*, p. IX, also p. 217.

[5] Joseph Fabre, *Réhabilitation*, p. 140.

the coronation, because they were seeking to clear the royal name? If Joan were a good girl up to the coronation, her pecca-dilloes later could not affect the royal repute. What of Quicherat's opinion, expressed in a private letter to the Marquis de Beaucourt:

Mon opinion est que la procès de réhabilitation a été dirigé et arrangé de manière à cacher les torts commis envers la Pucelle, et par le roi et par ses confidents, et par tous les personnages attachés ou ralliés à son gouvernement.[1]

To the writer, it would seem that there may be some merit in each of these opinions, and that none of them can be rejected absolutely. All must be taken together, in order to explain a complex phenomenon. Certainly, the judges must have thought that their case would be strengthened if they drew a veil over the later part of Joan's career, which was a period of growing failure and growing discredit, of declining fortunes and declining reputation, of decreasing popularity and decreasing support—a period in which many influential persons at court turned against her, among them the Chancellor of the Kingdom and Archbishop of Rheims, Regnault de Chartres, the ranking civil and ecclesias-tical personage at the court of Charles VII. We can realize from his letter to the good town of Rheims, after Joan's capture, and from her own earlier letter to Rheims, attacking and threatening to break the royal government's truce with Burgundy, that he found her proud and self-willed—an intolerable, over-enthusias-tic nuisance, impossible to control. Undoubtedly, many of the upper classes had always regarded her as a troublesome and perhaps dangerous upstart. She was no easily handled puppet, as M. Anatole France has suggested,[2] but a person of tenacious and dauntless will, even when, perhaps, mistaken in her views. She was, as Mr Shaw says, 'so positive', and success and public adulation had not made her less so. There is reason, too, to think that her capture and trial were preceded, and in a sense prepared

[1] 'Lettre du 17 novembre 1856,' cited in Richer, ed. Dunand, *op. cit.*, II, 453. Here we may trace surely the influence upon Quicherat of De Cagny, with his charges that Joan was the victim of certain personages at court influential with Charles VII. (See Chapter II, *supra*, pp. 40–6.)

[2] Anatole France, *op. cit., passim.*

for, by a period of increasing suspicion of heresy and witchcraft, directed against Joan. The Anglo-Burgundian propaganda had begun to affect the Armagnacs, especially in view of Joan's failure before Paris, before La Charité-sur-Loire, and elsewhere; this is a world where nothing succeeds like success, and there is evidence that defeat shook the soldiers' faith in Joan, so that they cursed her.[1] Perhaps success like hers could not be indefinitely maintained. Moreover, there was a number of compromising incidents, which emerged at Joan's trial: the breaking of her sword, the taking of the horse of the lord Bishop of Senlis, the attack on Paris on a feast day of the Church, the resuscitation of the 'dead' baby at Lagny, the execution of Franquet d'Arras, the apparent attempt at suicide,[2] the letter to the Count of Armagnac agreeing to decide the claims of rival Popes, and so forth. Even her ardent champion, Michelet, thought that her character deteriorated at this time; perhaps pride, luxury, and love of vainglorious display and popular reverence, grew upon her—a personality change which modern psychologists would find quite plausible, one may conjecture. Joan was haunted at this time by premonitions. and strange warnings of betrayal—premonitions and warnings which, one may well believe, had a solid objective base in the plots of those about her. She never lost a wide following among the people, however. There is evidence, also, that Charles VII remained personally friendly throughout; she herself made clear at her trial that he financed her final expedition,[3] which could not therefore have been undertaken against his will, as De Cagny has led many historians to believe.[4] But we may conjecture that Charles could not give her the same countenance as formerly, in view of widespread attitudes at court. No wonder the Rehabilitation preferred to concentrate upon the earlier, golden time, the time of unbroken success, before she became an embarrassment to the court, before she was eclipsed by gathering

---

[1] *Supra*, Chapter III, pp. 75–6.

[2] See Barrett, Articles of Accusation, and Joan's replies, pp. 140–224.

[3] Barrett, pp. 96, 204–5. She had ten or twelve thousand *livres* at the time of her capture, and 'what she had is her king's own money'.

[4] *Vide supra*, Chapter II (De Cagny).

doubt and controversy, and partially discarded, her emergency usefulness past.

We may conclude our consideration of the Rehabilitation by quoting the opinion concerning it of a modern American writer, Mr Milton Waldman:

> A whole new batch of miracles was submitted to the scrutiny of the commissioners and the legend regilded as bright as ever—none assisting more wholeheartedly than various of the clerics who had once voted with equal enthusiasm to burn her. In the end the dead Joan was so thoroughly rehabilitated that there could never in the future be the slightest danger of confusing her with the living Joan who had sat for Cauchon.

And further;

> The legend is now too old, too rugged, even too hallowed ever to be seriously modified.[1]

Perhaps so. But nothing that is human ever assumes final form; no crystallization is exempt from the flux and flow that is life itself.

---

[1] Milton Waldman, *Joan of Arc* (Boston, 1935), p. 5.

VII

EPILOGUE

Since the Rehabilitation of Joan of Arc, completed in 1456, more than five centuries have passed. We cannot here attempt to achieve more than a bird's eye view of the vicissitudes of her reputation during this great period of time. In portrait and ballad and mystery play,[1] the fifteenth century presents us with a folk-heroine; the view of her is sometimes primitive, often artlessly imaginative and fanciful. In François Villon's simple and profoundly moving allusion to her, we have the comment of high art.

> *Et Jehanne la bonne Lorraine*
> *Qu'Englois brulerent a Rouan;*
> *Ou sont ilȝ, ou, Vierge souvraine?*
> *Mais ou sont les neiges d'antan?*[2]

We have seen that the contemporary source-material relating to Joan of Arc fall sharply into two main groups, which interlace, sometimes alternate, in their influence, through succeeding ages. One main group consists of the Armagnac chronicles and the record of the Rehabilitation. The other consists of the record of Joan's original trial, and the Anglo-Burgundian chronicles; here we have Joan of Arc the virago, the strumpet, the heretic and witch, perhaps a puppet, perhaps an impostor; this is the Joan of Arc of the French Renaissance, of the earlier English tradition, of

---

[1] See François Guessard and Eugène de Certain (eds.), *Le Mystère du siège d'Orléans* (Paris, 1862), in *Recueil des documents inédits relatifs à l'histoire de France.*

[2] From 'Des Dames du temps jadis', quoted in *Oxford Book of French Verse, XIII Century–XXth Century.* Chosen by St. John Lucas, second edition, edited by P. Mansell Jones (Oxford, Clarendon Press, 1957).

Shakespeare in *Henry VI, Part One*, and, at least in some aspects, of Voltaire and Hume and other less eminent thinkers of the eighteenth-century Enlightenment. The memory of the 'false Pucelle' is one ingredient in this image of the *egregia bellatrix*, which, in Renaissance courtly literature, displaces the folk-heroine of the fifteenth century.

Joan of Arc was not of great interest to the Renaissance humanists of that century and the next. She was, indeed, 'too gothic' for their tastes; too plebeian in origin, we may conjecture, for an era of aristocratic culture; too nationalist for an age still, in large part, cosmopolitan in its cultural ideals. No great statues were dedicated to the Maid in this period, no great dramas were written about her. She is assimilated, however, in tapestry and in Latin epic, to the tradition of the Biblical and classical heroines; she is Deborah, she is Jael, she is Judith, she is Esther; she is the Sibyl of France; she is Cassandra, she is Velleda, she is Semiramis; she is Camilla, or Hippolyta, or Penthesilea, queens of the Amazons; or, she is Bellona, goddess of war. Her sacrifice rivals that of Iphegenia. She has the courage of Clelia, perhaps the virtue of Lucretia. She is even compared to Hector or Achilles or Hercules! Her virginity, however, is sometimes questioned, her supernatural inspirations generally ignored, her military and political judgement often denied, directly or by implication.

The Protestants of the sixteenth century saw Joan of Arc as the Joan of the Rehabilitation, 'tainted with idolatry', identified with Church and King. They destroyed every representation of her upon which they could lay their hands. Swedes in the service of France, who ravaged Lorraine, even cut down the fairy tree near Domrémy, *l'arbre charmine faée de Bourlemont*, which was prominently mentioned at Joan's trial.

Later generations of Protestants, however, have often adopted quite other attitudes. Some of them have accepted as valid the original view of Joan, arrived at by the Church court which tried her and condemned her to death; the view, namely, that she was a heretic. As such, she has been regarded by some Protestants as a forerunner of the later Protestant movement. German writers,

notably the theologian Karl Hase,[1] have been to the fore in express-
ing this view; but it is George Bernard Shaw,[2] in his play *Saint
Joan*, who has rendered familiar to the modern world the concept
of Joan as a nationalist heretic, a champion of the right of private
judgement.

The Protestants of the sixteenth century, in any case, disliked
Joan because, not having the benefit of Mr Shaw's views, they
accepted as valid at certain essential points the Armagnac conception of her, embodied in the Armagnac chronicles and in the
Rehabilitation. The conception therein embodied was, in fact,
usually dominant in the France of the *ancien régime*. In the
Armagnac 'sources', as we have seen, we encounter the 'illustrious
shepherdess', saintly heroine of the religious, romantic, and
French patriotic traditions, made familiar to us, in various guises,
by many modern biographers. These traditions are, it is true, still
rather undeveloped under the old régime. To its poets and artists,
Joan is, above all, the *preux chevalier*, or else the court lady, full
of plumes and poses—seen in due subordination to the monarch
whom she helped to crown, and to whom she was devotedly loyal.
The influence of the Renaissance view is still felt here.

It is felt, too, in the work which best sums up the courtly point
of view of the *ancien régime*—Chapelain's monumentally mediocre
epic, *La Pucelle*,[3] famous above all for having inspired Voltaire's
brilliant satirical pastiche of the same name.[4] Chapelain's poem
killed Joan of Arc as a serious literary subject for a century. She
who had suffered an ordeal by fire had now to undergo an ordeal
by laughter!

To the *philosophes* of the Enlightenment Joan was, at best, a
skilfully dressed *machine de guerre*; at worst, something of a fraud.
Of course, the writers of the eighteenth century did not have the
documents before them, so it was the easier to minimize the Maid's
qualities of mind and will, which showed themselves so clearly in

---

[1] See his *Neue Propheten, drei historisch-politische Kirchenbilder* (Leipzig, 1851).

[2] Shaw, *op. cit.*, pp. 118, 119, and Preface, *passim*.

[3] *La Pucelle d'Orléans, ou, La France délivrée, poème héroïque de Jean Chapelain, de
l'Académie Française, avec les figures de Bosse* (Paris, 1656).

[4] Voltaire, *La Pucelle d'Orléans; poème héroi-comique...Première édition* (Paris, 1755).

her trial. Joan stood identified with the Church which had rehabilitated her, and the monarchy which she had so stoutly championed; and she shared in the disfavour of these two increasingly unpopular institutions in an age which was notably deficient in historical imagination, and saw the Middle Ages as an era of dismal gloom. Joan's role as nationalist avatar could have but little meaning to the cosmopolitan and often rather pro-English thinkers of the French Enlightenment. In fact, she made more appeal to the Scottish philosopher, David Hume, who, in his *History of England*, reflecting the humanitarian outlook of the age, condemns her treatment by Bedford as 'barbarous and dishonourable'. 'This admirable heroine,' he says, 'to whom the more generous superstition of the ancients would have erected altars, was, on pretence of heresy and magic, delivered over alive to the flames, and expiated by that dreadful punishment, the signal services which she had rendered to her prince and to her native country.'[1]

The French Revolution was a decisive event in the development of the reputation of Joan of Arc, as it was in the development of everything else in France. In its immediate effect, it was a further blow to her reputation, already badly battered by the assaults of the Enlightenment on the eve of the Revolution. Whatever 'pasts', real or fictitious, or half one, half the other, were being resurrected by the various partisans, the Gothic age was not one of them; no revolutionary party looked back to it. The thinkers of the preceding century, who had traduced the Maid, now reigned in their glory; and when Voltaire's mortal remains were borne in a triumphal car to a resting place in the Panthéon, it was not to be expected that his verdict on the *Pucelle* would be widely discounted. Later Republicans might see in her 'the revolutionary gunneress and captain of the National Guard' in Anatole France's phrase; but this conception was not the dominant verdict of the great Revolution itself, though it was not an idea completely unfamiliar at the time. In the main, the Revolution viewed Joan with hostility, seeing in her the prop of Church

[1] David Hume, *History of England, op. cit.*, II, 357.

and King, the beatifically smiling heroine of the Rehabilitation. Her relics and her monuments were swept away; though her devoted city of Orleans insisted on naming after her one of the cannon cast from her bronze image.[1]

The way was therefore open for reviving conservatism to appropriate Joan unchallenged, and to make of her one of its icons.

In another respect, the Revolution contributed, in the long run though not immediately, to Joan's reputation. She was, above all, the inspired heroine of French nationalism, and the French Revolution immensely strengthened nationalistic impulses in France, and, both by French example and French pressure, throughout Europe.

It is not surprising then, that under Napoleon I, when many of the discarded ideas and institutions of the old régime began to reappear, in a new and rather unstable synthesis with the creations of the Revolution, Joan of Arc came back into fashion. Napoleon aimed at national unity against the English, and she was surely its appropriate symbol. The First Consul sought to detach her from her ties with the *ancien régime*, and to convert her into a support of the new and more splendid throne which he planned. He could find a use for the 'Gothic' Joan of Arc and for her religious associations. His official reconciliation with her was proclaimed by him in the *Moniteur*, the official gazette, dated 10 *Pluviôse*, Year XI of the revolutionary calendar (January 30, 1803). The decree restored the annual Orleans fête on May 8th, the anniversary of the raising of the English army's siege of the city in 1429, owing largely or entirely to Joan's intervention. Soon after the restoration of the fête, a new monument to Joan was erected with the approval of Napoleon. This new monument,[2] a ridiculous work, and a travesty upon its subject, faithfully reflected the artificiality of the attempted Joan of Arc revival, as well as the atmosphere of military emergency which had largely inspired it.

The nineteenth century has been called, by a German writer,

---

[1] See Joseph Fabre, *Réhabilitation*, II, 262.
[2] See Le Nordez, pp. 133, 167, 196, 351.

'the century of the *Pucelle*'.[1] Indeed, from 1815 onward the increase of interest in the Maid of Orleans was almost continuous, especially in France. The Restoration brought one great upsurge of this interest, the advent of the Second Empire another; and in the years after the defeat of France in the Franco-Prussian War, Joan again gained a new importance, as a symbol of France's unconquerable will for survival and glory, as well as for *revanche*.

It was inevitable that the restored monarchy after 1815 should find Joan of Arc useful. Before the Revolution the French monarchy had sustained Joan's reputation because she had been instrumental in the crowning of the King. After 1815, however, it was rather the other way about; it was Joan who sustained the reputation of the French monarchy. Her loyalty to the monarchy, in her time often looked upon by the people as their champion against the nobility, could never be questioned; and she could still be useful to monarchy in a later age when it was allied with a nobility on the defensive against popular forces. The monarchy had few claims to military glory, at least in more recent times; and it had to compete with the military achievements of the French Revolution and Empire. The martial exploits of Joan of Arc were, therefore, important as a source of military distinction, traditionally linked, as they were, with the monarchy. Joan was, moreover, not only associated with the King, and with the Church which, after 1815, was a main support of the King; she also had ties with the aristocracy, since she had been ennobled by Charles VII. Above all, she was a patriotic and popular figure, peasant-born; although in the Restoration period there were not lacking those who tried to show that she was really of noble or even of royal descent—perhaps a bastard princess. Her remarkable career seemed, perhaps, to require an equally remarkable explanation. In the main, however, the French Revolution had made her peasant origin and her patriotic creed great assets to her reputation, which flourished accordingly. A spate of books, learned and popular, appeared, in which she was dressed out,

---

[1] Von Jan, *op. cit.*, p. 143, *Mit Recht hat man das 19. Jahrhundert das Jahrhundert der Pucelle genannt.*

quite literally, in the elaborate habiliments, the plumes and furbelows of a great lady of the Restoration.[1] Her home in Domrémy, and other places associated with her, for the first time became objects of pilgrimage and popular interest.

The monarchists continued in France throughout the nineteenth century to make use of the memory of Joan of Arc; and they sought, in such writings as those of the Marquis de Beaucourt,[2] to link Joan's reputation with that of Charles VII, and to rehabilitate the memory of that monarch, so fortunate in his own time but so subject to the detractions of later historians. In the twentieth century French monarchist literature assumes increasingly a proto-fascist form, but in this form it continues to find Joan of Arc useful. She, who was burned as a heretic, becomes, ironically enough, the heroine of the Right.

Another movement which, after 1815, contributed no less than did monarchism to the growing interest in the Maid of France, was the Romantic Movement. This movement in France stemmed largely from the writings of Rousseau, and it came to its full development at the hands of the leaders of liberal thought in France just prior to the Revolution of 1830. It would seem to be associated with the new and less formal culture of the lower middle classes. It expressed their revolt against aristocratic formalism, their demand for the liberation of the emotions from the constraints which society had imposed upon them. The Romantic Movement was associated, too, with humanitarianism, with the cult of the common man, and with the return to nature. It would seem, therefore, that it grew out of the Enlightenment and was not essentially a reaction against that movement as it is so generally supposed to be.

There were many reasons why the Romantics should have been interested in Joan of Arc. She was to them the child of nature, the

---

[1] See, e.g., Philippe Alexandre Lebrun des Charmettes, *Histoire de Jeanne d'Arc, surnommée la Pucelle d'Orléans, tirée des ses propres déclarations, de cent quarante-quatre dépositions, de témoins oculaires, et des manuscrits de la Bibliothèque du roi et de la Tour de Londres* (Paris, 1817), *passim*; also, by the same author, *L'Orléanide* (Paris, 1820); see also Jacques Berriat-Saint-Prix, *Jeanne d'Arc* (Paris, 1817).

[2] Marquis G. L. E. du Fresne de Beaucourt, *Histoire de Charles VII* (6 vols.; Paris, 1881–91), vol. 2; and numerous other writings.

daughter of the people. She was viewed as the 'Déesse des Champs', and as a rebel, a tender-hearted humanitarian; yet she was also the embodiment of national tradition. Believers in salvation through scenery projected her against the background of her native fields and forests. It was in this light that she was seen by English Romantics such as Southey, De Quincey and Landor, no less than by the great German Romantic Schiller or a French Romantic such as Alphonse de Lamartine. Michelet gave a romantic historian's interpretation of Joan in some of the most celebrated pages of his *Histoire de France*. Verdi and Tchaikovsky presented Joan as she appeared to the romantic musician. A famous passage in Tchaikovsky's opera gives us her farewell to her native woodlands, *Adieu, Forêts*; in this, Tchaikovsky follows Schiller closely. Conservative opinion, after Chateaubriand, 'took up' the Romantic Movement and gave it a Gothic turn; romantic painters presented Joan against a Gothic background. Such sculptors as Dubois, Frémiet and Anna Hyatt Huntington also exploited this theme. Others, such as Chapu and Rude, continued the trend of the earlier romanticism in presenting Joan as a peasant maid. (See Plate 14, facing page 112.)

Many and complex are the uses of Joan in the nineteenth century as a symbol of French nationalism. French nationalists debated with the Germans over the possession of Joan, for some German writers claimed that, since she had been born in Lorraine, then part of the Holy Roman Empire, she was not really French at all. Natives of Champagne, and other French patriots, maintained that she was really born in that province, and that therefore, as a 'Champenoise', she was indisputably French.

For the Germans, 'unsere Johanna' took her place beside 'unser Shakespeare'; on the other hand, many French writers, following in the footsteps of Henri Martin,[1] elaborated Celtic theories of Joan of Arc—theories which saw in her an embodiment of the older Celtic tradition, which had never been obliterated by the pressure of Rome. This Celtic theory, originally strongly popular and republican, inspired by antipathy to the

---

[1] *Histoire de France*, tome 6 (Paris, 1865).

Roman Church and to Roman traditions of authority, becomes later a part of a nationalist *mystique*, allied with reactionary and even fascist tendencies.

It is easy to understand how Joan, as a Lorrainer, became, after 1870, emblematic of those lost provinces, Alsace and (in part) Lorraine, which many Frenchmen wished to redeem from the national enemy. In her pride and in her suffering, Joan became the very symbol of a bruised and suffering but invincible France which 'stared hypnotized at the gap in the Vosges'. The spirited monuments erected at this time in Nancy and even on the Ballon d'Alsace were symbols of this Irredentist sympathy. In the eighties there begins an arduous and pertinacious struggle, finally successful, to make the anniversary of Joan's triumph a *fête nationale*. She continues in our own time to be a rallying point for French nationalism of all types. Dahl's novel, *Jeanne d'Arc Revint*[1] . . . even pictures Joan's return for the purpose of chasing the Americans from Paris!

Joan's English reputation has passed through many vicissitudes; there have been several very distinct phases in the course of the centuries. The English chroniclers of the fifteenth and sixteenth centuries, followed by Shakespeare, in *Henry VI, Part One*, held to what the Chanoine Dunand has called the 'English theory', the theory that Joan was a witch and strumpet, justly condemned. This theory, of course, was, as we have seen, derived from the Burgundian chronicles. In the seventeenth century, with the growth of secularism, it tends to give way to the theory of the Enlightenment—the theory that Joan was really an impostor. Only gradually do more favourable attitudes appear.

Perhaps the original revisionist of the traditional views was John Speed, who wrote in 1611; but it is only with the young Southey's epic, at the time of the French Revolution, that Joan's apotheosis may really be said to have begun. We can trace the change in attitude toward her through successive editions of the *Encyclopaedia Britannica*. In the nineteenth century she becomes an object of romantic adulation, a favourite with peers such as

[1] A. Dahl, *Jeanne d'Arc Revint* . . . (Paris, 1929).

Earl Stanhope and Lord Gower, and with Victorian ladies, who wrote numerously concerning her, finding in her exploits a decorous encouragement for the nascent feminism. English opinion was influenced by French conservative opinion, especially in periods when relations between England and France were quite good, as they were during much of the nineteenth century. The national conflict in which Joan was involved was by now so distant in time that it ceased to excite nationalistic passions in England, and seemed only a remote and glamorous pageant. The formation of the *Entente cordiale*, and partnership with France in World War I, produced in England new manifestations of enthusiasm for Joan of Arc, often combined with contrition for the part which British authority had played in her fate.

It is only in our own century that the 'English theory' has been revived in new forms by the British anthropologist, Dr Margaret Alice Murray,[1] and by the French publicist, Henri de Rigné.[2]

The Scots, of course, were allies of the French Crown in Joan's own day, and favourable views of her are reflected in their contemporary records, such as the *Scottichronicon*. The tradition of friendly admiration for the French heroine is continued through the *History* of David Hume[3] down to the twentieth century where it finds expression in Mr Andrew Lang.[4]

Irish writers, too, usually take a favourable view of Joan.

The nineteenth-century upsurge of national feeling in Germany was bound to be reflected in various attitudes towards Joan of Arc. In Schiller's play, the *Jungfrau von Orleans*, Joan is used as a symbol of national devotion. Some Germans, as we have seen, even tried to claim that Joan of Arc was of German origin, just as some Italian nationalists endeavoured to claim that she was of

---

[1] See her *Witch-Cult in Western Europe, a Study in Anthropology* (Oxford, 1921); and *God of the Witches* (London, 1933).

[2] R. de Rigné, *La Clef de l'erreur judiciaire de Mgr. Pierre Cauchon* (Paris, 1928); *Jehanne d'Arc, Héroine du Droit, op. cit.*

[3] David Hume, *History, op. cit.*, II, 343–57.

[4] Andrew Lang, *Maid, op. cit.*

Italian extraction.[1] Another element of German opinion sought systematically to denigrate the reputation of the French national heroine.[2]

In general, we find that Joan of Arc all over the world is to many peoples a symbol of nationalism. We find her presented in this light in the national literatures of peoples as remote from France as Latvia and Poland and Brazil. Even in Maltese there are books which present Joan as a nationalist symbol.[3]

There have even been Jewish theories of Joan of Arc, which have, explicitly or implicitly, identified with Joan the Jewish people, suffering and persecuted through the centuries;[4] Joan thus appears again, in yet another role, as champion of the downtrodden. It is interesting to contrast the 'Celtic theory' which, inspired by chauvinistic nationalism, suggests, absurdly enough,

[1] L. R. Ghislieri, *Cenni sull'origine bolognese di Giovanni D'Arco* (Lodi, 1908); see also, J. S. Stuart-Glennie, *An Italian Claim to Jeanne d'Arc* (Rome, 1909).

[2] Richard Mahrenholtz, *Jeanne Darc in Geschichte, Legende, Dichtung auf Grund neuerer Forschung dargestellt* (Leipzig, 1890). See also *Jeanne d'Arc, eine Heilige? Skeptische Studien zum Kanonisationsprozess* (Munich, 1893). This work is anonymous; but it has been plausibly suggested that Richard Mahrenholtz was the author, whose non de plume is 'Quis?'

[3] G. Muscat-Azzopardi, *Guanna Darc xoghol Zgheir fuk Ittalien ta. F. Lodi* (Malta, 1894); Agostino Levanzin, *Guanna d'Arc; jiu, Ix-xbeiba ta Orleans* . . . (Valetta, 1894).

For a Latvian view, see Andréjs Upits, . . . *Zanna d'Ark: tragédija* . . . (Riga, 1930). A Polish book, also produced at a period of nationalist upsurge and tension: Wlodzimierz Dzwonkowski, *Portrety dziejowe* (Poznań, 1928).

For a Norwegian play, from the period of growing Norwegian national consciousness, see the anonymous work, *Johanna d'Arc, eller Frankrigs Skytsengel*, a tragedy in 5 acts and in verse (Christiania, 1870). Compare, from Finland, newly arrived at independence: J. Lindblom, *Jeanne d'Arc, En skiss till det profetiska själslivets historia* (Helsinki, 1927).

As for Brazil, see Erico Verissimo, *Avida de Joana d'Arc* (Porto Alegre, 1940).

In this connection, one may note also Kingsley Martin's comparison between Gandhi and (Shaw's) Saint Joan in *Mahatma Gandhi, Essays and Reflections on His Life and Work, Presented to Him on His Seventieth Birthday, Oct. 2, 1939; together with a New Memorial Section* (London, 1949), ed. by Sir Sarvepalli Radhakrishan.

[4] See Endore, *op. cit.*, pp. 396–8; Darmesteter, *op. cit.*, p. 54; Edmond Fleg, 'Le Cinquième Centenaire de Jeanne d'Arc,' *Revue Hebdomadaire*, VII (July, 1929), 5–42; Abbé Joseph Lémann, *Jeanne d'Arc, récompense des croisades. Discours prononcé dans la cathédrale de Reims, le 24 juillet, 1887* (Paris, 1887); *Jeanne d'Arc et les heroïnes juives, 1873* (Orléans, 1891); *Jeanne d'Arc, restauratrice de l'unité française* (Orléans, 1891); *Jeanne d'Arc, conservatrice du coeur de la France. Panégyrique prononcé dans la cathédrale d'Aix le 8 mai, 1894* (Lyon, 1894). The brothers Lémann were converted Jews who attained positions of considerable prominence in the Roman Catholic Church, and pleaded at the Vatican Council for missionary work among the Jews. Joseph Lémann devoted himself to Joan of Arc's cause and delivered a number of panegyrics on the Maid

that Cauchon was a Jew, and makes Joan a symbol of opposition to Jews!

American biographies, plays, histories dealing with Joan of Arc were in the nineteenth century usually echoes of their European counterparts. In the work of Mark Twain,[1] however, we may catch an authentic reflection of the rough, brawling exaggerations of frontier humour, and of the sentimental frontier attitude toward women, who have, in a new country, a scarcity value! Joan of Arc, too, was a favourite with pioneer American feminists, such as Miss Grimké.[2] To Fentonville,[3] writing in Richmond as the shadows of defeat closed about the Confederacy, Joan was the embodiment and the inspiration of a national *guerre à outrance*. Albert Bigelow Paine produced a more sober version of the sentimentalism of his friend, Mark Twain, whose biographer he was.[4]

Francis Lowell, a judicial-minded Bostonian, provided, however, in his *Joan of Arc*,[5] what we must esteem the most solid historical work upon the subject of the life of the Maid in our language.

In the period of World War I, Joan of Arc, to Americans, was the sentimentalized symbol of the Franco-American alliance, and of the cause of the *Entente*. Popular ballads,[6] bric-à-brac, medals, art exhibitions, alike expressed this sentiment; so did the noble monument, the work of Anna Hyatt Huntington, which stands on Riverside Drive, in New York City. W. P. Yancey's *Soldier Virgin*[7] catches the mood of the period.

In Day's *Joan of Arc of the North Woods*,[8] and the popular

---

[1] Mark Twain, *Personal Recollections of Joan of Arc* (New York, 1896).

[2] Sarah Moore Grimké, *Joan of Arc, a Biography* (Boston, 1876). This work is really a translation from the French.

[3] John Fentonville, *Joan of Arc: an Opinion of her Life and Character Derived from Ancient Chronicles* (Richmond, 1864).

[4] See his *Joan of Arc, Maid of France* (New York, 1922); also *The Girl in White Armor* (New York, 1927).

[5] Francis Cabot Lowell III, *Joan of Arc* (Boston, 1896).

[6] See the song, *Joan of Arc They Are Calling You*, composed by Jack Wells (New York, 1917). See also *Joan of Arc*, composed by James Kendis, words by Robert Roden (*World War Songs*, Vol. 5). First line: 'I hear the bells at twilight chime.'

[7] William Paul Yancey, *The Soldier Virgin of France; a Message of World Peace*, by a soldier of the A.E.F. (Gainesville, Florida, 1926).

[8] Holman Francis Day, *Joan of Arc of the North Woods* (New York, 1922).

songs, *Joan of Arkansaw*, and Jerome Kern's *Joan of Arc Was On Her Own When She Was Quite a Child*,[1] we hear a raw and raucous note distinctly North American.

Following World War II, there has again been a revival of the Joan of Arc cult in the United States, appearing even in women's clothes, and in advertisements of the most varied sorts. The revival, this time, has had little to do with Franco-American relations. Perhaps there is something somewhat synthetic about this new phase of the perennial interest in Joan of Arc; it has centred about Maxwell Anderson's rather shoddy play, *Joan of Lorraine*,[2] which had a good run in New York, with Ingrid Bergman in the leading part; and it has centred, also, about the expensive but rather unsuccessful film which was inspired by the Anderson play, and which also 'featured' the Swedish actress.

The fortunes of Joan's reputation have in recent times been much affected by the policy of the Roman Catholic Church. The 'fille de Dieu', as we have seen, played her part in the Catholic revival which accompanied the Restoration in France. The Neo-Catholicism of the period following 1848 further elevated Joan's reputation, and the number of works appearing which were devoted to her steadily increased. Finally, in 1869, the celebrated cleric, Mgr Dupanloup, Bishop of Orleans, the city which was always the centre of the 'Joan cult', launched the movement for Joan's canonization. The defeat of 1870, weakening the position of France very greatly, may have delayed the canonization; it would appear that a party at Rome, backed undoubtedly by German and other influences of the Triple Alliance, long delayed action of Joan's cause, which, however, moved deliberately through its various stages. Meanwhile, in France, Joan was the focus of a tremendous outpouring of scholarship designed to support the cause of canonization.[3]

France, with her allies, was victorious in World War I, and she

---

[1] Goodhart and Hoffman are the composers of *Joan of Arkansaw* (New York, 1933), whose first line is 'I went down to Arkansaw and met a girl named Joan'. The Jerome Kern song here cited by its first line, bears the title '*You Can't Keep a Good Girl Down*'!

[2] Maxwell Anderson, *A Play in Two Acts* (Anderson House, Washington, 1946).

[3] See, e.g. the works of Father Ayroles, Chanoine Dunand, Mgr. Touchet and others.

emerged for the time as the dominant power on the continent, linked to the Church in new compromises by the new fear of Bolshevism, and by the problem of Alsace-Lorraine, in the main a devoutly Catholic region, and now returned to France. The victory of France was echoed in the final triumph of Saint Joan, admitted in 1920 to the full glory of sainthood, at once national and universal, in stately ceremonial at St Peter's. Since the *fête nationale* in her honour was also established, she was now, in every sense, the Saint of France.

Charles Péguy's 'Catholic Socialism', expressed in his works about the Maid,[1] and more recently, Paul Claudel's mystic drama,[2] are significant modern variations upon the Joan theme.

English Catholics, such as Hilaire Belloc and G. K. Chesterton, and American Catholics, such as Riggs and Monahan, have added added comparatively little to French views of the saintly Maid.

French anticlerical republicanism, centring in the Masonic lodges, was formerly very hostile to the Joan of Arc cult; from French secularist scholars in the nineteenth century there emanated much criticism of legends and miracles associated with the name of Joan of Arc. Vallet de Viriville, for instance, contributed extensively to this literature. M. Siméon Luce dissipated by his researches a traditionally idyllic picture of the childhood and youth of Joan.[3] The anticlerical offensive was resumed after the defeat of French monarchism in the seventies of the last century; writers such as Thalamas endeavoured to divest the Maid of her aura of mysticism. The climax of this anticlerical literature is reached in the brilliant work of Anatole France.[4] For him, Joan of Arc is essentially a visionary, who is not different from other visionaries who appeared from time to time in the history of the ages of faith, and who is used as a *mascotte* for the Armagnacs, under the supervision of designing clerics. Anatole France

[1] Charles Péguy, *Oeuvres complètes*, esp. Vol. V, *Lé Mystère de la Charité de Jeanne d'Arc* (Paris, 1910, 1921).

[2] See Paul Claudel, *Jeanne d'Arc au bûcher* (Paris, 1939).

[3] Siméon Luce, *Jeanne d'Arc à Domrémy; recherches critiques sur les origines de la mission de la Pucelle* (Paris, 1887).

[4] Anatole France, *op. cit.* For the views of Thalamas, a Professor at the Sorbonne, see his *Joan of Arc, History and Legend*, lecture at Tours, 29 April, 1905.

seems, as we have observed, to ignore the evidence, to be found even in the record of her trial, of her high intelligence. His entire work may be regarded as an anticlerical tract, suggestive though it is in his treatment of many controversial problems. It was fortified by the profound scholarship of M. Pierre Champion, who was consulted by its author.

After 1908, the year of the appearance of Anatole France's book, there began to manifest themselves certain indications of a *rapprochement* between French anticlerical republicanism and the memory of the Maid. For this *rapprochement* much credit must be assigned to Senator Joseph Fabre, a moderate French Republican who was an indefatigable champion of the cause of Joan, and who sought to unite all elements of French national opinion in support of the establishment of a *fête nationale* in her honour. As we have already seen, he was finally successful in this; and following World War I the controversy about Joan of Arc in France died down, and she was increasingly accepted as a national figure and a symbol of national unity, although each party continued to give its own interpretation to her.

Meanwhile, in the course of the nineteenth and twentieth centuries, various new sciences were contributing new views of Joan of Arc. Modern scientific historiography was first to the fore in this difficult field. The labours of many scholars, of whom perhaps the most notable was J. E. J. Quicherat, brought to light the buried 'sources' and placed them in print, duly edited and annotated. Every step of Joan's career was made the subject of varied and multitudinous researches. There were translations of leading source-materials, such as the trial and Rehabilitation, into French and into English. In the works of Francis Lowell and Andrew Lang, cited above, the scholarship of the Anglo-Saxon world made its contribution; and a number of leading German scholars, of whom Prutz was perhaps the foremost,[1] also contributed notably; but all these multitudinous labours have brought little diminution of the controversy about the Maid.

---

[1] See Hans Prutz, *Bayerische Akad., der Wissenschaften Sitzungsberichte Philosophische-philologisch und historische Klasse* (Munich, 1911, 1913, 1914, 1917, 1920, 1923).

We have already mentioned the extraordinary contribution of modern British anthropology through the work of Dr Margaret Alice Murray. The psychologists, too, had something to say about Joan of Arc from the standpoint of their fast-growing science. Various theories of hysteria and of objectification, of schizophrenia and paranoia, were advanced.

Dr Murray's work on the witch-cult, with which she has sought to link the Maid, reminds us of those modern necromancers, the Spiritualists, who have not been slow to claim her, and to make much of her reported feats of clairvoyance, clairaudience and prophecy; at the same time, the Spiritualists carry on the tradition of antagonism toward the Church on the part of her old enemy, the wizard. Léon Denis, in a work translated into English by the celebrated Spiritualist, Sir Arthur Conan Doyle, has well stated the contention of this school of thought:

> A constant stream of inspiration flows down from the invisible world upon mankind. There are intimate ties between the living and the dead. All souls are united by invisible threads, and rhythm of the universal life. So it was with our heroine.[1]

The great loss of life in the first World War gave such views an increased currency; men and women turned to the occult for a species of pseudo-scientific consolation through the alleged achievement of communion with the dead; the work of Lady Grey of Fallodon (cited above), affords an example of this.

[1] Denis, *op. cit.*, Introduction, p. 9; see also Andrew Lang, 'The Voices of Jeanne d'Arc,' *Proceedings of the Society for Psychical Research*, XI, 198–212; J. A. Petit, 'Communication médianimique attribuée à Jeanne d'Arc' (edited by J. A. Petit), *Revue spirite-* Année 57 (1914), pp. 410–23; F. Fielding-Ould, 'Jeanne d'Arc,' *Occult Review*, XXXIV (1921), 74–9; R. Sudre, 'The Clairvoyance of Jeanne D'Arc,' *Journal of the American Society for Psychical Research*, XII (1927), 157–65; Peg Miller, 'The 10 Proofs of Joan of Arc,' *Fate*, V (September 1952), No. 6, 14; Théodore Bouys, *Nouvelles considérations puisées dans la clairvoyance instinctive de l'homme, sur les oracles, les sibylles et les prophètes, et particulièrement sur Nostradamus* . . . (Paris, 1806), gives an early treatment of the theme of clairvoyance, with extensive reference to Joan of Arc. See also F. W. H. Myers, *Human Personality and Its Survival after Bodily Death* (London, 1920), and 'The Daemon of Socrates,' in *Proceedings of the Society for Psychical Research*, V, Part XIV (1899), 522. A mystical interpretation, influenced by Spiritualism, is that of Lady Grey of Fallodon; see 'The Story of Joan of Arc Retold' in a volume of essays, *Shepherd's Crowns* (New York, 1923), in which Joan is pictured as

> An angel-watered lily that near God
> Grows, and is quiet.

Modern art movements, too, contributed new and often start-ling interpretations of the Joan of Arc theme. Realism, im-pressionism, post-impressionism, cubism, surrealism—all of these have commented upon her. The painting of Touchages, the sculpture of Barrias, the modernist music of Honnegger, and the expressionist drama of Georg Kaiser—each of these presents Joan in a light which is new and somewhat strange.[1] But it is, above all, Jean Anouilh who has achieved a brilliant triumph of experimental technique in the drama.[2]

Various modern radical movements have expressed points of view about Joan of Arc, but for the most part their discussions have contributed little that is new. L. Martin[3] has criticized her from an internationalist point of view. Mary Beard[4] has given us a feminist interpretation. Eugène Sue[5] and others have expressed socialist views; and there have been Marxist commentaries from Ribard,[6] Anna Seghers,[7] Morton,[8] Lawson[9] and others. The only notable work, however, which modern Leftist thought has con-tributed is the great play of George Bernard Shaw, who may be taken as presenting in the Preface to his *Saint Joan* the point of view of an intellectual leader of British Fabian Socialism.

In our own day, in the mighty crisis of World War II, the 'Joan legend' has undergone a new and startling development. The Vichy regime in France, continuing the long-established tactic of French reaction, sought to use Joan of Arc as a weapon against Britain and against the cause of democracy. Some of the most effective posters of Vichy recalled to the French that the wicked

---

[1] Georg Kaiser, *Gilles und Jeanne* (Potsdam, 1923).

[2] Jean Anouilh, *L'Alouette* ed. Merlin Thomas and Simon Lee (London, 1956); *The Lark*, trans. by Christopher Fry (London, 1955).

[3] L. Martin, *L'Erreur de Jeanne d'Arc* (Paris, 1896).

[4] Mary Beard, *On Understanding Women* (New York, 1931); *Woman as Force in History*, *A Study in Tradition and Realities* (New York, 1946).

[5] Eugène Sue, *Jeanne Darc* (Paris, 1865), translated by Daniel de Leon as *The Execu-tioner's Knife* (New York, 1910).

[6] André Ribard, *La France, histoire d'un peuple* (Paris, 1938).

[7] Anna Seghers, 'Der Prozess der Jeanne d'Arc zu Rouen 1431, Ein Hörspiel'. *Inter-nationale Literatur* (Moskau 1937), Jahrg. 7, Heft 5, pp. 74–90.

[8] A. L. Morton, *People's History of England* (rev. ed., London, 1949).

[9] John Howard Lawson, *The Hidden Heritage* (New York, 1950).

British burned Joan of Arc and exiled Napoleon to Saint Helena. She was used by the Pétainists in an attempt to discredit altogether the British alliance, and any dependence on the perfidious Anglo-Saxon powers. On the other hand, General de Gaulle and other patriotic leaders saw in Saint Joan of Arc the protagonist of their own crusade, which fought for the liberation of France from the foreigner. Gaullist Catholic writers, such as Jacques Maritain and Georges Bernanos,[1] turned to Joan with an especial eagerness as the appropriate emblem of the nation's struggle for freedom, and it was owing to this that the Cross of Lorraine, from the coat of arms of Joan's own province, became the symbol of the Gaullist movement for national independence, and for the restoration of the territorial integrity of France, from which Alsace-Lorraine had again been wrested. Each side in the great struggle, in other words, sought to appropriate the story of Joan of Arc as its own weapon. World War II closed, therefore, with Joan of Arc established in a new and a more exalted sense as the patron saint of France. In contemporary France, the tradition of the Maid is securely identified with the *mystique* of General Charles de Gaulle, the Liberator who now, as President of the Fifth Republic, rules and leads the France which he seeks to regenerate and restore to her former glory. Whatever future vicissitudes France may undergo, we may be sure that Joan of Arc will have a part in them, and that her reputation, though it may and will undergo new metamorphoses, will always, in France, be secure. For all time, Joan is France. The world at large, too, will admire her heroism as long as heroic courage is respected; it will accept her as the symbol of a struggle for national liberation as long as national liberties are treasured; and it will reverence her as a saint as long as saints are reverenced.

---

[1] Georges Bernanos, *Sanctity Will Out, An Essay on St Joan*, translated by R. Batchelor (New York, 1947).

1338   Outbreak of the Hundred Years' War. French support of of the Scots and threat to Aquitaine, English alliance with Flemish cities, contributing factors; England opposes French trend toward national consolidation. Edward III's claim to French throne (in right of his mother, Isabella) an afterthought.

1340   English naval victory of Sluys, gives command of the Channel.

1346   Great English victory at Crécy; the role of the longbow.

1347   The English capture Calais.

1356   Battle of Poitiers—another great English success.

1358   Jacquerie, uprising of French peasantry.

1360   Peace of Brétigny; France surrenders sovereignty of Aquitaine.

1364–1380   Charles V (the Wise), King of France, establishes strong monarchy, based on popular support.

1372   Naval battle of La Rochelle, French recover control of Channel.

1376   Death of Black Prince. Du Guesclin reconquers English holdings in France, save for some seaboard enclaves.

1377–1399   Richard II, King of England.

1380–1422   Charles VI, King of France. Government intermittently paralysed by royal insanity. Rivalry of the 'Princes of the Lilies', Dukes of Anjou, Berry and Burgundy, King's uncles; later rivalry of Burgundy and Orleans.

1381   Peasants' Revolt in England.

1396   Twenty-year truce between France and England.

1399   Henry IV chosen King of England by Parliament, after revolutionary overthrow of Richard.

1404   Jean sans Peur, Duke of Burgundy—able, seeks popular support.

1407   Burgundy's orders lead to assassination of Louis, Duke of Orleans—Armagnac and Burgundian parties.

1411–1412   January 6 (?). Birth of Joan of Arc at Domrémy.

1413   Cabochian revolt—popular reform movement in Paris, pro-Burgundian; Cabochian Ordinance; Armagnacs regain power in Paris, effect a feudal reaction.

1413–1422   Henry V, King of England; policy strongly friendly to the Church.

1415   Henry V, invading France, victorious at Agincourt; takes advantage of French divisions, errors of French feudal nobility, which is in ascendant.

1415–1419   The reconquest of Normandy by Henry V.

1418   Dauphin Charles flees to south of France, Armagnacs in Paris massacred.

1419   Assassination of Jean sans Peur, Duke of Burgundy, on the bridge of Montereau, by the henchmen of dauphin Charles—Anglo-Burgundian alliance renewed.

1420   Treaty of Troyes. The dauphin Charles disinherited; Henry V, regent of France and heir-apparent, in control of northern France, marries Catherine, daughter of mad King Charles VI of France.

1422   Death of Henry V; also, soon after, death of Charles VI; Henry VI, son of the late King Henry V, nine months old, proclaimed King of France and England. His uncles, Dukes of Gloucester and Bedford, regents in England and in France. Charles VII, the dauphin, becomes 'Roi de Bourges'.

1424   Bedford's victories at Cravant, Verneuil.

1424 (?)   Joan's first visions; her sojourn at Neufchâteau.

1428   May (?). Joan's first visit to Vaucouleurs. The English begin the siege of Orleans.

1429   February. Joan's second visit to Vaucouleurs. Visit to Duke of Lorraine.
February 12. Battle of the Herrings.
February 23. Departure from Vaucouleurs.
March 8. Interview with the King at Chinon.
April 29. Arrival at Orleans.
May 8. Raising of the Siege of Orleans.
June 18. Battle of Patay.
July 17. Coronation of Charles VII at Rheims.
August 28. Secret treaty of Charles VII and Burgundy.
September 8. Attack on Paris.
September 18. Second treaty with Burgundy.

1430   May 23. Capture of Joan of Arc beneath the walls of Compiègne.
November. Joan sold by Jean de Luxembourg.

1431   January 9. First day of the trial of Joan of Arc.
February 21. First Public Examination, in the Chapel-Royal.
March 27. Trial in Ordinary begins, with a solemn sitting in the Great Hall of the Castle of Rouen.
May 9. Joan is threatened with torture.
May 19. Solemn assembly in the Chapel of the Archi-episcopal Manor. The Resolutions of the University of Paris are read, and the opinions of the Assessors taken.
May 24. Joan's abjuration, and sentence.
May 29. Decision to deliver Joan up to the secular arm as a relapsed heretic.
May 30. Joan burned in the Old Market Place of Rouen.
August 8. Sentence pronounced against a monk who had spoken ill of the judges.

1432   Charles favours the Council of Basel, against the Pope. Death of Bedford's wife, Burgundy's sister, weakens Anglo-Burgundian alliance.

1435   Treaty of Arras; reconciliation of Charles VII and Philip of Burgundy.

1437   Charles VII enters Paris in state.

1438   Pragmatic Sanction of Bourges; autonomy of the Gallican Church.

1440   Release of the Duke of Orleans by the English. Praguerie; uprising of great nobles against Charles VII, with support from the dauphin.

1442   French conquest of Gascony, except Bordeaux and Bayonne.

1444   Truce of two years.

1445   Marriage of Henry VI and Margaret of Anjou.

1445–1446   French army reforms, establishing standing army; royal finances reformed under Jacques Coeur.

1450   February 13. Declaration of Charles VII empowers Guillaume Bouillé, one of his counsellors, to enquire into the conduct of Joan's trial.
April 15. Last stand of the English in Normandy, at the battle of Formigny; Normandy completely conquered by Charles VII.
Jack Cade's rebellion in England.

1451   Charles VII gains Bordeaux and Bayonne.

1452   April, Enquiry at Rouen of Cardinal d'Estouteville and Jean Bréhal.

1453   Death of Talbot at Castillon. English attempt to recover Gascony fails; end of the Hundred Years' War.

1455   March. Death of Pope Martin V; succeeded by Calixtus III.
June 11. Rescript of Pope Calixtus III, designating a tribunal to reopen Joan's case.

December 7. Solemn session, at the Cathedral of Notre Dame in Paris, under authority of Rescript of Calixtus III. Petition of Joan's mother and brothers.
December 12. Rehabilitation process begins.

1456   July 7. Formal Sentence of Rehabilitation, in the Hall of the Archiepiscopal Palace of Rouen.

1909   Beatification of Joan of Arc.

1920   May 16. Canonization of St Joan of Arc, at St Peter's in Rome.

INDEX

Abbeville, 68

Abbreviator of the Two Trials, 53

Academy, French, *see* French

Achilles, 155

Acton, Lord, 26

Adieu, Forêts, 161

Aeneas Sylvius Piccolomini, *see* Pius II

Africains, rue des (Orleans), 110

Agincourt, 71, 82, 173

Albigensian heresy, 116

d'Alençon, Jean, duc, 19, 40–6, 50, 66, 102, 140*n*.; duchesse, 42; *see also Bailli, under* Glasdale

Alespée, Jean, 104

Alexander, 29

Alsace, 87, 162

d'Alsace, Ballon, 162

Alsace-Lorraine, 167, 171

Amazons, 110, 155

American theories, 165

American writing, 59

Amiel, Henri-Frédéric, 33

Amiens, 68

Amnesty, 137

Ancien régime, view of Joan dominant in, 156, 158

Anderson, Maxwell, 166

Anglo-Americans, 114

Anglo-Burgundian alliance, 77, 106, 111, 115–16, 173–4; chronicles, 154; propaganda, 152; territory, 59; *see also,* Burgundy

Anglo-France, 112

Anglo-Saxon powers, 171

Anglo-Saxon scholarship, *see* scholarship

Anjou, 46; duc d', 172; Margaret of, Queen of England and France, 114, 175

Annales d'Aquitaine, 53

Annales de Flandre, 53

Anne of Brittany, Queen of France, 54, 92

Anthropology, British, 169

Anticlericalism, middle-class and legal, 125; twentieth-century, 58

Antoninus, Saint, *see* Florence

Anouilh, Jean, 170

Aquitaine, 172; *see Annales* d'

Aragon, 97; King of, 115*n*.

l'Arbre charmine faée de Bourlemont, *see* fairy tree

d'Arc, Lanéry, 17, 142; family, 127, 131;

Isabel, mother of Joan, *see under* Joan of Arc; Jean, *see* Du Lys; Jeanne, *see* Joan of Arc; Pierre, *see* Du Lys

Aristocracy, English, 60

Aristocratic formalism, *see* formalism

Armagnac, 21, 31, 36–7, 69, 74, 77, 90, 100, 108, 116–17, 141, 152, 167; chronicles, 37ff., 46, 55, 62, 154, 156; count d', 115*n*., 152; credulity, 78; freebooters, 60; materials, 70; opinion, 61; outpost, 72; party, 82, 104, 120, 173; Thibaut d', 145; tradition, 59; *see also* Paris

Armoises, Jeanne des, 79, 109

Arouet, *see* Voltaire

Arras, 114, 125; Franquet d', 60–1, 80–1, 152; Peace Conference of, 112; Treaty of, 61, 68, 90, 111, 113, 175; *see also* Vaudois of

Articles of Accusation, 72

Assessors at trial, 144, 174

Astrology, 89, 94

d'Aulon, Sieur Jean, 71, 119, 144, 145, 150

Auxerre, 50

Avignon, 96, 115

Ayroles, Father Jean Baptiste Joseph, SJ, 48, 116*n*.

Bailli of Rouen, *see* Rouen, *Bailli* of

Ballon d'Alsace, *see* Alsace, Ballon d'

Barbarossa, Frederick, 79

Barrias, sculptor, 170

Basel, 87

Basel, Council of, 102*n*., 107*n*., 115, 474

Basin, *see* Lisieux

Baudricourt, Robert de, Provost of Vaucouleurs, 72–3, 110

Bavaria, Isabel of, *see* Isabel of Bavaria

Bayonne, 55, 175

Bear Inn, landlord of the, 81

Beard, Mary, 170

Beatification of Joan, 176

Beatrix, 146*n*.

Beau procès, 129

Beaucourt, G. L. E. du Fresne, Marquis de, 151, 160

Beaupère, Maître Jean, 64, 130*n*., 131*n*., 144

Beaurevoir, Castle of, 71, 150

Beauvais, 105*n*., 123; diocese of, 106; Pierre Cauchon, Bishop of, 19, 82,

101–3, 105–6, 115, 118, 125, 129–39, 142–3, 153; character of Cauchon, 106–7; theory that he was Jewish, 164
Beckmann, P., 37, 87
Bedford, John, Duke of, Regent, 68, 70, 73, 77, 83, 111–13, 139, 157, 173–4; Duchess of, 139
Belle Dame sans Merci, La, 57
Belleforest (*Histoire des neuf Charles*), 53*n*.
Belloc, Hilaire, 167
Bellona, 155
Bergamo, Giacomo Filippo Foresti of (Philip of Bergamo), *Universal History, De claris eclectisque mulieribus*, 92
Bequest of Kingdom; see Charles VII
Bergman, Ingrid, 166
Bernanos, Georges, 108, 171
Berni, Guarneri, 94
Berri, Duke of, 56, 172
Berri, Herald of, see Le Bouvier, Gilles
Bertrand, Louis, 146
Black Prince, The (Edward Plantagenet), 172
Blois, 99
Boccaccio, *Griselidis*, 53*n*.
Bois-chesnu, le, 93, 145
Boisguillaume, 99*n*., 131
Bologna, 91
Bologna, University of, 113
Bolshevism, 167
Bonne Lorraine, la, 79
Bordeaux, 55, 60, 114, 175
Borgia, Alphonsus, see Calixtus III
Bosquier, Pierre, 101
Boswell, James, 32
Bothwell, James Hepburn, Earl of, 149
Bouchard, Alain, advocate at the *parlement* of Rennes, *Croniques*, 53
Bouchier, Jacques, 41
Bouillé, Maître Guillaume, 118, 121, 136, 175
Bouligny, Dame Régnier (Réné) de, see La Touroulde
Bourgaut, Abbé, *curé* of Domrémy, 77
Boulainvilliers, Perceval de, 57, 66, 140
Bourbon, Duke of, 46
Bourchier, see Bouchier
Bourgeois of Paris, see *Journal*
Bourges, 139*n*.; Pragmatic Sanction of, 115, 175;
'Bourges, Roi de', 173
Boutet de Monvel, Louis Maurice, 69

Bouton, 82
Brazil, see Nationalism
Bréhal, Jean (Grand Inquisitor), 119, 122–4, 128–9, 136, 140, 145, 175
Bréhal's *Summarium*, 122
Bretagne, Les Grandes croniques de, 53
Brétigny, Peace of, 172
Breton language, 54
Breviarum historiale, 57
Brézé, 46
British alliance (with France), 171
Brittany, 45, 92; Anne of, see also Anne of Brittany; Duke of, 66
Bruges, 95
Buchon, Jean Alexandre, 47
Buonincontro, Lorenzo, 94
Burgundy, Burgundian, 21, 31, 37, 45, 90, 108, 112; Burgundians, 69; Burgundian chronicles, chap. iii, 58ff., also 23, 38, 162; Burgundy, Dukes of, 82; John the Fearless (Jean sans Peur), Duke of, 84*n*., 128, 172–3; his murder, 37, 59, 112; Philip the Good (Philippe le Bon), Duke of, 36, 46, 61, 68–70, 77–8, 83, 85, 88, 103, 106, 111, 113, 174–5; death of Duke Philip's sister, 174; loyalty of Paris to (Burgundy), 81; (Burgundian) party, 60, 173; Charles VII's truce with (Burgundy), 43, 151; wine merchants of (Burgundy), 60; see also Domrémy, feudal
Bury, Baron Henri Blaze de, 30
Butterflies about Joan's standard, 38
Butti, Adele, 94

Cabochien (Burgundian) opinions, 74
Cabochian Ordinance, 173
Cabochian revolt, 173
Caddy, Mrs Florence, 39, 93
Cade, Jack, rebellion, 175
Caen, University of, 113
Caesar, Julius, 29
Cagny, Perceval de, 39–43, 45–6, 67, 70, 82, 151*n*., 152
Calais, 114, 172
Calixtus III (Alphonsus Borgia), Pope, 123–4, 137
Calmet, Dom, 56
Calmette, Joseph, 143
Camilla, 155
Canon Law, 134–5

Canonge, General Frédéric, 143

Canonization, 21, 34, 84, 120–1, 166, 176

Cardinals, College of, 115*n.*

Carolingians, 112

Cassandra, 155

Castile, 97

Castillon, 114, 175

Catherine, Queen, *see* Katherine

Catholics, 21; American, 167; English, 167; Writers, 171; *see also* Gaullist

Catholicism, Neo-, 166

Cauchon, Pierre, *see* Beauvais

'Celtic theory', of Joan of Arc, 161–2, 164

Champagne, 161

'Champenoise', Joan as, 161

Champion des Dames, Le, 101

Champion, Pierre, 20, 38, 42, 53*n.*, 66, 70, 101, 107, 116*n.*, 134, 139, 168

Chancellor of France, *see* Rheims

Channel, English, 172

Chapel of the Archiepiseopal Manor of Rouen, 174

Chapel Royal of Rouen, 174

Chapelain, Jean, 25, 156

Chapu, Henri, 161

Charlemagne, 79

Charles V (the Wise), King of France, 172

Charles VI, King of France, 37, 59, 172–3

Charles VII, King of France, 36–7, 41–6, 48–50, 52–5, 57–61, 66, 68, 70, 77, 80–1, 89–93, 96–7, 99, 102, 107–8, 111–22, 127, 147–51, 156, 159–60, 173–5; attempt at ransom of Joan of Arc, 96; bequeathes the Kingdom to Joan, 57; as dauphin, 173; financed Joan's final expedition, 152; secret treaty with Burgundy, *see* Burgundy, Duke of; *see also* coronation campaign; Coronation

Charles VIII, King of France, 55

Charles XII, King of Sweden, 29*n.*

Chartier, Alain, 52, 57

Chartier, Jean, precentor of St Denis, *Chronique,* 47, 49, 51–2

Chartier, Guillaume, *see* Paris

Chartres, Captain of, 110

Chartres, Regnault de, *see* Rheims

Chastellain, Georges, *Chronique,* 78–80

Chateaubriand, François, Réné de, Viscount, 161

Cherbourg, 114

Chesterton, G. K. ,167

Chinon, 65, 72, 145; Joan's interview with the King at, 174

Christ, Jesus, 21, 23

Christendom, 133

Chronicle Concerning the Deliverance of Orleans and the Holiday May 8, 55

Chronicles: *see* chaps ii, iii, iv; *see also* Anglo-Burgundian alliance; *Annales*; Armagnac; Bouchard; Burgundian; degli Ariente; Dynther; *Eugubinum*; Florence; German; *Gestes*; Italy; *Journal(s)*; Le Bouvier; Le Fèvre; *Livre(s)*; Lorraine; Metz; Mont-Saint-Michel; Morosini; Nangis; Register, *Registre*; Richemont; *Scottichronicon*; Tournay

Chronique: de la Pucelle, 46–8, 51, 54, 146; *see also,* Chartier, Jean; Chastellain, Georges; Cochon; Cordeliers; *Croniques*; Wavrin

Chuffart, Jean, 74

Church, Holy Roman Catholic Apostolic, 34–5, 109, 111*n.*, 113, 117, 120, 155, 162, 169, 173; of France, 116, 120; law of the, 130 (*see* canon law); *see* Gallican church; Inquisition; Pope of Rome

Classidas, *see* Glasdale

Clelia, 55

Clement V (Bertrand de Gouth), Pope, 115

Clement VII (Giulo de' Medici), Pope, 115

Clermont, Charles de Bourbon, Count of, lieutenant-general (Sept. 7, 1429), 44

Class, lower middle, 160

Claudel, Paul, 167

Clopinel, 66

Clovis, 112

Cochon, Pierre, *Chronique normande,* 82

Coeur, Jacques, 46, 175

Collaboration: *see* Germans; Vichy; Pétain, Pétainists

Colles, Guillaume (*see* Boisguillaume), priest, notary public, 139*n.*

Cologne, University of, 88

Commentaries, see Pius II

Commines, Philippe de, French chronicler, 67

Common man, *see* cult of the

Compiègne, 21, 43–4, 61, 69, 71, 82, 110, 127*n.*, 150, 174

Conciliar movement, 104, 115

Confederacy, Southern, 165

Constance, Council of, 115

Constantinople, 85, 122–3
Contes, Louis de, *see* Coutes, Louis de
Council of Basel, *see* Basel
Council of Constance, *see* Constance
Corbie, 68
Cordeliers, Chronique anonyme dit des, 69–70
Coronation campaign, 50, 96
Coronation of Charles VII, 49, 96, 116, 119, 151, 174
Courcelles, Thomas de, 92, 107, 132, 137
Cousinot, Guillaume, 47
Coutances, Richard de Longueil, Bishop of, 124, 127
Coutes, Louis de, page of Joan of Arc, 41, 42, 145
Cravant, 174
Crécy, battle of, 172
Croce, Benedetto, 22, 32
Croniques, see Bouchard
Crown, French, *see* French
Crusade planned by Pope against the Turks, 122
Crux honesta, 127
Cubism, 170
Cult of the common man, 160

Dahl, A., 162
Darmesteter, James, 21
Darnley, Henry Stuart, Lord, 149
Dauphin, 90, *see also* Charles VII
Dauphiné, 55
David, King, 94
Day, Holman Francis, 165
De claris eclectisque mulieribus, see Bergamo
De Quincey, Thomas, 161
Deborah, 155
Déesse des Champs, 161
Degli Ariente, Giovanni Sabadino, 91
Denis, Léon, *The Mystery of Joan of Arc,* 169
Des Ursins, *see* Rheims
Deschamps, 67
Digne, Bishop of, *see* d'Estouteville
Dominican Order, 76, 87, 129
Domrémy, 72, 77, 111, 144, 155, 160, 173; Burgundian raid on, 62; curé of, *see* Bourgaut
Doyle, Sir Arthur Conan, 169
Dreyer, Carl, 101
Dubois, Abbé F. N. A. (1752–1824), 52
Dubois, Paul, sculptor, 161

Du Desert, Maître Guillaume, Canon of Rouen, 130n., 131n.
Dufour, Antoine, *Livre des femmes célèbres,* 92
Du Guesclin, Bertrand, 172
Du Haillan, Bernard de Girard, Sieur, 23
Du Lis, *see* du Lys, below
Du Lys (or Dulys), 110, 111n.; Jean, Joan's brother, 110, 126n., 127; Pierre, Joan's younger brother, 110, 126n.; Pierre's son Jean, seigneur de l'Isle aux Boeufs, 110n.
Dunand, chanoine, 114–16, 162, 166n.
Dunois, Jean Count de, Bastard of Orleans, 41, 46, 48, 67, 127n., 140, 145
D'Urfé, M. S., 107, 126n., 131
Dynther, Edmund de, 83

Edward III, King of France and England, 172
Egregia bellatrix, 55, 109, 155
Emotions, liberation of the, 160
Emperor, Holy Roman, of the German nation. 90, 97, 112, 115n., 133
Empire, Holy Roman, 88, 161
Empire, Napoleonic, 159
Empire, Second, 159
'En nom Dieu', 47
Encyclopaedia Britannica, 162
England, 22, 35–6, 122–3
English, 42–4, 46, 48–50, 52–3, 56, 59, 62, 67–9, 77–8, 83, 89, 91, 96–8, 103–4, 110–13, 115–16, 119–20, 129–31, 138–9, 157–8; army, 158; chroniclers, 58, 162; cloth, 112; court, 148; government, 108; pressure, 142; reputation of Joan of Arc, 163; 'theory', 162–3; tradition, 154; *see also* aristocracy; Channel; historians; scholarship
Enlightenment, 23, 32, 58, 65, 73, 125–6, 155–7, 160, 162; *see also philosophes,* Rationalist views
Entente cordiale, 163, 165
Epic, Latin, 155
Érard, Maître Guillaume, 149
d'Escouchy, Mathieu, 71
Estates of the realm, 60
Esther, 155
d'Estivet, Canon Jean, Promoter of the trial of Joan of Arc, 99, 102n., 137–8
d'Estouteville, Cardinal Guillaume (Car-

dinal St Martin-les-Monts), Bishop of Digne, 122, 175

Eugenius IV (Gabriel Condulmieri), Pope, 106, 112, 115

Eugubinum, Chronicon, 94

Evreux, 131*n*.

Executioner, 148

Expressionist drama, 170

Eymeric, Nicolas, 135

Fabre, Senator Joseph, 40, 52, 150, 168

Fairy tree, or ladies' tree (*l'arbre charmine faée de Bourlemont*), 140, 155

'False Pucelle', 56, 79, 108–11, 127, 155

Falstaff, Sir John, 73

Fascist theories, 162

Fastolf, Sir John, 73, 74

Fauquembergue, Clément de, notary of the *Parlement* of Paris, *Journal* (Register), 80–2

Fauquembergue sketch, 49, 81

Fave, Maître Jean de, 130*n*., 138*n*.

Feminism, 163, 165, 170

Fentonville, John, 165

Ferrara, 92

Fête nationale, 162, 167–8

Feudal; anti-feudal character of Burgundian party, 75; disturbers, 74; French nobility, 173; warfare, laws of feudal, 60; uprising of nobles, 175; *see also* France

Feudalism, 28, 36, 45–6, 59–60

Fierbois, 94; *see also* Joan of Arc, sword; St Katherine of

Fifth Republic, President of the, 171

Flanders, 59–60, 95, 97, 112

Flandre, Annales de, see Annales de Flandre

Flavy, Governor Guillaume de, 53

Flavy, Mémoire sur Guillaume de, 84

Flemish cities, 172

Florence, St Antoninus, Archbishop of, *Chronicle*, 94

Folk-heroine of the fifteenth century, 155

Formalism, aristocratic, 160

Formicarium, 87; *see* Nider

Formigny, battle of, 114, 175

France, 10, 17, 21–2, 24, 35–7, 42, 49, 64, 77, 83, 87, 95–6, 100, 103*n*., 109, 112–14, 116–17, 119–20, 122, 125, 133, 158–60, 164, 170, 172–3; marshals of, 20; nobility and higher clergy of, 19;

territorial integrity of France, 171; third estate, 114; *see also* French

France, Anatole (Jacques Thibault), 18, 23, 28, 32, 41, 51, 73, 86, 115–16, 118, 124, 140*n*., 149, 151, 157, 167–8

France, King of, 49, 56, 90, 112, 120, 129, 155

Francis I, King of France, 53

Franciscan Order, 94

Franco-American alliance, 165

Franco-American relations, 166

Franco-Prussian war, 159

Frankish kingdom, 112

Freemason, 21

Frémiet, Emmanuel, 161

French, 21, 23, 32, 35–6, 43, 48, 57–8, 93, 95, 107, 111, 113–15, 118, 167–8, 170–3; Academy, 20; army reforms, 175; monarchy, 111*n*., 125; nobility, 111*n*., 159, 172; *see also* France; historians, Renaissance

French nationalism, 21, 22, 26, 31–2, 40, 48, 59, 62, 84, 104, 111–12, 120, 125, 155–6, 158–9, 161–2, 164, 168, 170–2, *see also* France

French Revolution, 136, 157–9, 162

Froissart, Jean, French historian, 71

Frontier views of Joan of Arc, 165

Gallican Church, 107*n*., 115, 175; *see also* Church of France

Gamine de France, 39, 120

Gandhi, Mohandas Karamchand, 164*n*.

Garivel, Maître François, 140*n*.

Garter, Order of the, 73

Gascony, 175

Gaucourt, Sieur Raoul de, 44, 139*n*.

Gaulle, General Charles de, 120–1, 126–7, 171

Gaullist: Catholic writers, 171; movement, 171; patriot, 21

Germain, Jean; *see* Nevers

German: chroniclers, 37; nationalism, 161, 163–4; pressure, 120; sources, *see* chap. iv; writers, 155; *see also* Empire; scholarship

Germans, 77; collaboration with, 138

Germany, 97

Gerson, 104, 107*n*., 121, 134

Gestes des nobles françoys, 47

Gevaudon, shepherd of, 117

Gien, 50

Gilles, Nicolas, 53n.
Gilles, see Sainte Trinité de Fécamp
Girault, Guillaume, 85
Glasdale, William (Classidas), *Bailli* of Alençon, 48, 77
Gloucester, Duke of, Regent, 112, 173
Gobelins, 33
Godefroy, Denis (*historiographe de France*), *L'Histoire du Roi Charles VII*, 46
Godons, 68
Golden Fleece, Order of the, 82–3
Golden Legend, 95
Goodhart and Hoffman, 166
Gorckum, Heinrich von, 88
Gothic age, 157
Gower, Lord Ronald Charles Sutherland, 25, 162
Grandes annales et histoires generalles de France, Les, see Gilles, Nicolas
Grandes croniques de Bretagne, Les, see Bretagne
Grand Inquisitor, *see* Bréhal
Graverent, Jean, 135n.
Graville, Mallet de, 53
Great Schism, 104, 115
Green, John Richard, 61
Greffier of La Rochelle, *see* Notary
Grey, Lady, of Fallodon, 169
Grimké, Sarah Moore, 165
Grouchet, Maître Richard, 130n., 131n.
Gruel, Guillaume, 39, 55–6
Guasche, Guillaume, 93
Guesdon, Lawrence, deputy of the *Bailli* of Rouen, 134
Guienne, 114
Guizot, François, 98

Hardiesses des grands rois et empereurs, see Sala
Hase, Karl, 156
Hector, 155
Henry IV, King of England and France, 173
Henry V, King of England, Regent of France and Heir-Apparent, 82, 113, 117, 173
Henry VI, King of England and France, 60, 101–3, 106, 114, 133, 147, 173; marriage of, 175
Henry VI, Part One, see Shakespeare, William
Herald of Berri, *see* Le Bouvier, Gilles

Herald, Joan's, 52
Hercules, 155
Heresy, 23; *see* Joan of Arc, as alleged heretic
Heroines, Biblical, 155
Heroines, classical, 155
Herrings, Battle of the, 174
Hippolyta, 155
L'Histoire de France, see Mézerai; Michelet
L'Histoire des neuf Charles, see Belleforest
L'Histoire du Roi Charles VII, see Godefroy
L'Histoire et discours au vray du Siège, 53
Historians, English, 32; French, 58
Historiography, scientific, 168
Holinshed, 58
Holland, 88
Holy Roman Emperor, Empire, *see* Emperor, Empire
Honegger, Arthur, 170
Hordal, Étienne, 93
Hordal, Jean, 92
Hotot, Saturnin, 51
Howe, Nathaniel, 20
Hozier, 82
Huguenot, 21
Huizinga, J., 79
Humanitarianism, 157, 160
Hume, David, 65, 70, 76, 95, 155, 157, 163
Hundred Years' War, 36, 97–8, 112, 172–5
Huntington, Anna Hyatt, 161, 165
Hysteria, 169

Imposture theory, *see* Joan of Arc
Impressionism, 170
Inquisitor of the Faith, *see* Lord Inquisitor
Inquisition, Holy, 123–5; in Italy, 125; in Spain, 125; *see* Bréhal; Le Maistre; Lord Inquisitor
Internationalist view of Joan of Arc, 32, 170
Iphigenia, 155
Ireland, William Henry, 38
Irish views, 163
Isabel (Isabeau) of Bavaria, Queen of France, 37, 59
Isabella, mother of Edward III, 172
Isabellette, 146n.
Italy, 141; Italian chroniclers, 37; cities, 112; nationalism, 163; sources, *see* chap. iv; troops, 97; *see* Inquisition

INDEX

Jack Cade, *see* Cade
Jacob, 94
Jacoby, J., 34
Jacquerie, 172
Jael, 155
Jan, Eduard von, 80
Jargeau, 42
Jeanné, Égide, 87
Jeanne d'Arc Revint . . ., 162; *see* Dahl, A.
Jeannette, widow of Thiesselin de Viteau, 146*n.*, 147*n.*
Jesus Christ, *see* Christ
Jewish theories of Joan of Arc, 164
Joan of Arc: age, 76; alleged abjuration of, 23, 30, 129, 142, 149, 174; alleged desire to go home, 48; her amazing story, 29; apparent attempt at suicide, 152; appearance, 93; attack on Paris, 75; attempt at ransom of, *see* Charles VII; banner of, 38; baton, 42–3; and the birds, 77; birth (January 6, 1412), 56, 140, 173; brothers, 71, 176, *see* Du Lys; Burgundian view of, 60; burned at the stake, 71, 171, 174; called the Angelic, 83; capture of, 83, 150–1; Cauchon charged with showing too much favour to, 131*n.*; brings miraculous change of wind on the Loire, 140; character alleged to have deteriorated, 152; as *chef de guerre*, 82; as child of nature, 160; childhood, 57; and the Church, 157, 159, 166–7; and clairaudience, 169; and clairvoyance, 140, 169; costumes of, 41; courage of, 26, 80; as court lady, 156; as cowherd, 146; credibility of, 63–4; critics of, 22–3; cult of, 166; death of, 141; delivered to the secular arm, 174; as daughter of the people, 161; drowning of the man who insulted, 140; effects on morale of, 69; as an enigma, 30; entry into Compiègne of, 71; excommunication of, 127*n.*; English reputation of, 162; final expedition of, financed by Charles VII, *see* Charles VII; first visions of, 174; as fraud (alleged), *see below*, impostor; 'Gothic' Joan of Arc, 158, 161; as heretic (alleged), 152, 154–5, 157, 160; as heroine of the Right, 160; home of, 111*n.*; horsemanship of, 41, 62, 65–6, 93; as humanitarian, 161; impostor theory about, 23, 31, 37, 60, 152, 154, 156; interview of, with King at Chinon, *see* Chinon; kingdom bequeathed to, *see* Charles VII; last day of, in the field, 69; leap of, from the tower, 71, 150; lease of the house of, in Orleans, 49; 'legend' of, 170; letters of, 37; male dress of, 73, 89, 91, 103; as *mascotte*, 167; as military leader, 42, 50, 52, 57, 140, 150, 155, (at Montepilloy), 68; miracles of, 140; miraculous prediction of arrow wound by, 140; miraculous prediction of the Battle of the Herrings by, 52; mission of, 49; was mission of, complete at Rheims, 96; and monarchy, 157–60; monument of, at Orleans, 127; mother of, 110, 124, 126, 137, 146, 176; as French nationalist avatar, 156–7; as nationalist symbol, 164; neighbours of the family of, 148; nineteenth-century increase in interest in, 159; peasant-born, 159; penance, 130; plans for crusade of, 49; pledge of faith in surrender, 70, 80, 84; as polymorphous genius, 140; posthumous reputation of, 15–24, 30–2; premonitions of, 152; as *preux chevalier*, 156; pride of, 80; property of, 127–8; prophecy of, 169; prophecy to Glasdale, 77; as rebel, 161; in Rehabilitation, 139; relapse (alleged) of, 23, 142; represents new national codes of values, 61; resistance movement and, 31; sale of, 174; second recantation (alleged) of, 76, 132; secret of, told the King, 91; secular sentence of, omitted, 133; sentence of, 174; as shepherdess, 39, 95, 140, 156; sign of, to the King, 53; and the Social Sciences, 30; standard, 42; story of, concerning the crown brought to the King, 64, 99; as a subject for the dramatist, 24–26; supernatural inspirations of, 155; sword of, 50, 54, 94, 140–1; sword broken, 152; as symbol of *revanche*, 162; as symbol of struggle for national liberation, 171; threatened with torture, 174; trial of, *see* Trial of; uses of the study of, 32–4; as virago, 154; virginity of, 62–3, 155; as visionary, 167; 'Voices' of, 76, 93, 132, 140–1; as witch, 157; *see also*, American theories; Beatification; butterflies; Canonization; 'Celtic theory'; champenoise; Coutes;

Coronation campaign; Coronation; *egregia bellatrix*; Executioner; Fascist theories; Frontier views; *gamine de France*; Irish views; Internationalist views; Pasquerel; Poitiers; Protestant theories; puppet theory; 'Sainte de la patrie'; Scottish theories; strumpet theory; Socialist views; witchcraft

Joan of Arc of the North Woods, 165

Joan of Arc Was On Her Own When She Was Quite a Child, 166; *see* Kern

Joan of Arkansaw, 166; *see* Goodhart and Hoffman

Joan of Lorraine, 166; *see* Anderson

Johnson, Dr Samuel, 32

Journal, *see* Fauquembergue

Journal d'un Bourgeois de Paris, 43, 74–8, 141

Journal du Siège d'Orléans et du Voyage de Reims, 47–8, 51

Joyart, Mengette, 139*n*.

Jove, 39

Judith, 155

Jungfrau von Orleans, 163; *see* Schiller

Justiniani, Pancrazio, 95

Kaiser, Georg, 170

Kaiserstuhl, 79

Katherine, Queen of England and France, Henry V's Queen, 60, 173

Kenyon College, Gambier, Ohio (Conference on the Heritage of the English-speaking Peoples), 61

Kern, Jerome, 166

Koerner (Cornerius), Hermann, *Universal History*, 90

La Broquière, Bertrandon de 85

La Charité-sur-Loire, 44, 150, 152

La Curne de Sainte-Palaye, Jean Baptiste, 67

Ladies' tree, *see* fairy tree

Ladvenu, Martin, 132, 138, 140*n*., 149

Lagny-sur-Marne, 44, 61, 150; resuscitation of 'dead' baby at, 152

La Hire, Maréchal, 42

Lami, 88

Lancaster, 112, 114

Landor, Walter Savage, 161

Lang, Andrew, 20, 49, 140*n*., 149–50, 163, 168

La Pierre, Isambard (Ysambard) de, 129, 138

La Rochelle, 54; naval battle at, 172

La Rochelle, Catherine de, 117

La Rousse, woman, 62, 65

La Saussaye, in diocese of Evreux, 131*n*.

La Touroulde, Dame Marguerite, 140*n*., 145

La Trémoïlle, Seigneur Georges de, 43–5, 50

Latin epic, *see* epic

Latvia, *see* nationalism

Laval, Lord Guy de, 85, 93

L'Averdy, Clément-François de, 92

Law, Canon, *see* canon law

Lawson, John Howard, 170

Le Barbier, Robert, 104

Lebouchier, Messire Pierre, 130–1*n*.

Le Bouvier, Gilles, Herald of Berri, *Chronicle*, 52

Lebrun des Charmettes, Philippe Alexandre, 33, 93

Lebuin, Michel, 139*n*.

Le Crotoy, 41

Le drapier, Perrin, *see* Perrin le drapier

La Fèvre, Jean, seigneur de Saint-Remy, *Chronique*, 67, 78, 82

Lefèvre-Pontalis, Germain, 87

Le Franc, Martin, 101

Leftist thought, 170

Legate, papal, 113, 122

Léliis, Théodore de, 134

Lémann, Joseph, 164*n*.

Le Maistre, Jean, Vice-Inquisitor of Beauvais, 101, 104–5, 125, 135*n*., 137

Lenglet-Dufresnoy, L'Abbé, 92, 125

Lenozoles, Maître Jean de, 131*n*.

Leo X (Giovanni de 'Medici), Pope, 115

Leonard, Brother, 119

Libre-penseur, French, 35

Ligeur, 21

Lille, 71

Lionel, 70; *see* Lyonnel, below

Lisieux, Thomas Basin, Bishop of, 53*n*., 54, 135*n*.; cathedral of, 107; diocese of, 106

Literature, *see* Renaissance; Romances; Romantic; Writers

Livre de la Pucelle natifve, 53

Livre des femmes célèbres, *see* Dufour

Livre des Trahisons, 83

Longbow, 172

Lord Inquisitor of Heretical Error, by

apostolic authority in the Kingdom of France, 76, 105, 135*n.*, 136; *see* Bréhal

Lorraine, 62, 65–6, 95, 99, 107, 155, 161–2, *Chronicle of,* 155; coat of arms of, 171; Cross of, 171; Duke of, 55, 66, 174; *History of,* 56

Louis XI, King of France, 54–5, 58, 89, 92, 111*n.*; as dauphin, 175

Louis XII, King of France, 53, 92

Louvre, 46

Low Countries, 36, 112

Lowell, Francis Cabot III, 98, 139, 145, 149, 165, 168

Lowell, Abbot Lawrence, 149*n.*

Lower middle class, *see* class

Luce, Siméon, 101*n.*, 147, 167

Lucretia, 155

Luxembourg, Jean de (John of Luxembourg), 53, 103, 174

Lyon, 144

Lyonnel, Bastard of Vendôme (Wandonne), 70, 80

Machine de guerre, 156

Mahrenholtz, Richard, 23

'Maid of France', 66

'Maid of Orleans', 66, 117

Mailly, Jean de, Bishop of Noyon, 130*n.*

Mâle, Émile, 33

Maltese nationalism, *see* nationalism

Manchon, Guillaume, 130–3, 138*n.*, 145

Marcel, Jean, 130*n.*

Margaret of Anjou, *see* Anjou

Marguerie, André, 130–1, 144

Maritain, Jacques, 144, 171

Mark Twain (Samuel Langhorne Clemens), 15, 165

Martin V (Otto Colonna), Pope, 106, 115*n.*, 121, 123, 175

Martin, Henri, 131, 161

Martin, L., 170

Marxist comment, 170

Masonic lodges, 167

Massaeus, 53*n.*

Massieu, Maître Jean, 130–2, 145, 149

Maugier, Pierre, 137

Melun, 150

Metz, 110; Chronicle of, 56

Metz, Sir Jean de Novelemport, called Jean de, 71

Meung, 42

Meyer, Jacques, *see Annales de Flandre*

Mézerai, Eudes de, 53*n.*

Michelet, Jules, 20, 47, 74, 77, 84, 152; *Histoire de France,* 161

Middle Ages, 157

Midi, Maître Nicolas, 130*n.*

Migier, Prior of Longueville, 130*n.*, 131*n.*

Milan, 85, 94; Duke of, 56, 97

Minerva, 33, 39

Miracles, 153; *see also under* Joan of Arc

Models, French, 59

Modern art, 170; modernist music, 170

Monahan, Michael, 15–16, 108, 167

Monarchy, French, *see* French

Monarchism, 21–2, 32, 59, 167

Moniteur, 158

Monstrelet, Enguerrand de, *Chroniques,* 61–70; *also,* 23, 58, 71, 76, 78, 80, 82

Montepilloy, 68

Montereau, 37, 112, 173

Montigny, Jean de, 123

Montreuil, 47

Mont-Saint-Michel, Chronicle of, 55

Monvel, Boutet de, *see* Boutet de Monvel

Morel, Jean, 139*n.*

Morosini Chronicle, 94–6

Morton, A. L., 170

Murray, Dr Margaret Alice, 23, 127, 163, 169

Murray, T. Douglas, 29

Museum, British, 9, 17, 77, 134

Mystère du Siège d'Orléans, 24, 51–2, 127, 154

Mystery of Joan of Arc, see Denis

Mystery on the Death of Charles VII, see Chastellain

Myth, 31–2

Nancy, 55, 162

Nangis, Guillaume de, *Chronicle* of, 56

Napoleon I, 111, 140, 158, 171; coronation of, 126

Nationalism: of Brazil, Latvia, Malta, Norway, Poland, 164, 171; *see* French, German, Italian nationalism; *see under* Joan of Arc, for her use as a nationalist symbol

Nativity of the Virgin, feast of the, 75

Natural law, 125*n.*

Necromancers, modern, 169

Nemus canutum, see Bois-chesnu

Neufchâteau, 62–3, 65, 77

Nevers and Châlons, Jean Germain, Bishop of, 83

Nevins, Allan, 19

New York, 166

Nider, Johann (*Formicarium*), 87–8

Nobility, French, *see* French

Norman, 122; conquest, 60

Normandy, 42, 44, 55, 113–14, 173, 175; reconquered, 137

Norwegian nationalism, *see* nationalism

Notary (greffier) of La Rochelle, Relation of the, 54

Notaries at the trial of Joan of Arc, 132–3, 144

Noyon, Cathedral of, 121

Nuremberg, 87; trials, 61

Objectification, 169

Order: of Preaching Brothers, 101, 136; *see* Dominicans, Franciscans, Garter, Golden Fleece

Orleans, 21, 49, 88, 101, 109, 111, 126, 144, 158; archives of, 51; Chronicle Concerning the Deliverance of, *see Chronicle*; Duke Charles of, 36, 40–1, 46–7, 49, 66, 110, 114; released by the English, 175; Duke Louis of, 172; assassinated, 173; Félix Antoine Philibert Dupanloup, Bishop of, 166; Joan's entry into, 51, 174; financial records of, 52, 142; fête of May 8 at, 52, 110, 118, 120, 127, 158; House of, 41; livery of, 41; Maid of, *see* Maid of Orleans; Mgr Touchet, Bishop of, 166n.; relief of, 72, 74, 85, 96; siege of, 38–9, 41, 47–8, 51–3, 55, 67, 77, 79, 145, 158, 174

Paine, Albert Bigelow, 19, 42, 165

Painting, 170

Panthéon, 157

Papal legate, *see* legate, papal

Papacy, 112–13

Paranoia, 169

Paris, 21, 59, 68, 70, 74–7, 85, 103, 106–7n., 144, 150, 152, 173–4, 176; Armagnac attack on, in 1429, 43, 81, 152; Armagnacs in, 81; Cathedral church of Notre Dame de, 124, 126–7, 137, 176; clergy of, 81; Charles VII's state entry into, 175; episcopal palace of, 124; Guillaume Chartier, Bishop of, 124–7; miseries of the people of, 78; *parlement* of, 59–60;

125; public opinion in, 124; University of, 74–5, 81, 86n., 88, 101–5, 108, 115–16, 121–3, 136; University of, Faculty of Theology, 102n.; University of, Resolutions, 174

Par mon martin, 42–3, 47, 82

Parton, James, 148

Pascal, Blaise, 22

Pasquerel, Brother Jean (Joan's confessor), 71, 140, 145, 150

Passion of Joan of Arc, The, 101

Patay, battle of, 56–7, 67, 72–4, 145, 171, 174

Peace conference of Arras, *see* Arras

Peace of Brétigny, *see* Brétigny

Peasantry, French, 172

Peasants' Revolt, 172

Péguy, Charles, 167

Penthesilea, 155

Perrin, le drapier, 139n., 146n.

Pétain, Marshal, 116, 120

Pétainists, 171

Petitot, Claude B., 47

Philip of Bergamo, *see* Bergamo

Philip the Fair, King of France, 115

Philosophes, 156

Picardy, 68, 82; archer of, captor of Joan of Arc, 70; clerk of, 70–1

Piccolomini, Cardinal Aeneas Sylvius, *see* Pius II

Pius II (Aeneas Sylvius), Pope, *Commentarii*, 90–1, 107n.

Plutarch, 39

Poitiers, 101n.; assembly of the doctors at, to give a hearing to Joan of Arc, in the spring of 1429, 21, 146n.; battle of, 172; Book of, 87, 100, 101n., 115; church of, 100; Joan's vindication at, 90

Poland, *see* nationalism

Political excursions, 22

Pontano (Pontanus), Paul, 134

Pontius Pilate, 107

Pont l'Évêque, 82

Pope of Rome, 90, 97, 103–4, 108, 113–16, 122, 124, 141, 174; rival Popes, 152; *see* Clement V; Clement VII; Eugenius IV; Martin V; Pius II; Leo X; *see also* Church; Great Schism; Legate; Papacy; Rome; Vatican Council

Posthumous Information, 132–3

Post-impressionism, 170

Poulengy, Bertrand de, 71

INDEX

Progmatic Sanction of Bourges, *see* Bourges

Praguerie, 46, 175

Priam of Troy, 47

'Princes of the Lilies', 172

Promoter of the trial of Joan of Arc, *see* d'Estivet

Protestantism, 128; *see* Heresy, Huguenot

Protestant views of Joan of Arc, 155–6

Proto-fascism, 160

Provost of Vaucouleurs, *see* Baudricourt, *also* Du Lys, Jean, *also* Vaucouleurs

Prutz, Hans, 168

Psychology, 30, 169

Pucelle, 66, 92

Pucelle, *Chronique de la, see* Chronique

Pucelle d'Orléans, La, see Voltaire

Puppet theory of Joan of Arc, 23, 31, 72–3, 154

Quicherat, Jules Étienne Joseph, 36, 40, 43, 47–9, 51–2, 56, 70, 79, 83, 87, 91, 95–6, 102, 107, 118, 123, 128, 131–2, 135, 142, 144*n.*, 150–1

Quintilian, 27

Quintus Fabius Maximus, 73

Rabateau, Jean, 41

Rabelais, François, 62

Radical movements, 170

Raimondi, Cosmo di, of Cremona, 94

Ransom, attempted, of Joan of Arc, *see* Charles VII

Rationalist position, 142, 147; *see also* Republicans (French)

Realism, 170

Reason, Goddess of, 126

Régime, ancien, see Ancien régime

Register, *see* Fauquembergue

Registre Delphinal, 55

Regnault de Chartres, *see* Rheims

Rehabilitation of Joan of Arc, chap. vi, *also* 38, 42, 55, 58, 64, 69, 91–2, 94, 96, 99*n.*, 101*n.*, 105*n.*, 108–11, 116, 124, 154–6, 158, 168, 175–6; Proceedings, 21, 29–30, 37, 47, 49, 52–3, 62, 72, 103*n.*

Relapse (alleged) of Joan of Arc, *see* Joan of Arc

Relation of the Notary of La Rochelle, see Notary

Renaissance, 23, 32, 58, 62, 65, 73, 90, 93–5, 110, 141, 156; courtly literature, 155; French, 154; poetry, 55

Rennes, 53

Republicans (*in France*) and Joan of Arc, 21, 32, 43, 157, 161; anticlerical, 167; their *rapprochement* with the memory of the Maid, 168; *see* Anticlericalism; *libre-penseur;* Rationalist position

Respublica Christiana, 116–17

Restoration, 33, 159–60

Return to nature, 160; *see* Romantic

Reuchlin, 115

Revanche, 159

Revolution, 136; French, of 1789, *see* French; of 1830, 160

Rheims, 37, 43, 48, 96, 102, 111*n.*, 174; Cathedral of, 116, 119; Jean Jouvenel des Ursins, Archbishop of, 46, 99, 119, 124; Archbishop's letter to, 157; Joan of Arc's letter to, 151; Regnault de Chartres, Chancellor of France, Archbishop of, 44, 102, 115–16, 151

Ribard, André, 170

Richard, Brother, 80, 117

Richard II, King of England and France, 172

Richemont, Arthur Count of, Constable of France, 19, 45–6, 56, 111, 113

Richemont, Chronicle of Arthur de, 55

Richmond, 165

Riggs, T. Lawrason, 167

Rigné, Raymond de, 34, 163

Riom, 93

Romances of chivalry, 95

Romantic movement and Joan of Arc, 26, 40, 57, 59, 66, 74, 84, 140, 156, 160–2; *see also* English romantics

Roman traditions, 126

Rome, 102, 115, 121, 125, 135*n.*, 176; Cathedral of St. Peter's in, 176

Rommée de Vouthon, Isabel, Joan's mother, *see under* Joan of Arc

Rose, Philippe de la, 122

Rouen, 55, 59, 71, 79, 82, 98–9, 101–6, 113–14, 121–2, 175–6; Archbishop of, 127; archiepiscopal palace of, 127, 176; archiepiscopal see of, 130; *Bailli* of 50, 134; castle of (Great Hall), 174; Old Market Place of, 174; *see also* Chapel(s)

Rousseau, 160

Rouvray, 68; clairvoyant prediction of, 140

Royal Council, 50

Roye, Gilles de, 71
Rude, F., 161

Sabadino, *see* degli Ariente
Sackville-West, Victoria, 126, 146
St Aignan, 127
St Antoninus, *see* Florence
St Denis, 49, 50
St Eusebius, Cardinal of England, *see* Winchester
St Florent, 42
Saint Helena, 171
Saint Joan, see Shaw
St Katherine of Fierbois, church of, 54
St Katherine's sword, *see* Joan of Arc, sword of
Saint-Martin-des-Champs, 76
St Martin-les-Monts, Cardinal, *see* d'Estouteville
St-Ouen, Place, 127
St Quentin, 68; Burgundy's letter to, 69
St Sauxon, church of, 110
St Thomas, 89
Sainte-Beuve, Charles Augustin de, 25–6, 40, 124
Sainte-Croix, Cardinal Albergati de, 115
'Sainte de la patrie', 124
Sainte-Trinité de Fécamp, Gilles, Lord Abbot of, 102
Sala, Pierre, *Hardiesses des grands rois et empereurs*, 53
Samaran, Charles, 47
Sarmaize, Maid of, 109
Saumur, 42
Scherrer, J. J., painting, 'Entrée Triomphale de Jehanne d'Arc dans Orléans', 51
Schiller, Johann Christoph Friedrich von, *Die Jungfrau von Orleans*, 24–6, 69–70, 161, 163
Schism, *see* Great Schism
Schizophrenia, 169
Scholarship, Anglo-Saxon, 168; German, 168
Scholastic, 125*n*.
Scotland, 97; Scots, 172
Scottichronicon, 163
Scottish theories, 163
Sculpture, 170
Seghers, Anna, 170
Séguin de Séguin, Dean Pierre, 101*n*., 146*n*.

Seine, 21
Semiramis, 155
Senlis, 150; *Bailli de Senlis*, 61; horse of the Lord Bishop of, 152
Sepet, Marius, 79
Shakespeare, William, *Henry VI, Part One*, 23–6, 58, 69, 73, 76, 154, 162; 'unser Shakespeare', 161
Shaw, George Bernard, *Saint Joan*, 15, 73, 151, 156, 170
Shepherd of Gevaudan, *see* Gevaudan
Sibyl of France, 155
Sibylla Francica, 88–90
sibyls, 89
Sigismund, Holy Roman Emperor, 87
Sluys, 172
Socialist views, 170; British Fabian, 170; Catholic, 167
Soldier Virgin, 165; *see* Yancey
Soubsdan (Soudan), 51–2
Southey, Robert, 161–2
Spain, Inquisition in, *see* Inquisition
Speed, John, 162
Spire, clerk of the diocese of, 88–9
Spiritualism, 169
Stanhope, Earl, 162
Stoic, 125*n*.
Strachey, Lytton, 28
Strumpet theory, 154
Sue, Eugène, 170
Sully, flight from, 44
Surrealism, 170
Swedes, Swedish, 93, 155, 166
Sword, breaking of Joan's, *see* Joan of Arc, sword broken

Taft, Senator Robert, 61
Talbot, John, Earl of Shrewsbury, 73, 114, 175
Tapestry, 155
Taquel, Nicolas, assistant notary at trial of Joan, 107*n*., 129–30, 131–2
Taylor, Coley, 18, 21
Tchaikovsky, 161
Te Deum in Notre Dame de Paris, in celebration of Joan's capture, 126; in honour of General de Gaulle, 126
Templars, 115
Thalamas, Professor, 167
Thiesselin, Jeannette, 111*n*.
Thomassin, Mathieu, 55

INDEX

Tolstoyan Christian philosophical anarchism, 128

Touchages, L., 170

Touchet, Mgr, 166n.

Toul, 144

Tourelles, 77, 85, 145

Tournay, Chronique de, 54, 87

Toynbee, Arnold, 120

Treaty: of Arras, see Arras; of Brétigny, see Brétigny; of Troyes, see Troyes

Tressart, John, 141

Trial of Joan of Arc, 21, 36, 50, 72–3, 91, 99, 102, 105, 110, 128, 144, 148, 149, 151, 154, 157, 168, 174; Trial Record, 30, 37–9, 53, 64, 96–7, 100–1, 103, 107, 118, 121, 131, 133–4, 137, 142–3; see also, Articles of Accusation, assessors, beau procès, Beauvais, notaries

Tringant, 39

Trithemius, 87

Troyes, Treaty of, 59, 74, 113, 173

Tuckey, Miss Janet, 75

Tuetey, A., 74

Turks, 122

Twain, Mark, see Mark Twain

Twelve Articles, 136–7

Twenty-year truce between France and England, 172

Universal History, see Bergamo; Koerner

Vatican Council, 164n.

Vaucouleurs, 65, 72, 110, 144; Joan's visits to, 174; provost of (Jean d'Arc, Joan's brother), 126n.; see also Baudricourt

Vaudemont, Comte de, 101n.

Vaudois of Arras, 125

Velleda, 155

Velly, see Villaret

Vendôme, see Lyonnel

Vendôme, Count of, 46

Venice, 94–5

Verdi, 161

Vermandois, Bailli of, 110

Verneuil, 41, 174

Versailles, 33

Vertot, Abbé, 38

Vice-Inquisitor, see Le Maistre, Jean

Vichy régime, 21–2, 31, 116, 121, 170–1

Victorian ladies, 163

Vienna, University of, 87

Villaret, M., continuation of Velly's Histoire de France, 48, 92

Villon, François, 154

Vincennes, 77

Vinci, Leonardo da, 30

Virgil, 27

Virgin Mary, 96, 127; see Nativity of the Virgin

Virginity, 139

Viriville Vallet de, 47, 167

Visconti, Bonne, 85

Voltaire (François Marie Arouet), La Pucelle d'Orléans, 15, 24–6, 31, 33, 38, 65, 155–7

Vosges, 162

Vouthon, Isabelle Rommée de, see Joan of Arc, mother of

Waldman, Milton, 153

Wallon, Henri, 48, 93

Wandonne, see Lyonnel

'War party' at the court of Charles VII, 43

Warwick, Earl of, 130–8

Waterin, Jean, 139n.

Wavrin, Robert de, knight, Lord of Forestel, 71

Wavrin, Jean de, de Forestel, son of Robert (Chronique d'Angleterre), 71–5

Well of the thorn, 140

Winchester, Cardinal of (St Eusebius, Cardinal of England), 102, 130n., 131n.

Windecke, Eberhard von, 87

Witchcraft, see chap. iii, 'The Witch of the Armagnacs', 58ff.; chap. vi, 'Witch Unwitched', 118ff.; 23, 28–9, 31, 37–8, 45–6, 49, 63, 76, 87–9, 94, 97, 107–8, 113, 116, 141, 145, 152, 154, 157, 162–3, 169

World War I, 163, 166

World War II, 170–1

Writers, English, French, 23; see also, Catholics; American writing

Yancey, W. P., 165

York, 114

189

GEORGE ALLEN & UNWIN LTD
London: 40 Museum Street, W.C.1

Auckland: 24 Wyndham Street
Bombay: 15 Graham Road, Ballard Estate, Bombay 1
Buenos Aires: Escritorio 454–459, Florida 165
Calcutta: 17 Chittaranjan Avenue, Calcutta 13
Cape Town: 109 Long Street
Hong Kong: 1/12 Mirador Mansions, Kowloon
Ibadan: P.O. Box 62
Karachi: Karachi Chambers, McLeod Road
Madras: Mohan Mansions, 38c Mount Road, Madras 6
Mexico: Villalongin 32–10, Piso, Mexico 5, D.F.
Nairobi: P.O. Box 12446
New Delhi: 13–14 Ajmeri Gate Extension, New Delhi 1
Sao Paulo: Avenida 9 de Julho 1138-Ap. 51
Singapore: 36c Prinsep Street, Singapore 7
Sydney, N.S.W.: Bradbury House, 55 York Street
Toronto: 91 Wellington Street West

THE YORKIST AGE

PAUL MURRAY KENDALL

The Yorkist Age unfolds the panorama of daily life during the Wars of the Roses. This first full-length study of English society in the fifteenth century draws upon contemporary narratives of travellers, the Paston Letters and other less widely known collections of correspondence, observations of French and Italian diplomats, town records, ecclesiastical reports, the literature of the age, chronicles, household and estate accounts, wills, chancery proceedings, and other revealing sources, in order to recreate the substance and the flavour of the life of the time.

Ideas, attitudes, fears, aspirations, the 'olde daunce' of love and death, as well as the dress of the age, housekeeping in town and country, recreation and the state of business and the way of courtship are caught in action, as they display themselves in the histories, proud and humble of hundreds of people.

The Yorkist Age deals with pirates and members of Parliament, with merchants, minstrels, lords and lawyers, with ladies in love, ambitious yeomen and bored nuns.

Contrary to Shakespeare and popular belief, the Wars of the Roses had comparatively little effect upon the lives of the people as a whole and represented rather a recovery from than a descent into anarchy. The story of modern England opens not with the Tudors but in this Yorkist realm, a fascinating period of beginnings-and-endings, prosperously balanced between the upheavals of the late fourteenth century and the hard times and hard feelings of the early sixteenth.

'It may even be that we shall find in the reign of Edward IV the Age that subsequent centuries looked back to as Merrie England.'

Demy 8vo   35*s net*

DAILY LIFE IN FRANCE
UNDER NAPOLEON

JEAN ROBIQUET

Demy 8vo   35*s net*

THE TIDES OF HISTORY

Volume 1. From the beginnings to Islam

JAQUES PIRENNE

'History', the author writes in his Preface, 'is essentially a continuity and a unity; a continuity that goes on, without men being able to escape it, from generation to generation, and which links our own times to the most distant epochs; a unity, since in any society the life of each man is bound up with the lives of all others, even as, in the community of nations, the history of each nation develops, without even being aware of it, as a part of the history of all the nations of the universe. . . .

'Confronted by the abyss into which humanity has fallen, should we not take stock and examine our consciences? There is no other way to do so, in my opinion, than to follow the long adventure of humanity. Only universal history, by comparing all civilizations, can cause some sort of philosophy of history to become apparent, and thus lead to sociological, scientific and moral conclusions. It alone is capable, by revealing to us that neither our country nor our race nor our age has achieved a civilization in all ways superior to all that has gone before, of eradicating those prejudices of religion, race and language, of political, social or mystical ideologies, that have not ceased to drive men into vain massacres and to degrade, by hatred, all ideals, even the noblest and those which have no other aim than the triumph of tolerance and love. Universal history also is alone able, by developing before our eyes the great cycles of human evolution, to make us understand at what point in evolution we are today. That, I think, is the essential question. For it is on knowledge of the necessities and possibilities of our time that the value of future peace depends.'

Jacques Pirenne, the distinguished Belgian historian, and son of the equally distinguished Henri Pirenne, has now completed a study of universal history in seven volumes, covering the whole of civilization from the beginnings to the most recent events of the 1950's. The first volume to be published in English, which ends with the advent of Islam, includes all the civilizations of antiquity from the earliest movements on the deltas of the Nile, the Indus, the Euphrates and Tigris, through the histories of Ancient Egypt, Babylon, Assyria, Persia, Greece, Rome and China and other parts of Asia. Gigantic in its scope, this study is remarkable for its lucidity, its comprehensiveness and its great readability.

Demy 8vo. Illustrated with 33 maps. About 50s net

GEORGE ALLEN & UNWIN LTD